To Rosen

C000000280

SQUAD
AVERAGE

I hope you enjoy

Mark Invicon

SQUAD AVERAGE

MARK INMAN

The Book Guild Ltd

First published in Great Britain in 2018 by
The Book Guild Ltd
9 Priory Business Park
Wistow Road, Kibworth
Leicestershire, LE8 0RX
Freephone: 0800 999 2982
www.bookguild.co.uk
Email: info@bookguild.co.uk
Twitter: @bookguild

Typeset in Aldine401 BT

Printed and bound in Great Britain by CPI Group (UK) Ltd, Croydon, CR0 4YY

ISBN 978 1912575 442

British Library Cataloguing in Publication Data.
A catalogue record for this book is available from the British Library.

In memory of the men I served with and lost.

*Dedicated to the brave men and women who are plighted
with PTSD – post-traumatic stress disorder
"You have the ability to beat it!"*

*Dedicated to my Angels:
Donna, Bethan,
my heir
Charlie-Jack (CJ)
&
Cassius*

CONTENTS

An outstanding solider, Corporal Inman was one of the best I have had the privilege to command. Right from the outset, he stood out among his peers; not just for his physical ability and accomplished fighting skills, but for his compulsion to do the job he was trained to do. A genuine 'soldier's soldier', Inman thrived on operations. Professional and focused, he had an ingrained sense of courage and commitment. I relied on him to deliver and he invariably did.

Lt Col J Green, 1 STAFFORDS

There are many top soldiers that I have been proud to have worked with over the twenty two years I have served in the STAFFORDS, but I have to say Corporal Inman is one that sits at the top of that list. His name is one of the chosen few that are on the distinction board in the corridors of Junior Division at the Infantry Battle School Brecon, having achieved a distinction on Section Commanders Battle Course. This man is a true Stafford. Extremely loyal and one of the best.

WO2 Derry, 1 STAFFORDS

Imagine being back in the school playground. Two captains picking from the best of the bunch. My first pick would be "Inman". Nobody comes close to his diligence, professionalism, confidence and ability. He brought the aggression to the fight, which gave myself and the team that feeling of invincibility.

Richard Moon, Close Protection Officer 2005–2008

1

THE ROCKING CHAIR

My grandfather was my world, my idol. I would be around eight years of age and I would often be so excited to be stopping with Grandad Charlie. It was my little adventure, my treat. I got to sleep in his room by the side of his bed. He would buy me sweets and pop. On Saturday evenings we would watch *The A-Team* together. Grandad reminded me of an older Hannibal, but he was cool. My grandad was the best. A very handsome man, he always took great pride in his appearance. A true gentleman through and through! On Saturday afternoons we would venture into Tamworth and go to the pub. He would have half a bitter and would treat me to a cola and a packet of nuts. He would pop his coins into the fruit machine and let me press the buttons, the ones I could reach anyway. He seemed to be a very popular man around town. "Hey up, Charlie," you would often hear as we paced through the centre of town. I remember one day going into a newsagents. He was chatting to the gentleman behind the counter while purchasing his racing news.

"Who's this then?" Gesturing towards me.

"This is my grandson, Mark," he said with visible pride. The nice gentleman proceeded into the back of his store and brought out a huge assortment of comics. It was stacked so high that string had to secure the bundle.

"I was waiting for someone special to come so I could give this to them." I placed my tiny arms out and collected the package.

"Thank you very much," I said. My grandfather also thanked his friend. Charlie purchased some pipe tobacco and we continued on our adventure. I loved the smell of Grandad's pipe. When I'm lucky enough to catch a whiff now and again, I will automatically think of Grandad.

Charlie served in the RAF during his National Service and, of course, the war. He would tell me stories about things he got up to and the friends he had, and shared his adventures with me. He would tell me of times he would be in a plane and the pilot would swoop low towards the sea and then rise again and continue the process in order to make the men in the back feel ill. He had so many stories to tell me, and I loved every one of them. I tried to imagine him as a younger man. What would he look like? How scared must he have been? Grandad would always have a smile on his face when telling the stories. He without doubt must have loved his time serving his country.

Grandad would let me stay up late when I stayed with him. He wanted to spend as much time with me as possible. I enjoyed being his centre of attention. We definitely had a special bond, a bond which I will never forget and feel blessed to have had in our short time together. I don't recall my grandfather being religious or ever going to church. However, I do recall him every morning saying the Lord's Prayer the second his feet hit the ground on rising from his pillow. I am pretty sure also that I heard him cry after saying it on numerous occasions. Maybe Grandad had some bad memories also?

As my grandparents become progressively older and my

grandmother sadly passed away, Charlie moved into a care home. It was a decent place. He enjoyed his independence still. He had his own room with his TV set and his rocking chair. He loved that chair, and it did look comfortable. The care home was a fifteen-minute car journey from our home in Whittington. The family together would drive over on either a Saturday or Sunday morning and visit Grandad, and take him for a beer at The Green Man pub in the nearby village. As I grew older I would often cycle on a Sunday morning to visit him. Charlie would be looking out for me from his room window. As I would cycle into the grounds I would see his handsome face waiting for me. He was so happy to see me. I do recall once telling him I would see him the following week. For some reason I didn't go. When I finally did see him he told me how disappointed he was that I didn't go. It made me feel terrible.

Again, when I was in his company he would tell me about his life, continue with the stories of the war and his military career. At this point in my life, I decided what I wanted to do with my life. I wanted to follow in my father's footsteps and join the police force. I loved the stories Charlie would tell me; I would be gripped. I could see also that he obviously enjoyed telling them to me. It must have been a way of reminding himself of the person he was proud to have been. Then he dropped something on my lap that would stick with me until this very day.

"Son," he began, "promise me you will have no regrets in life. We are blessed with one life – you must live it to the fullest. Have adventures and fun. I'm sitting in this rocking chair and have the privilege of telling you all the stories of my life. One day you will be sat in a rocking chair similar to mine. I hope you have stories to tell your grandson."

Immediately I understood. I had to live life in the way my grandfather did. I didn't want to sit in my rocking chair having nothing to pass on to my grandson. I want my grandson to look to me like I did to Charlie. I think I knew what he wanted for me without telling me. He wanted me to join the military. I will never forget the way he told me. It was with real feeling. I was thirteen, going on fourteen, but understood that life was for living and creating memories, and more importantly I wanted to be the man one day in my chair that rocked! Thank you for that advice, Grandad.

A matter of months later, my Grandad passed away. It hit me quite hard. All of a sudden I went from a hardworking school boy to one who didn't give a fuck. I stopped trying so hard. My education was the least of my worries. I began to hate school and it showed in my grades and annual reports. I would dread taking them home. *Mark must try harder, Mark must concentrate, and Mark needs to put more effort in.* You get the picture. I knew that when it came to sitting my GCSEs it would come back to bite me, and it did. I failed the fucking lot. Reality struck. What was I going to do?

As previously mentioned, we lived in Whittington. Dad was the village copper so we lived in a police house opposite the village church and village hall. A huge car park was situated directly opposite my bedroom. Often on Saturday mornings you would hear a platoon of recruits marching past our house with all their kit on. You would hear the shouting from the instructors: "Get up the front." I would often look out the window crawling from my bed, observe the brutality and think *Fuck that!,* then turn my TV on and spend the next hour or two chilling, a typical teenager's behaviour.

Whittington Barracks was close by. It was a small infantry training barracks. Young recruits started what's called their basic training there before moving on to further infantry training. They would transition from civilian and go through a tough 10-week process learning the pure soldiering basics.

Every Bonfire Night the barracks would put on a great event. The bonfire was huge and the fireworks were spectacular.

The barracks would invite all the locals from the nearby village of Whittington. My parents would take us kids every year. That was the closest I was ever going to get to a barracks!

After receiving my disastrous GCSE results I decided I wasn't going back to school. To be honest, I wasn't sure what I was going to do. I got the odd job working as a labourer but that didn't last. I was lucky to walk away without knocking someone out to be honest. I quit while I was ahead. I went to the job centre week after week but nothing took my fancy. My parents started to get on to me about money and what I was going to do. I started to feel the pressure from them and also felt their disappointment in me. I failed all my exams, couldn't hold a job down and refused to sign on the dole.

I went to pay my grandfather a visit, something I'm ashamed I didn't do enough of, especially as he was only buried in the church yard across from our house a matter of 200 yards away. So I guess you can add terrible grandson to that list of failings. I sat down next to his headstone. *What shall I do, Charlie Boy?* I thought to myself. I remembered all the good times we spent together. They were such special times in my young life. I didn't realise this growing up business would be so difficult. It just gradually crept up on me. I thought I would be that young boy forever. Then I remembered what he had said to me. He looked me deep in the eyes that day and gave me the answer. I remembered him talking about the rocking chair that one day I would be sat in. I was to have no regrets and live an adventure, just as he had. There it was, clear as day. I needed to join the military. I proceeded to go home and inform my parents of my decision.

My father wasted no time. The next day I was in his car on the way to the Careers Office. I walked in and sat down. There was a fierce-looking Colour Sergeant sat at the desk.

"What do you want to join?" he asked.

"The Paras," I responded.

"No you don't! You want to join your local regiment, the Staffords." (The Staffordshire Regiment). He proceeded to tell me that this was the best option, as by the time my training was complete I could be posted to Hong Kong. Those two words sold it straight away. As the reason for joining was to have an adventure, it seemed to be the perfect choice.

Things proceeded quicker than I anticipated. Within weeks I had an enlistment date and venue to report. Whittington Barracks, only a short distance to travel.

I used to frequent my local pub, The Dog. One of the barmaids there was a beautiful-looking girl who was, unfortunately for me, married to a soldier based at the barracks. He also used to pop in on occasions and have a drink, often to check she wasn't being chatted up by some civvy. He was very protective over what appeared to be his prized possession. His name was Freddy. At a stretch he was five foot six inches small, and a lot older than her. He walked around the bar like he owned the place and thought he was hard as fuck. By all accounts he fancied himself as a bit of a boxer. Little did the prick know that his good lady had the eye for me, or did he? He knew of me at this point. I don't particularly know why, but he used to stare a bit and often drop a sarcastic one-liner in my earshot. It made the temptation of sleeping with her a little more attractive than it already was. Luckily for him I refrained from making any advance, which I have no doubt she would have welcomed. I appreciate I must sound arrogant, but the purpose of this journal is to provide the truth.

The day of my reporting came. Sunday 5th November 1995 by 16:00hrs. I had my kit packed and threw it into the car. I said goodbye to my mum, then Dad drove me the 3-minute journey to the barrack entrance. He got out of the car with me, grabbed my bag and, for the first time that I can remember, hugged me. I had never had this before, but I would never forget it. I felt his pride for the first time in a long time. I couldn't let him down. I had to see this through at all costs.

I walked through the barrack entrance and reported to the guardroom. A runner escorted me to my lines, which would be home for my basic training that lasted for 10 weeks. I was a new member of Gulevant Platoon. I walked into the lines to find my name and which room I should wait in. I walked into my section room. Whose was the first face I saw? Only fucking Freddy's. He must have been expecting me, waiting like a vulture to intimidate his prey. That's exactly what I became over the next 10 weeks.

From Day 1, I was the scumbag recruit who tried to bang Freddy's precious wife. That must have been what he told the other three section commanders and Platoon Sergeant. I was picked out immediately to do all the shit jobs. I was a ten-week brew boy. Whenever the platoon staff wanted a brew, it was dickhead here they would shout to do it. "INMAN!" they would shout. I knew what they wanted. I must have made over 10,000 fucking coffees for those wankers. I would often take great pleasure in saying I would wash the mugs out before making their fresh brews, only to go into the washroom and 'rim' (rub my dick around the edge of) Freddy's mug. I knew it was his as he was the only Devon & Dorset instructor who was the proud owner of a regimental mug. On offering the staff their brews, I would linger to witness Freddy take his first sip. Isn't it ironic?! It was him that got closer to my knob than his wife.

I was bullied 7 days a week for 10 weeks. The instructors would jump on any minute error I would make and hammer me into the ground. I would be on 'staff parade' every night. Staff parade was a punishment that nobody wanted because it was a pure fuck around. You had to parade at 22:00hrs in front of the guardroom to be inspected in your smartest dress (uniform) by both the regimental orderly sergeant and orderly officer.

My locker layout was immaculate due to my long suffering from OCD. The instructors would still find a speck of dust or something to justify ripping my complete locker out, trashing it, so I would spend my free time (what little we had) re-doing it. I would often come in from a lesson and find my bed turned over and ragged about. No one else's, just mine. The staff tried their utmost to make me quit. This was never going to happen. The more they did to try and bully me out, the more I thought *Fuck you! I'm going to finish this ten weeks with my head held high.* Little did the 'bed wetters' know, they were encouraging me to stay. I was becoming more and more stubborn. Freddy and the other section commanders could see I was tough. I would not break. I often got a cheeky slap around the head or a distinct punch to my chest. They couldn't leave signs of bruising now, could they?! I never retaliated. That's what they wanted. If I gobbed off or offered them something back then they could put a case over to the Commanding Officer that I did not show soldier qualities and I could have been discharged. I had no option. Take the shit. It's only for 10 weeks.

I, to this day, wear contact lenses. My section commander found out and arranged for me to have an eye test. I was prescribed glasses that they ordered me to wear. They can only be described as the old NHS glasses that poor unfortunate kids had to wear. Another tactic to try to belittle me and make me quit. The good-looking lad who they made look like "Adrian fucking Mole".

Weeks were going by and the section commanders were failing in their efforts to make me submit. Halfway through the training we had the opportunity to go home for the weekend. We were all so excited. I couldn't wait to meet up with my mates and Vicki to go for a beer. Our bags were packed. My section commander kicked the door to the section room through. He appeared to be fuming. He was not happy with the state of the block jobs (cleaning of the lines). He felt as though it was not up to standard. It clearly was, due to the effort we had put in.

"None of you are going on your long weekend," he announced. He continued to ask who was responsible for the mirrors.

"I was, Corporal," I said, standing to attention as I responded. He frogmarched me to the toilets and showed me the smeared mirrors. "They were immaculate when I had finished them, Corporal!" He didn't take that. I knew that he knew that they had been sabotaged. Nice one, Freddy!

"You will stay here until the block is immaculate." I wasn't going anywhere. The remainder of the platoon were fallen out and went on their way to enjoy their much-deserved time off. I was left scrubbing the toilets. That was probably the closest I got to throwing the towel in. I was broken. Maybe, though, this was their final push? If I got through this maybe they would start respecting the fact that I had taken everything and still refused to give in. Surely I was showing a soldier's, a fighter's, spirit? Corporal said that he would be back to inspect the mirrors the following day (Saturday) to see if they were to his expectation. Saturday came and went. I had no TV or radio. All I had was the block jobs and a book to read while sat on my own in a twelve-man room, knowing my peers were probably in a pub or nuts deep. Sunday afternoon came. The door opened and in came my section commander.

"I've checked the mirrors. You can go. Be back for 6pm." *Thank you, Corporal.* He was kind enough to give me 6 hours. Was it worth it? *No,* I thought. *I'm staying put.* The lads came back one by one and were talking about what they had been up to. The lads discovered I had been there all weekend. A few of the brighter lads started to ask questions. "What have they got in for you?" The penny was beginning to drop. I lived in Whittington and so did the Corporals. Something must have happened previously to me joining up. I denied anything.

"However, I will tell you something when we're out of here," I promised.

Training continued to be a nightmare. My brew-making ability was top-notch. Even if I did add a little extra flavour to Freddy's brew a little bit too frequently. I mean, what a thick bastard, would you give someone you are giving the world of shit to the job of making you a drink or food? That's how dumb the prick was. Generally speaking, I was winning the other Corporals around by about Week 7. They could see I wasn't going anywhere, coupled with the fact that I was producing some good results. I was fitter than any other recruit in the platoon. I had good intelligence, was always well turned out. My weapon handling was excellent and my performance on the drill square was impressive. I was beginning to feel that I was the best recruit there. The Corporals could see this too. This must have got poor Freddy's back right up. He must have hated me. The lad they set out to break was becoming the best recruit in the platoon. This gave me re-energised efforts to cross the 10-week finish line.

In Week 8 we took a short break from the grind of military training and had some adventure training. The platoon did some walking in the Lakes, coupled with some map-reading, orienteering and some potholing. I was pretty much left alone by the staff during this time. May I add at this point that potholing is fucking shit scary! Out of everything I have done in my life, which I will come on to, of course – white water rafting in Kenya, skydiving in Canada… oh, and all the contacts (fire fights) I have been involved in – this is the most frightening thing I have ever done. I fail to see any fun in jumping down a wet, dark cave and crawling on your belly through some tight rocks! For all you people that spend your free time doing this activity, you need to get your nut looked at.

On returning to Whittington Barracks we had one final activity to look forward to. The instructors set up some clay pigeon shooting on the local ranges. This, I believe, was an interest of my favourite instructor Freddy. He seemed to know what he was doing, clearing the guns before using them, setting up the shooting safe area and arranging the clay pull machine. The Platoon Sergeant went through a teaching induction while Freddy drove off in his flash blue Escort XR3I, grabbing our attention as he wheel-spun off. All he needed was a spoiler on the back. Tit. He returned 10 minutes later with a passenger in his prickmobile. It was only his wife. I noticed her immediately. Freddy was about to show off his wife to the remainder of the platoon. I didn't want to look at the car. They both got out as I watched through my peripheral vision. I did not want Freddy or the other instructors to see me looking towards his wife. After all, she and Freddy's insecurities led me to be bullied from Day 1. Was this Freddy's final attempt to alienate the rest of the staff? Remember, I was now becoming the best recruit in the platoon and his attempts at making me quit had failed up until now.

One by one we took control of the shotgun and attempted to shoot the clays. Freddy was bouncing around like Zebedee and making a poor attempt at coming across as the alpha male, gobbing off and swearing at recruits, showing his wife that he had some sort of power over us young lads. Inevitably, it was my turn to take centre show. I didn't give a fuck that Freddy's Mrs was there or watching. She was probably having a good look at my arse as I took the alert stance.

"Pull," I shouted. I pulled the trigger twice, missing my desired target both times. Well, it was my first attempt and many of the other lads had failed miserably to hit also. With me, of course, missing meant that Freddy could try to belittle me in front of his darling wife.

"Inman, you fucking mong." I gritted my teeth and tightened my frame, an action that I would use to portray control. "You're fucking shit. Haven't we taught you the Marksmanship Principles?"

"Yes, Corporal."

He continued, "Get in the press up position and begin." I had been in this position many times over the last 8 weeks; this was not strange for me, just another form of punishment.

"What are the 4 Marksmanship Principles?"

I started reciting them;

- The position and hold must be firm enough to support the weapon;
- The weapon must point naturally at the target without any undue physical effort;
- Sight alignment, i.e. aiming must be correct;
- The shot must be released and followed through without any disturbance to the position held.

(Bloody hell. That's the first time I have recited that in approximately ten years. Shows it never leaves you)!

Anyway, I continued with my press ups and simultaneously shouting the Marksmanship Principles. This went on for approximately 2 minutes. Then I heard my Platoon Sergeant tell me to get up. I rose to my feet and stood to attention.

"Fall back in, Inman," I was instructed. As I rejoined the group I noticed Freddy's wife was sat in the car. I noticed my section commander speaking to Freddy. It started to get a little heated. Was my Corporal sticking up for me? Freddy continued to his car and got in the driver's seat. I couldn't help but look. I saw his wife going off at him and him in return arguing with her. He glanced towards me. I could see he was angry. Again, he quickly sped away like a typical boy racer. He had just made himself look a right prick not only in front of his wife but his colleagues and us recruits. That was it. The platoon knew there was some history between Freddy and I. I wasn't going to say anything until I left those gates after our passing out parade.

We made it into the final week. We had our final test exercise and returned to camp to clean all our kit. The hard work had been done. All we had to look forward to was preparing for our upcoming parade in front of our family and friends. One by one we were ordered into our section commander's office where he read us our personal reports that would be sent to our next instructors at ITC (Infantry Training Centre) Catterick where our training would continue for a further 12 weeks. I was the last of the section to have his report read.

"Come in, Inman." My Corporal was sat behind his desk. He invited me to sit down and relax. "Before we go any further I want you to tell me about Corporal Tarvey (Freddy) and his wife."

"There is nothing to tell, Corporal," I responded. He went on to tell me that Corporal Tarvey had wanted me out and that they had all tried their best to achieve that goal. Corporal Tarvey had led them to believe that I had made advances to his wife. I told my section commander that this was definitely not the case at all. I said I had spoken to her on many occasions because I was a local at the bar where she worked and we got on well and regarded each other as friends. I continued to say that it was obvious that they all wanted to break me because of that reason but that was never going to happen. I had done nothing wrong and it was Corporal Tarvey's insecurity that made him feel anger towards me. I honestly believe at that point he believed me. My section commander went on to read my final report. I was expecting it to slate me because of what I had been through over the last 10 weeks, but this was not the case. My report was really good, but it was the truth. I had worked hard, excelled in my fitness and pursued for excellence on the drill square, and my knowledge of the basics was impressive. I had done incredibly well. My hard work and stubbornness had paid off in the end. I had earnt the respect of my section commander.

He shook my hand and told me, "I would have you in my section in battalion tomorrow." This was the highest compliment he could have given me. I walked out of his office knowing I had earnt that respect.

Passing out day came. We were all excited as we would get a week's leave before reporting to Vimy Barracks in Catterick. I got out of bed and made my way to the shower to prepare myself for my first formal parade. My parents and Vicki would be there to see me graduate. After my shower I made my way back to my section room. Freddy was laid on my bed. I didn't want to, but I stood to attention.

"I tried to break you from Day 1," he informed me.

"I know, but that was never going to happen," I responded. He went on to say that he had a little respect for me as I took a lot of shit, more than any other recruit that had been through Gulevant Platoon's door. I think that this was his way of acknowledging my efforts. He went on to say that should he see me near his wife again, I would regret it. *Fuck it,* I thought, *what can he do to me now?* My report was written and it was pass out day. There was only him and me in the room, no witnesses. I went on, "I will be in the pub tonight. If you want to go, we can go?" This was me offering a confrontation with him. "I don't give two fucks about your wife. It's you that has the issue, not her or me." I'd had enough. All the fucking grief this prick had given me over the last ten weeks and he was still threatening me, thinking I would bow down to his demands. No way! *He had his time, it's my turn.* "If you're there then I know we will be dancing." I meant every word. Before he had time to respond to my offer the door to the room opened. The lads started to enter. He got up, stared into my eyes, a gesture which for the first time I returned, he walked away. *Do I have a date tonight?* I thought. I truly hoped so!

We passed out as a platoon and met up with our family and friends. We all went to the NAAFI (Navy, Army, Airforce Institute (Bar)) and had a couple of drinks. It was time to leave Whittington Barracks, basic training complete. We were to report in 7 days' time for Phase 2. I walked out of the gates with my head held high.

As promised, I went to the pub that night with Vicki and some friends. Freddy's young wife was not there. I found out she had left her job. Not only her job, but had left Freddy and moved back south. What a result. I couldn't help but laugh. Was a contributing factor that put the nail in the coffin her witnessing how he tried to belittle me on the clay pigeon shoot? I will never know. My gut feeling is yes. Freddy never came to the bar that evening. What a fucking pussy. If some recruit had offered a showdown with me then I would have made sure I would have been there. Showed his true character! Isn't that what bullies do? Abuse their position of power? And when it came to a level playing field, he couldn't show his face. I would have fucked him up that night for sure. Revenge would have been sweet. I never saw him again. Mark my words, if I ever do see him, he will regret what he put me through.

I thoroughly enjoyed my Phase 2 training at Catterick. It felt completely different. I had a good relationship with my new section commander. He quickly saw that I was a competent soldier who had promise. I continued to be diligent and enthusiastic. I wanted to be regarded as the best recruit in the platoon. I had broken from the shackles of Gulevant Platoon; this enabled me to fly and finally start enjoying my time as a soldier. The following 12 weeks quickly went by. I had the privilege of being awarded 'Best Recruit' on my pass out parade.

On my final night of training before all of us separated to go to our battalions, I told the background story of why the instructors hammered me in Whittington. The lads knew something must have happened. They thought it was piss funny. "I bet you wished you'd shagged her, hey?" one of the Neanderthals piped. I wasn't going to answer.

I left Vimy Barracks. Little did I know that one-day, I would return. Next stop, battalion. I was to report to Clive Barracks, Tern Hill in seven days' time.

I reported to my new battalion. The Staffordshire Regiment (The Prince Of Wales'). Things were very different from training. I was fully trained and embarking on my new career. I still had much to learn but was looking forward to it immensely. I initially worked with the Quartermaster's Department, helping with packing up camp and organising the movement of stores to Hong Kong. Battalion were about to leave but I wouldn't be far behind. I could hardly contain my excitement.

2

BIG TROUBLE IN LITTLE CHINA

I spent my last evening with Vicki, doing the normal stuff that an 18-year-old couple get up to while her parents are downstairs! If I'm to be honest with myself and her, all I wanted to do was to get to the other side of the world. It was all I was thinking about. I was like a child on Christmas Eve. My excitement level was through the roof. All my hours of training and pure bullshit had been for this moment. I felt like I was going on a lads' 18–30s holiday; Hong Kong, the skyscrapers, the lights, the food, the nightlife, and of course the local women. My true army adventure was about to begin. My first tour, a place I could talk about with fondness in years to come when I was in my rocking chair. *All the other lads in the area are just pissing their 9–5 money up the wall on a Friday and Saturday night. I'm the man.* The soldier who thinks he knows it all and is as hard as fuck is representing his country on a foreign patch. *You better be ready for me,* I thought to myself. My bags had been packed for days. I was counting the hours down until my father was to pick me up from Vicki's and make my way to Tern Hill.

The morning came. I'd hardly slept due to the anticipation of my journey ahead. This was not a bad thing as I was about to endure a thirteen-hour flight. I'd be getting ample sleep. I embraced Vicki at the door. Saying goodbye was emotional for Vicki more than me. She was being left behind to continue with her nursing training and I was off on a holiday of a lifetime. I chucked my kit into the boot of my old man's Vauxhall Astra, jumped in and the journey began. A usual forty-minute journey takes the ex-copper, a sensible driver, a generous one hour. We talked on the way about taking care of myself and if I got into any shit then call home immediately. *Yes, yes,* I thought in my head. *Stop going on! What trouble am I going to get into? I'll be safe as houses. I'm a soldier. The army look after me, it's as it is. If one of us is in trouble, we all are. What trouble could I possibly get in? There he goes again, talking shit.* We arrived at the front gates. We both got out, I grabbed my kit and made my way to him to say goodbye. We had only embraced once beforehand, I supposed we should again. We did. *Goodbye, Dad. See you in 5 months.* I don't know how my father was feeling at that moment in time, watching me walk through those large opened gates with the guard asking me for ID as I walked away. Was he upset, proud? I'm not sure. To be honest, I didn't care.

I did not go with the main party. I flew out a few weeks later due to some hospital appointments in regards to my knees. I recall five of us throwing our kit into the back and climbing into a minibus provided by the MT department. We were off. The duty driver was taking us on the road for a few hours to get to Heathrow. We arrived several hours later. Found our check-in gate and booked in. The flight was a civilian British Airways flight. 13 hours 55 minutes later, I was in Hong Kong. The first thing I remember was the smell. It had a real city stench to it, a musty, dirty smell. I walked out of the airport with the other four lads and the first thing I saw was a McDonalds. *Great,* I thought. *If all else fails I will survive on that.* I looked around and saw the locals busy rushing around, pushing, shouting, scurrying around. It was like something I had only seen on the TV. Before this, the busiest thing I had seen was New Street Station in Birmingham. We were greeted in the main terminal by the duty driver this end. We all piled into a DPM pattern Land Rover; making it obvious we were British Forces. Not like this mattered. We had no enemies over here. This tour was a luxury. It was the dream tour that every unit wanted; bit of guard duty, bit of live firing, bog standard exercise and, most importantly, R&R (rest and recuperation). I would have paid thousands for this experience. I was the lucky one. I was getting it courtesy of the army. It was a warm evening in September. I was looking out of the back of the Land Rover as we made our way to camp, a base called Stonecutters Island – a military base used by the British Army for over a century. It was small and well maintained, and far away from the hustle and bustle of Hong Kong Island and Kowloon. To get to the mainland we would have to jump on a small power boat provided by the navy to ferry us to and from camp. The short journey would take thirty minutes. A journey I would embark on hundreds of times during my stint at Stonecutters. Sometimes on the journey I'd be pissed, other times tired, going on shopping trips, sightseeing, sometimes on a run for the NCOs wanting me to get them a McDonald's. Every time though I would enjoy the journey, looking at the ferry and small traditional boats in the huge harbour, observing the lights on the tall skyscrapers, trying to take in everything and place it into my memory bank.

On arriving at Stonecutters we were dropped off at the guardroom. I was shown to my platoon lines. I was a new member to C Company 7 Platoon. I seemed to fit in well. As well as it can go being a CROW. This is the name for a new bloke. Fresh meat. A new dogsbody to do all the shit jobs. Senior soldiers used to get a buzz from calling you a crow. They would never use your real name. All they could do was look at you and shout demands with the word 'crow' at the end. *Polish my boots, crow. Run to the NAAFI, crow. Give me a fag, crow.* You get the picture. It's a phase all new soldiers have to go through; you need to gain respect not only from the NCOs but also the senior private soldiers. Once the respect was gained you began to fit in. Then when the next crow would join the platoon you advanced a step, and there was some other poor crow to do the shit jobs. One day I could shout my orders at the crow. As I was the current crow who had just flown in to Hong Kong, I was the fresh meat for a while that did ALL the shit jobs. It was a heavy burden as I would not have anyone to replace my title as crow until we returned from Hong Kong. *It is going to be a long five months,* I thought. *Maybe not the luxury holiday I was expecting after all?* On receiving my daily orders with the word 'crow' at the end, I would just carry out the task, no questions asked. I knew that if I should gob off and tell them to fuck off, the shit would really fall. You risk consequences of not fitting in with the rest, like getting a banging (punch or kick). I just kept it in my head that my turn would come. *I will be the senior soldier in a year or two. Ride it out, keep my head down, do as I'm told and everything will work out like it should do.* I think in *The Lion King* they call it the circle of life. That's probably the best way to explain the pecking order and how you are expected to behave when joining a tight-knit platoon like mine. All in all, they were good lads. I would have to iron uniforms, polish boots, do NAAFI runs, and jump on that boat for thirty minutes to get my section commander a large Big Mac meal. And if it came back cold I'd be fucked. Work that one out. One-hour round trip and bring the fries home warm!!!! Because I loved the boat trip and wanted to take as many of the sights in as I could, I would do it without complaint. Plus, if I was not in the platoon lines, it meant I couldn't be ordered to do anything else.

As time went by and I started to prove I wasn't a fucking mong (a word used to show little intelligence), the platoon quickly came around. I was not seen as the enemy but just a hard-working young 18-year-old who had ambition and potential. I was showing evidence of good intelligence, diligence, enthusiasm, maturity, and excellent soldiering in battlefield skills, and my fitness level was through the ceiling. I was without doubt growing to become an impressive individual. With this new notoriety I was growing in confidence. I took immense pride in my cap badge, regimental history, the platoon, my uniform and what being a soldier meant. It was not just a job to me. It was *me*. It was who I was supposed to be. It was all in all my DNA.

After a month or so of settling down and becoming inaugurated into the platoon, I really started to enjoy the experience. I felt a belonging. I genuinely felt liked by my peers, but still needed to know my place as the crow. The platoon went about its guard duties of looking after the Prince of Wales' building, the head office of the British Army, located in Victoria Harbour. This is now known as The Chinese People's Liberation Council of Hong Kong and is overlooked by The Peak on Hong Kong Island. We also guarded a number of military bases in the region, including a base/airfield in Shek Kong amongst others, and protected the Governor of Hong Kong's residence. During our guard stint of a month we worked hard. Sections of the platoon were broken down and located in various locations. We would work 24-hour shifts and then take 24 hours off, known in the trade as day-on, day-off. We would guard premises then come off guard, have a quick shit, shower and shave then hit Hong Kong Island or Kowloon: either on a shopping spree, taking in the local sights or hitting the bars. Planet Hollywood was always popular due to good food and cocktails. It was also a place where we could frequent with Western girls. The lads in battalion would often hit an area called Wan Chai. It's a well-known busy commercial area. During evening times it would be packed with local food stores. At night is when Wan Chai really comes to life. Crowds of people would descend onto Lockhart Road to get to the bars and nightclubs. The most popular spots were Carnegie's, China Jump (ask the England football team. Remember the dentist chair? I sat in it before Gazza's escapade), Rick's Café, Joe Bananas, Mad Dogs and the Big Apple. The famous Happy Valley Racecourse is also close by.

One day, after completing our day-on at the Prince of Wales' building, we ran back to our barracks and went through the 3 'S's. A group of us hit the town. We went through the normal routine; hit the bars, had some food and went back home for a bit of sleep before hitting it again in the evening. Four of us found a bar that we had not heard of before. On entry we paid a set price but didn't have to pay for individual beers. A one-off payment, but that was it, waitress service and unlimited booze. Perfect. The four of us sat down on a circular table and started downing the Buds. The group of us were later joined by two girls. One girl was beautiful, she really stood out. Even though I had good looks and was getting a reputation as a ladies' man, I didn't think this girl was into me. To my delight, I was wrong. I thought I'd hit jackpot. She made it perfectly clear it was only me she was interested in. I felt like king dick. Approximately an hour later we were joined by another two lads from the platoon, one being an NCO. Lance Corporal Giuseppe. He was a bully. He didn't like me and, to be perfectly honest, my gut feeling in regards to him wasn't positive. I have always had a sixth sense when it comes to what my gut says. They joined us at our table and continued to drink. The Buds were going down well and the company, apart from L/Cpl Giuseppe, was cool. He noticed that the stunning long-haired blonde was into me. Red mist must have come down. He, of course being an alpha male, thought he could knock me down and run away with the girl. She wasn't having it, and to be honest nor was I. I was the crow but when it comes to it, she was with me. He was showing me disrespect but also her. He crossed the line. However, instead of me putting him in his place, she did. I spent that night in her company and the rest of the lads made their way back to barracks.

"Make sure you're back for guard in the morning, Inman."

"Yes, Corporal," I said. *Fuck off,* in my head. This is why I was in Hong Kong. *This is where the party starts.*

I made it to camp the following morning with plenty of time to spare to iron my stones (grey ceremonial uniform), have a shower and shave, and make myself presentable to the highest standard. On making sure my boots were immaculate before I placed them onto my Size 7 feet, in walks Giuseppe to the room. Four of us shared this room. We had four beds, four bedside tables and a wardrobe each. We attempted to segregate them slightly in order to have some own private space. On Giuseppe entering, I knew I had problems. The other lads went quiet but observed Giuseppe inform me that I made him look like a mug, and should I ever do it again, he would fuck me up. On completing the sentence he took the wide stance and threw a right hook. I saw it coming but probably due to the excess Budweiser intake, I failed to dodge. The strike hit me square on the side of my cheek. *Was that it?* I thought. *And you're supposed to be tasty.* I looked at him as if it didn't bother me. The strike itself didn't. He hit like a pussy. However, from this moment on I knew he and I would have problems. On returning to the UK, Giuseppe handed in his one year's notice and left. He would learn my name in the future due to upcoming circumstances. Last I heard, he became a smack head. Not surprised, the deadbeat. I could honestly say if I ever come across this c**t again, I would fuck him up. Stand over him and remind him of that cheap faggot punch. This happened in '95 and I would still like my revenge to this day. I didn't grass. I never mentioned it to anybody. It couldn't have been much; it didn't make a mark on my handsome face. It also demonstrated to the platoon that I could be trusted. There's no room for inside grasses in a platoon environment. We all needed to trust each other when it came down to it.

Time rolled on. We completed some jungle training followed by a 5-day exercise, had a little R&R and I was genuinely enjoying my experience. I would write to Vicki once weekly if I could be arsed, phone home occasionally. I was popular with my platoon and popular with the ladies when we went out in Wan Chai. Life was good. This is what I joined the army for, to live like this.

I recall going out one night with a few of us. We decided to hit a local nightclub. I got completely drunk and was busting some moves on the dancefloor like John Travolta. I noticed a beautiful girl at the bar, Chinese in orientation. She was wearing a traditional red Chinese dress with a very high neck, concealing her upper body modestly. She was to become my target. I noticed she in return was admiring my dance moves and was having a good look herself. This gave me the confidence to approach her with the aim of chatting her up. I wandered over and started to talk to the beautiful girl. The music was loud so I could barely make out what she was saying. After half an hour or so I found myself kissing the girl and thinking I had the winning lottery ticket. I looked over to the lads who were looking at the pair of us giggling like school boys.

"What you lot laughing at?"

"Inni, it's a bloke, mate. You're copping off with a geezer!"

I was drunk and adamant that I had the hottest girl in the club. I returned to her. I looked at her face closely. She was genuinely beautiful, but were the lads right? *One way to find out,* I thought. I would try my Crocodile Dundee trick. I decided to reach between her legs. I was met by a smile while holding a handful of meat. The lads were right. The tossers could have stopped me before I kissed him. I would never live this down.

Even to this day, my wife takes great pleasure in telling people that I kissed a bloke.

Our Platoon Commander arranged for us to go on a boat trip one afternoon. It was supposed to be a platoon bonding exercise. We would have a traditional Chinese fishing boat and travel from village to village, taking in the sights of a different side of the area. We met our boat and had a local fisherman escort us from village to village. The boat was stacked with crates of lager. We could drink as much as we wanted as long as we represented ourselves and the cap badge in the correct manner. It was a good day up until then. The sun was shining; we were seeing new things and enjoying food from different traditions. On returning to Stonecutters we all made it clear we wanted to continue with the drinking. We ran back to our rooms, went through the 3 'S's, got a new set of threads on and out we went to catch the boat to take us to Hong Kong Island and Wan Chai. Little did I know that this would be the last time I would see Wan Chai, most of my friends and any other set of civilian clothing until I reached UK soil.

As the night went on we would hit bar after bar, getting increasingly pissed. The lads were dropping off one by one. In the end there were two of us left, me, and a senior soldier by the name of Johnno. Johnno was a bit of a wide boy who had come from another regiment due to reasons I can't quite recall. He was a good soldier and respected in C Company and 7 Platoon. Because he was respected in the quarters, it meant I had to respect him also and probably strive to be like him. I suppose I looked up to him. We were in Rick's Café, dancing and enjoying ourselves. I personally had been frequenting this venue a lot and had got to know the bar staff and waitresses really well. The staff recognised me and showed me preferential treatment when ordering drinks. Johnno asked me, "How much money do we have between us?" I searched my pockets and realised very quickly that I had enough to cover the taxi fare back to

Stonecutters. "That's all we have, mate," I informed Johnno. *Looks like the night is coming to an end,* I thought. How wrong could I be?

Johnno looked disappointed. If I'm to be honest, I wasn't. I had had enough. To say I wasn't a big drinker, the day had taken its toll on me. At this point I witnessed an action that I genuinely believe wrote the path of my life. Johnno looked around the busy bar. He noticed a lady's handbag in his near vicinity. He glanced around again and then quickly, in a sweeping motion, dragged the said bag along the bar towards himself and disguised it under his jacket in one swift move. I froze. *What the fuck is he doing?* I thought. Johnno looked at me and made his way immediately out of the bar and on to the streets of Wan Chai. I couldn't believe what I was seeing. Within minutes I went from looking at this soldier with admiration and wanting to be like him to losing all respect. I didn't want to be like him. He could have got me right in the shit, and for what? A fucking handbag that might have some wedge in so we could have another drink? I didn't want to be a part of it. I didn't want to see Johnno again that night. I had enough in my pocket to get that taxi home to Stonecutters and that's what I was going to do. I thought if I stayed in the bar for 20 minutes, then by the time I left he would be fast gone. I would jump in a taxi and make my way home to camp. Simple plan. *My hands are clean. I've done nothing wrong.* I went along with my plan. I hovered around the bar for 20 minutes, making sure my drink lasted that long. Time went by and it was time to leave. *Here we go.* I walked to the exit and made my way outside. The street was almost empty. Almost. Johnno was in the alleyway waiting for me. My plan was compromised. Johnno had been patiently waiting for me to emerge from the club. He waited those 20 minutes clutching at the stolen handbag. As I saw him, my heart dropped. It was at this point I went into crow mode. Instead of doing what was right, I decided to revert back to being told what to do. I had in the past trusted the system. I needed to put my trust into Johnno that he would get us out of this situation. I could rest assured that I had done nothing wrong and played no active part in committing this crime. Johnno made his way across the road, approximately 200 metres to the Big Apple, a popular nightclub in the area, and very popular with the lads as they would often get lucky with the local girls. I myself had been in there many times. I knew the layout of the place.

"Come with me," he ordered. The entrance to the Big Apple was at ground level with a bouncer situated in the single doorframe, a typical neon light over his head with a huge red apple illuminated in the night. There were stairs that dropped away from the entrance into the club itself after making a right turn at the bottom few steps, making us feel that we were underground. As we entered the club we immediately found ourselves in a dark smoke-filled room with customers dancing to the latest Ministry of Sound tunes. Johnno instructed me to follow him again. He made his way to the toilets. He went straight into the one and only cubicle. I stood at the pisspot pretending to urinate, ironically shitting myself. Johnno spent moments rifling through the handbag. He opened the door and invited me in, making it feel as an order from a senior bloke to his crow. I made a huge mistake and entered, closing the cubicle door and locking it behind me. The handbag was placed on top of the toilet lid. Johnno opened it. I could see a purse with cards and cash in, a set of keys and ladies' toiletries. Johnno took the cash out and placed it into his pocket. As I turned to leave in a rush, leaving the bag behind, I was met face to face by an employee of Chinese origin peering over the top of the cubicle door. We were caught. I opened the door slightly and the discoverer yanked it open. There were two in total. They never said a word to us but grabbed me firmly by the right arm and frogmarched me to the centre of the dance floor with Johnno close behind. I could see the two Chinese men were signalling to the bar to grab the attention of what appeared to be the head barman. I later found out he was the owner, a tall white Englishman who I would later come to face.

I have always been taught to never run from anything. Face what you have done, be honest and truthful and things will work out. My gut feeling which, remember, is usually right and which I always go with told me different on this occasion. The Chinese glass collector who held me and marched me to the heart of the dancefloor momentarily let go of my arm. I didn't need to think twice. I ran. I knew they would have to be quick to catch me as my fitness level was outstanding, and coupled with the fear and adrenaline running through my veins there was only going to be one winner. I made my way like lightning to the staircase. I climbed the first two steps and turned to the left to navigate the remainder to get to ground level. I felt what can only be described as a rugby tackle attempt on my right foot. Whoever it was chasing me had missed and stumbled. This was my chance. I continued up the stairs with ferocious pace. Then I saw the bouncer. *Shit.* He was huge. Looking back, he reminded me of the chauffer-cum-bodyguard Oddjob from the James Bond film *Goldfinger*. There was only one way this was going to go. He had his back to me, but as he was alerted to my chase he turned to face me. I caught him off-guard. I punched him square on the chin. He stumbled back, giving me the adequate space to flee and make my way to relevant safety for the time being.

I ran down the street faster than I had ever moved before. I was wearing quite distinctive clothing at the time. Instinct kicked in. *I need to get out of these clothes,* I thought, *before the local police get hold of me.* Hong Kong's streets had market stalls all over, selling every kind of fake branded polo shirts you could imagine. If it was in the UK then HMRC (Customs and Excise) would have had a field day. It didn't stop us topping up on Ralph Lauren, Calvin Klein and Tommy Hilfiger the list goes on. I binned my black jacket in the nearest bin. This left me with a white T-shirt. This T-shirt had to be replaced. I went to the closest stall and purchased the cheapest red shirt, put it on and ditched the white one. I flagged down a taxi and offered him all the remaining money I had in my hand. Luckily, he accepted my offer and we made our way to Stonecutters Island. During the taxi journey I was wondering how Johnno was. What was I going to do when I returned to camp? Surely I would be safe and protected by the regiment?

By the time I got back to camp it was approximately 1am. I got to my lines and decided to wake my section commander and tell him everything. By this time I felt completely sober. He listened to the story and replied, "You're both fucked. Go to the guardroom and inform the Provost staff." I ran to the guardroom and asked the guard commander to wake the Provost staff (regimental police). The Provost Corporal was not happy that I got him up, so that didn't start well. Once he had his coffee, I explained what had happened that night. I felt safe and truly believed I would be fine now. The Provost Corporal telephoned the RMP (Royal Military Police), who quickly came and interviewed me and took a statement. The red cap monkey (nickname for RMP officer) bastard did me right in. He escorted me directly to Wan Chai Police Station. So much for being looked after. I wasn't cuffed but as I walked through the door of Wan Chai Police Station, I knew instantly I was proper in the shit. The station reminded me of something out of *Hill Street Blues*, the American police show. There was a reception area with locals waiting around. I was taken to the front desk; somehow the bastards were expecting me. Those fucking red cap monkeys gave them the heads-up. Immediately I was taken into the back, up some stairs and straight into an interview room. I was told to wait. The red cap had left by now, so I was on my own in a foreign police station. It felt like I had been fed to the lions. The locals didn't particularly like us

British soldiers. We got pissed, flashed the cash and thought we owned the fucking place. We must have looked like right arrogant twats. Therefore when they had the opportunity to fuck up a soldier, they jumped at the chance. A detective, maybe the equivalent of our CID, walked in and introduced himself in a professional manner. He spoke very good English so I was confident I could get my story across, get my hand slapped and be back for breakfast. The officer went through what had happened in the hours before and made notes.

Things then took a turn for the worse. I was not charged with anything but taken to the back of the station. I was frogmarched outside to where I entered a large courtyard. Lots of police vehicles were parked up, white with a prominent red stripe running horizontally. There were so many I couldn't count them. In the distance I could see what appeared to be a cage. It almost looked like a chicken coup. As I was being led towards it I recognised a face: Johnno. He glanced up and had the fucking audacity to smile at me. He was sat on the floor inside the cage. There were no chairs, no toilet, nothing, just a fucking chicken coup of a cage. We could stand up and take about 6–8 paces in length and maybe 2–3 paces in width. We were the only pair in there. Where were the rest of the prisoners? We couldn't be the only two? This was Wan Chai – the station looked buzzing – and this wasn't a proper cell that we were in, surely. We were in a cage in the station's car park. Not only that, but the cage could only fit approximately five people in at a push. This didn't add up. I sat on the ground next to Johnno and asked how he was. He told me that he had been brought straight to the station after being arrested in the Big Apple. He was interviewed and then placed in the cage. I told him what I had done and that the RMPs were aware of where we were. He then went onto apologise.

"I got you in this shit, I will get you out. It was my entire fault. Don't worry, I will tell them everything." This was music to my ears. That's all I needed to hear, it would be a matter of time before I would be released, especially when Johnno tells the authorities exactly what happened and it was all his doing.

After half an hour or so, I heard an engine start in the courtyard. I looked up and saw a large white van backing up towards the cage. A police officer got out of the passenger side, made his way to the rear of the van and opened the double doors. The van was empty. It had seats running down the sides from the double doors up to the driving compartment. There were steps up to the van. The same officer approached the cage and unlocked it. We were being moved, I thought. Another officer joined the first and proceeded to handcuff just one of my arms, leaving the other free. They did the same to Johnno. We were grabbed and shoved towards the van. That's where they wanted us, so that's where we went. There was a prominent chrome bar that ran above the seats near the roof of the vehicle. This bar also ran adjacent to the seats. I'm sure it's for the purpose to hold onto while travelling. In this case, it was for something else. The hand that was cuffed was raised above my head. The copper hung the cuffs over the bar and cuffed the other hand. My hands were now above my head and cuffed around the chrome bar. Simultaneously, the same had happened to Johnno who was sat opposite me. I felt exposed. I was then to see the scariest thing in my life. Two other officers, who before now I had not seen, joined the party. The original two got back into the driving compartment and the new pair of goons climbed into the back to join us. The four officers looked frightening. They were of Chinese origin, slim with quite fierce demeanours. My gut, again, was telling me this was not going well. Again, my gut was correct. The doors were closed and the engine started. We left the courtyard and made our way onto the streets of Hong Kong. The windows were quite large but tinted and in the night light I could see very little. The journey didn't last long, ten minutes maximum. Enough time for my arms to be aching like crazy. I kept moving my fingers to try to keep some blood flow. I could feel the blood pooling. During the journey not a word was spoken by Johnno, me or the coppers. I looked at Johnno and opened my eyes to him as wide as I could get them. I was trying to signal that this was going down. He returned the signal.

The engine finally came to a stop. I couldn't see a single street light. I don't know where we were, but my guess would be a car park or derelict area where the police van could not be seen. The driving compartment doors opened and the first two officers dismounted. Within seconds, the back doors were opened. The officers had batons, which were approximately fifty centimetres long and the diameter of a fifty pence coin. The batons were drawn by the two sitting in the back with us. My head went down with my chin on my chest. I crossed my left leg over the right to protect my bollocks. It began. Shots came raining down. Firstly on the rib cage. Shot after shot. I felt the batons at a frequent violent pace and then a break where punches were thrown. The punches would land on the face, chin, cheek and eye socket. Batons began on the legs. My legs soon went dead. I didn't say a word. I just wanted it over. If I gobbed off, I would get more. I wanted them to feel pity on me. That was round one. The first two fuckers had their shot at the British soldiers, now it was the other pair of bastards' turn. *Here we go again.* With every blow the pain became less and less. I must have just been going numb or maybe I was concussed. The main action was at the legs and rib cage, with the occasional blow to the head. I had my eyes closed for the majority of the rampage. I could hear Johnno whining and grinning and shouting the occasional "stop, stop". I'm not sure if I blanked out; I think I may have. It finally came to an end. My wrists were sore from the chafing of the cuffs. I was thankful that my bollocks were still intact. I didn't raise my head. I kept my chin on my chest and my eyes tightly closed. I felt the two scumbag motherfuckers get out of the back and a conversation happened in Chinese between the fuckers. I heard the driver's compartment doors open and felt the van suspension move as two coppers got in. The other bedwetters entered the van and sat next to us. Not a word was spoken. The double doors were shut and the engine started. We survived. I opened my eyes and looked opposite me towards Johnno. He was beaten up badly. I gathered I pretty much looked the same. I had the headache from hell, maybe a combination of the last 24 hours drinking and the fucking beating from hell from four bent coppers. The van made its way back to the station. How did they think they could get away with this? The coppers at the station must be in on it or it must be a done thing, an SOP (standard operating procedure) for these bastards. On returning to the station and the courtyard, the doors were opened. The officers released my hands from the cuffs and my arms dropped. They must have been elevated for at least 45 minutes. They were in agony. We were guided out of the van, thankfully being held up, because my legs had nothing in them, no strength at all. I felt like a boxer who had been knocked out and couldn't get up, no matter how hard I tried. We were gently placed back into our cage. I sat on the floor looking up at the sky. We were kindly thrown a blanket. Johnno and I cuddled up like a pair of kittens. We saw the rest of the night out in the cage. At that moment in time we had nothing. All we had was each other. We needed to stick together from this moment forward. We now had a bond. Proper, 'brothers in arms'.

Morning came. We had had a little sleep – an hour or two – maybe helped by some concussion. What was the day to bring? We were taken from the cage into the station. I started to feel a bit warmer. None of the police officers we saw that morning mentioned our clearly visible injuries. We were placed in an interview room and left alone. We were sat behind a desk on two plastic chairs. We were facing a door in a small room painted in a drab grey colour. I could hear talking. One accent was definitely of West Midlands origin. The door swung open and I could see initially DPM material walk in. That meant we were safe for the meantime. It was an officer from our battalion. His job role for that 24-hour period was orderly officer, in charge of any business outside normal regimental duties. I recognised his face but didn't know his name. Johnno and I simultaneously stood to our feet, with difficulty, and to attention. This movement was not executed as well as if on the drill square. We had been beaten hours before. He sat down in front of us and asked how we were.

"Sir, we have been beaten up by the police."

The orderly officer replied "Well, when in Rome, boys."

You bastard, I thought. *We have just been fucking beaten up and you are sat in front of us not giving two fucks, you wanker, probably only in the army in order to get Daddy's trust fund.* The officer went on to inform us that we were in a huge amount of trouble. However, battalion had bargained with the local force and they had agreed to release us into the care of the regiment as long as we were placed under close arrest in regimental custody. This had to be better than being in this environment. Within half an hour we were released. The orderly officer led us in the direction of the duty driver and Land Rover. We jumped into the back and watched the station disappear as we made our way home to Stonecutters. During the journey back, I spent time going through what had happened in my head. *Hold on a minute. Look at the worst-case scenario. If we do get done for this crime what would we be looking at? If it was back in the UK it would be a caution, maybe a fine or some community service. I'm not going to get sent down for this. It's a handbag, not the fucking Crown Jewels. This is, after all, still British Sovereignty. It's not China just yet.*

We made it back to camp. We entered the gates and the duty driver took us immediately to the guardroom where we dismounted. The Provost staff marched us at double pace directly to the RSM's (Regimental Sergeant Major's) office, where we were briefed that we were going in front of the Commanding Officer. We got marched in. We received the most almighty bollocking and were placed into regimental custody until our court date was announced.

Our time in battalion cells was rough. Our uniform was a dirty green boiler suit and boots with no laces. We were definitely not to wear our regimental headdress as we didn't deserve the privilege. We were treated like pure shit, spending days polishing brass and scrubbing floors. We had daily 'beastings' (excessive physical exercise), which took even me to the limit. We would be hammered until we were physically sick. We were in hell. When we dined in the cookhouse other soldiers would look at us, or should I say 'stare'. Our bruises were coming out nicely. You could clearly see the black, blue and yellow over our faces, and as for our ribs and legs – well, they were a different story. I wish to this day we had photographs of the injuries we sustained in that brutal attack. The bottom line is we were treated like the scum of the earth even by our own. Like I said, we only had each other. We were guilty before proven guilty. After five days we were marched up to the Adjutant's office. He informed us that we were in court the following day. We were to be released from detention and spend the evening preparing for our court appearance. We were told we needed to report to the guardroom at 6pm, 10pm and 6am the following morning. This was called open arrest. At least we were out of the cells. We were both handed our passports in case we were imprisoned by the court. Imprisoned? Surely this wouldn't be happening?

We made our way to our platoon lines and sat on our beds. The first thing I wanted was a shower and change. Everyone in the platoon wanted to know the story. I told them everything. In fairness, Johnno told his side too. Fair play, he didn't try and share responsibility, he took the lot. He told me that he would plead 'guilty' to any charge in court and then he could be a witness for me to say I had nothing to do with the theft. My confidence was growing that this experience was coming to an end, for me at least. Things were not going to turn out as I planned or expected.

I went onto the roof of the accommodation where we could sunbathe and look over Hong Kong. It was a good view. I had been on the roof for an hour when I was joined by a section commander in the company. He was from a different platoon but he was a good bloke. Cpl Bashford was his name. He had heard the story of events and felt for me that I had been caught up in these shenanigans. He didn't like Johnno and saw me as quite naive. He asked if I had my passport.

"Yes," I replied.

"Well, I have a friend who runs a scuba diving business in Macau." He offered to give me some cash and the name and address of his friend. He would look after me. He continued to suggest that when the regiment return to the UK, I could catch a flight home and report back to unit. I would obviously be done for being absent without leave but at least I would get home safe, serve a sentence for being AWOL, then crack on with my career. It was an option. I thought about it, if I'm honest. I would report to the guardroom at 10pm, then jump the fence, get to the airport and get a flight. I would have 8 hours to get out of Hong Kong before battalion realised I'd absconded when I didn't report back to the guardroom at 6am. It was an option. I would be lying if I said I didn't contemplate it. Would I get away with it? If I didn't, I would look even more guilty and probably be in even more shit. I have also previously mentioned that I was brought up to face my responsibilities and not run from them. *Thanks for the offer, Bash. I appreciate it, but I'm going to face this and plead 'not guilty'. Anyway, what's the worst that can happen? A fine? Community service?*

I got a little sleep that night. In the morning we both made our way to the guardroom, where we were driven to the High Court of Hong Kong. We were met by a solicitor that would represent us from the RAF. We went into the courtroom and proceedings began. The judge was British, which was a slight comfort. Our solicitor must have informed the court that Johnno was going to plead 'guilty' as he was first up. The judge stated the crime of theft and asked Johnno for his plea.

"Guilty," Johnno replied. He kept to his word so he could be a witness for me to say I had no part. All was going as planned. The shock came when the judge gave a custodial sentence of six months' imprisonment. What? Six months! He only stole a handbag. Six months! Our faces must have been a picture. Johnno was led to the side to witness my plea. The judge again stated the crime and asked me for my plea.

"Not guilty," I responded. A trial date was to be set in the future. In the meantime, I too would be imprisoned on remand while my trial happened. We were to be sent to Stanley Prison. Before we left the court I had a meeting with my solicitor to go through the process of my trial. I would be imprisoned in the same prison as Johnno. He would be serving a sentence but I wouldn't be. The solicitor wanted as much information as possible to prepare a case for my trial. I had Johnno to be my witness.

"It doesn't work like that here," my solicitor informed me. Johnno had in the eyes of the law committed a crime and admitted to it. Therefore, his witness statement was viewed as worthless. He was a proven thief and not of honest character. What he said in court was worthless. *Already my case is crumbling,* I thought to myself. That was all I had to go on. I asked about fingerprints. The bag would have nothing of mine on. The police did not check for fingerprints at all. Again, this was a blow for me. I had no Johnno to say I didn't take an active role in stealing the bag, and I didn't have physical evidence to back it up. Then I got hit with even better news. If, when my trial happened, I got found guilty, then I would be sentenced to a longer stint than Johnno's six months because it would appear that I had wasted time and resources. Not only that, but my time serving on remand did not count towards any sentence I might receive.

"So you're telling me I could serve longer than Johnno?"

"Yes." Why wasn't I told this before? Finally, there was no time off in Hong Kong for good behaviour. Six months for Johnno means six months. If you got sentenced, you would also receive the full custodial term. This just got better!

We were escorted through the court into a car park and into the back of a prison wagon. We were already handcuffed. We had a 30-minute journey to Stanley Prison. I told Johnno what the solicitor had told me.

"You've fucked me right up. I'm going to end up serving longer than you." Johnno held his head low and didn't respond. Little did I know I was about to serve 2 ½ months on remand.

It was a long journey to the prison. So much was going through my brain. *How did I get into this mess?* Then I thought about my parents. *How would they feel if they knew their son of 18 years of age was in a foreign prison and didn't know when he was getting out? Vicki. I haven't spoken to her since this whole escapade took place. They all must think I've vanished from the face of the planet. What's going to happen in regards to my military career? What's this place going to be like? I've seen the TV programmes about foreign prisons. Can I protect myself?* I knew that I had to go in with the attitude that I didn't give a fuck. Now I really needed to man up, show no signs of weakness and if I needed to fight, then god damn, I'd fight. I wanted to show I had some swagger. Even at 18 when we think we know it all, we know far from it. I needed to learn quickly and effectively otherwise this place would probably get the better of me. I was mentally preparing myself. I expected the worst, so anything better was a bonus.

We arrived. The engine stopped and the doors opened. I got

out and immediately looked around. The sun shone brightly so at first all I could do was squint my eyes because of the sun beaming down. I immediately became frightened. The vehicle we were escorted in had stopped on a road between two basketball pitches. The pitches were surrounded by extremely high fences. Inside these fences were the inmates, hundreds of them. They had stopped their recreation time of playing basketball and approached the fences to view the new detainees. It was a harrowing vision. Metres away from me were countless Chinese men staring. They all looked as though they could handle themselves. I had to start as I meant to go on.

"What?" I shouted. I was looking directly at one of them. He changed his facial expression and took a step back. I was agitated and the fear turned into aggression. I looked at Johnno and shrugged my shoulders. He must have thought, *what the fuck is he doing? Is he on a death wish?* The inmate's fingers were clenched at the fence. Eyes were piercing us. As though they had not seen a white guy in the prison before.

We were quickly processed by the prison authorities and introduced to our wing. I felt comfort from the fact that we were segregated. We were placed on a European wing, so we weren't going to be the only white lads in there. The wing didn't have many detainees and they all looked to get along OK. Our attire was a horrid boiler suit which rode above the ankles and a pair of white/cream plastic flip-flops. Everyone was dressed the same. I was given a badge which I needed to attach to my boiler suit. It was in both Chinese and English writing. It simply said 'European'. It was obvious I was fucking European, dickheads. The purpose though was for the cookhouse. There was one cookhouse so this was the point where all wings would meet and eat together. It showed, obviously, what wing I belonged to, but also served a purpose for the chefs to know what type of food I was to be given. Bonus – I didn't have to eat fish heads and rice after all. The food wasn't bad either to be honest. We had a decent variety and it tasted quite good. Portions were a little light, but I wasn't going to be burning the calories I was used to while back in the platoon. We had our exercise time also. As we were European, we got to play football. Bit of a bitch playing it in flip-flops, so as my feet got stronger I would play barefoot. We got to play for an hour a day. It was a bit of fun, nobody took it too seriously. We tried to create national teams, but the closest we got was two Englishmen, five Dutch, one Belgian, two French and an Irish dude. We must have looked like something out of *Escape to Victory*.

Sleeping arrangements were strange, but I quickly got used to it. We had large cells which held eight of us together. The beds were brought out at night and stacked on top of each other during the day in the corner of the cell. The beds were hard, flat plastic with four legs approximately 60cm high. Like a very cheap version of a sun bed. They were bastard uncomfortable. No mattresses, and bedding consisted of two blankets and a pillow (no pillow case). We would lay the beds out in the evening and try to get some sleep, wake in the morning, gather the bedding up and place it immediately into a laundry basket, then stack the beds away. Simple but effective, I suppose. Fresh bedding every night, but it was old and smelt a little musty. This process was purely for hygiene purposes and to keep things simple and orderly.

Another luxury, if you can call it that, was video time. We could congregate in a room with plastic chairs and gather around a small portable TV. We couldn't get a signal on it to watch any English-speaking channels. We did, however, have a video player. This is the shit part: we had one film. *Top Gun*! So to break it down, we had one hour a day to watch *Top Gun*; we would watch half one day and the other half the following. Then start the process again. Imagine that. I watched that fucking film so many times that I could recite every damn word. I fucking hate Goose! Two and a half months of watching Top Gun! If I ever have to sit through that film again I will scream. It may be enough to put me into a psychiatric unit.

All the inmates on the wing had jobs to do during the day. It wasn't like we just sat in the cells for hours on end waiting for the football and *Top Gun*. We would spend 5 hours at work. I worked as a pot washer in the kitchen. Johnno worked the laundry. Other tasks consisted of gardening, rubbish disposal, cleaning etc. It helped the hours go by. Washing the pots gave me the chance to run over what had happened during that night. Could I remember anything that would help my case? How were things at home? I just hoped my parents were not aware of where I was. It would destroy them. I was doing fine at the end of the day. I was getting by. I'm not saying I enjoyed it, far from it, but it wasn't as bad as I first thought.

I had two visitors while inside. The Commanding Officer who visited once to check we were OK and inform us that a custodial sentence meant we would be kicked out of the army on return to the UK. However, we were still classed as British soldiers until we hit UK soil, so the regiment had a duty of care over us. The wanker took great pleasure over telling me that. I responded by reassuring him that I was innocent and my time was not custodial because I had pleaded 'not guilty' and my trial was approaching. He smiled back as if to say, "OK, Inman. You're more fucked than your mate next to you." This, of course, meant that Johnno had no career in the military on return to the motherland. Being kicked out was the least of our worries at that moment in time. I was also informed by the Commanding Officer that should I receive a sentence longer than six months, I would be in the care of the British Embassy on release. There would be no British unit in Hong Kong as the Black Watch (Scottish Infantry Regiment) would be handing sovereignty over to China. So instead of being a prisoner of Her Majesty, I would be a prisoner of China. *This just gets even better. That's another guilt trip I can shove in Johnno's face.* The Commanding Officer got up, smiled at me through the glass dividing us and left. He must have thought, *I'm never seeing him again.*

The padre also visited on a couple of occasions, talking his nonsense. He informed me that he had brought some cigarettes and FHM magazines from the lads of 7 Platoon. *Fair play, lads. That's really good of them,* I thought. They were still thinking of us, even though it was forbidden to smoke in the prison. The FHM would go down well though. *Not seen a woman in weeks.* He told me that battalion were packing up and about to leave for the UK. This news made me feel really sad. *We're being left behind by the people who should have protected us,* I thought. I felt we were thrown to the slaughter. I truly felt that they didn't give a fuck if we were never to get out of this shithole. That was the last time I saw the padre. I was escorted back to the cell. Half an hour later, a prison guard approached the bars. He shouted towards me. I noticed he had the FHMs in his hand. I ran over to him. I noticed the twat smile as he handed them to me. I sat on the floor of the cell with my back against the wall in anticipation of looking at the girls in the magazines. There were 3 separate issues. As I continued to open them I quickly noticed that pages were missing. The fucking wankers had torn every page that contained a girl out. This pretty much meant there were hardly any damn pages left. That was the straw that broke the camel's back. I went fucking berserk. I started punching the walls, shouting as loud as I could. I wanted to hurt myself. I was determined to break a hand, or both. One of the Dutch lads ran over and bear-hugged me to try and stop me. For the first time in my life I knew how it felt to want to kill someone. During my life this feeling would become frequent. All this because I couldn't see a pair of Abi Titmuss' tits?

Days turned into weeks. All I was living for was *Top Gun,* football and washing pots. I then had a visit from my solicitor. "We go to court next week," he informed me. I was chuffed there was a chance. OK, it was a small chance but I had to hold some hope. He asked me if I could recall anything at all.

"No," I replied. He went on to tell me that one of the officers in my company had to stay behind to tie up some loose ends with Black Watch. This officer had offered to be a character witness for me. This was great news, finally something positive.

On the morning of my trial I got dressed into the clothes I was wearing on the day of the last court case. They had been stored away for me as well as 200 Benson & Hedges, the cigarettes from the boys. Before I was escorted to the sweat wagon I spent a few minutes with Johnno. He wished me luck. I hugged him. Part of me didn't want to leave him on his own for another 3 ½ months. Then again, if this didn't go as planned it would be him saying goodbye to me in the next 3 ½. I genuinely believe he hoped I would be free. After all, he was the reason I went through the beating, the time inside and facing longer if I was to be found guilty.

I left Stanley Prison, hoping I would not be returning soon. On arrival at the High Court I was greeted by my solicitor and the Platoon Commander from 9 Platoon. This was the decent fellow who volunteered to be my character witness. The only bloke who offered me any help in this whole story. I was briefed on what was going to happen and we made our way to sit outside the court. Other people soon gathered; the tall English bloke from the Big Apple club, a young Chinese girl who I didn't recognise although later became apparent she was the victim, an air hostess travelling through Hong Kong. Oh, and Oddjob. The bouncer I assaulted.

Proceedings began. I had the same judge as before. Prosecution began. There were statements from the said witnesses and questions asked of me by the prosecution barrister. I just told the truth, I had nothing to hide. I felt I came across well, showing sincerity and passion. We broke for lunch. Like I said, I thought things were going alright. But while sitting having a sandwich with my solicitor and the officer, the solicitor said it was not going well. *He knows better,* I thought. As soon as he said that I thought I'd better start preparing myself to go back to Stanley. I felt gutted. I knew this also meant my parents needed to be informed. I had got away without telling them until now, hoping that this trial would be my saving grace. *How will they deal with the news their son is banged up abroad in a Chinese prison? Not only that, he's been in almost three months already. This news would break their hearts. They are not particularly strong mentally either. I could tip them over the edge.*

We returned to the courtroom where proceedings once again began. The officer from 9 Platoon gave a fantastic character statement, telling the court that I had the potential to be a good soldier, that I was young but showed signs of being a future leader, and that I had never put a foot wrong before. He made me sound like Andy McNab.

"Would you please stand," I heard the judge say. I rose to my feet with my head down. *Here we go. Be strong, whatever happens.* "I find the defendant......... not guilty." I felt immediate relief. *I'm innocent. I'm going to be released. It's over.* The judge went on to say how he had considered doing me for aiding and abetting but he felt I had been through enough. He spoke some strong words too, reminding me how lucky I was, and then he wished me luck for the future. I was free to leave the court. I shook the solicitor's hand. I couldn't thank him enough. I did the same to the officer who gave up his time to help me.

"What happens now?" I asked.

"We go back to Stonecutters and wait for our flights home," replied the officer. We went down the stairs of the court and towards some large glass doors. I walked out into the open and raised my head to the sun. *It's over.* I remember thinking that nothing in life could ever get as bad as that. *Whatever life throws at me, if I got through that, then I can get through anything.* I spent a moment thinking of Johnno. I wondered how he would feel when he noticed I didn't return. I'm sure he would be happy for me. We would see each other one last time in the future. The officer came out to me and informed me he just needed to telephone camp to get the duty driver to collect us. He walked over to the pay phones in the entrance way.

As he did, he turned to me and said, "Do you want to phone home?"

"Yes please," I replied. He handed me a phone card. I used it to phone Vicki to start with. We had a brief conversation. I told her what had happened in a roundabout way. Most importantly, I told her I would be home very soon. I then proceeded to phone my mum and dad.

"Hello, stranger. We were getting worried about you."

If you only knew, I thought.

On arriving at Stonecutters I was given some accommodation and told I needed to do nothing but just wait for my flight home which would be in a few days' time. The Black Watch CSM (Company Sergeant Major) also informed me I was free to leave camp if I desired. *No way,* I thought. *I'm not leaving the security of this camp until I leave for my flight.* I was not risking anything. My flight was three days later. I got on the plane and couldn't wait to get into the air. I felt that once those wheels left the ground I was one hundred percent on my way home. Nothing could happen. I looked out of the window as the plane circled higher over Hong Kong and thought about the soldier I was leaving behind. I hoped he would be OK.

"See you soon, brother," I whispered. I closed my eyes.

3

HOMECOMING

It felt like a long flight home. All I had on me was a daysack
with some toiletries in, my passport and a little cash. As the
plane landed at Heathrow, I couldn't wait to feel the cold air
and for the smell of London. As I exited the door of the plane
I took a second to breathe in the night air. I walked down the
stairs and over to customs. I had no luggage to collect so made
my way through and looked around for a name plaque. I was
briefed the other side that a duty driver from Tern Hill would
be greeting me. True to the word, there was. I recognised the
driver who in return recognised me. I made my way towards
him. He shook my hand and said, "Let's go". It was a long
drive back to the Midlands. I arrived at Clive Barracks, Tern
Hill at approximately 2am. I booked in at the guardroom and
took a slow walk up to C Company lines. The COS (Company
Orderly Sergeant) was around. He showed me where my bed
space was. I noticed my MFO box (a wooden box which had
all my belongings in. This was packed by me before leaving for
Hong Kong). I didn't open it. I wanted to stay as quiet as I could
because there were 3 lads dossed down in the same room. My

bed was kindly made up. I stripped off and got into it. The next thing I heard was one of the lads: "Did you get bummed then?"

"Yes. Every night," I replied in a sarcastic manner. Then I heard giggles. I was back.

Morning soon came. I had some banter with the lads and rushed around trying to find an iron in order to press my uniform before surely going in front of the CSM, RSM and Commanding Officer. *I can't wait to see that tosser,* I thought. I met up with the rest of the company. Had a few interesting conversations. For some reason, they all wanted to know about bum sex. I assured them I had not had homosexual intercourse and that my bottom still operated as it should, I had not been turned by any lady boys and my fingers didn't smell of shit, I was still straight and they were safe to shower with me. However, keep their soap on a string.

After nominal roll I was ordered in to see the CSM. He welcomed me back and asked if I was alright. He spent half an hour with me asking questions about what actually happened that night and how prison was. How was I feeling now I was back? He showed genuine interest in and concern about my wellbeing. He then marched me to the RSM's office, where I was again questioned on what had happened during my holiday in Stanley Prison. He did, however, say I was going on 'orders'. This is being placed in front of the Commanding Officer, usually because you have committed some sort of petty misdemeanour, and where you have some privileges taken away, are fined or even serve some battalion prison sentence. I wasn't worried. *I'm home; I'm safe, what's the worst that can happen?* I was marched in front of the CO double time by the RSM. *Left right left right left right.* I stood in front of the Commanding Officer, saluted and smiled.

"Take that fucking smile off your face, Inman. You are in front of me charged with bringing the army into disrepute. You will serve 5 days imprisonment." *WHAT? Are you kidding me? I* have just spent 2 ½ months in civilian prison in a foreign country, got found 'not guilty', got home and you want the last laugh by putting me back in the clink? I wanted to jump the fucking desk and grab the fucker by his scrawny neck. I'd learnt some tricks while inside though. Stay calm, show no emotion, grit your teeth and pretend you don't give a fuck. That's exactly what I did. *Shit, I have turned into one emotionally tough motherfucker. You won't beat me,* I thought.

"Take him away, RSM," he shouted his order. The RSM marched me double time out of the CO's office where I was greeted by the Provost staff, the same bastard who telephoned the RMPs back over there. He in turn marched me to the guardroom and booked me in. *Here we go again,* I thought. When was this fucking nightmare going to end? I knew the drill of battalion nick. I'd been in it only 3 months prior. I was going to be again polishing brass, cleaning my cell floor, walls and probably ceiling and, yes, getting beasted into the ground by the PTI (Physical Training Instructor) staff. *See it out for 5 days,* I thought to myself. *Could be worse, I could be over in Hong Kong with Johnno doing the pots, playing football in my flip-flops and, don't forget, watching* Top Gun. I was once again given another boiler suit to wear. *I'm not going to be winning any GQ style awards, am I?*

I banged those 5 days out with absolute ease. When I was marched double time around Clive Barracks I held my head high. I had done nothing wrong but just been in the wrong place at the wrong time. *I could use this to my advantage though,* I thought. *All these soldiers and NCOs know I'm the lad that's come back from Hong Kong late because he's been banged up in civvy nick. He's now getting fucking beasted by every man and his dog. Everyone must know me. I must be getting talked about in the lines and the cookhouse as the poor bastard that's been through the mill. So when I get out of here I'm going to use this fame as a stepping stone.*

A weekend had passed during those 5 days, another

opportunity gone of seeing my parents, sister and Vicki. *Maybe next weekend hey, if I'm not banged on guard duty.* I was released from nick on a Monday at 5pm. I was handed my beret and told to fuck off. I walked up to C Company lines with the intention of emptying my MFO box, settling back in and getting all my kit in order. I would go down to the stores the next day and sign out all my kit. Bergen, webbing, body armour etc. As I walked through the barracks, soldiers I didn't know acknowledged me. Remember, I was still a crow. I must have had an aura about me of invincibility. That is how I felt. *Keep throwing me the shit and I will take it. It won't ever break me.* I got to my room and sat at the end of the bed. First thing I did was laugh.

"Fuck 'em," I said to the lads in the room. "I need a drink." The room lit up. A penny dropped. One of the lads suggested, "Let's go on the piss". *Oh no,* I thought. *Look what happened last time.*

"Come on, Inni, you deserve a break." *Yes, I suppose I do. And, again, what's the worst that could happen? I'm back in the UK.* I knew I would have to take it easy as I hadn't had a beer since that fateful night quarter of a year back. The lads in the room spread the word that we were going out. This quickly gathered some interest and others agreed to join us. Lads from 8 and 9 Platoons also wanted a bit of the action. It ended up that around 20 of us were hitting Market Drayton's nightlife. Which isn't all that great – probably 5 different pubs, and the women had buckteeth and hairy legs. We all gathered outside the lines and made the 5-minute walk to the guardroom where I had just been released not an hour ago. Before we left in countless taxis which were waiting outside the front gates, we needed to book out. This is a process that everyone in the military, no matter where in the world, has to do. It's a formality. It's making sure they know where you are at all times. Are you in camp or not should a bomb scare happen or a fire start, for example? We queued up patiently, one by one, signing out – date, time, name, rank, number, where you were going, and your signature. We got into the taxis, RV'd in the centre of Market Drayton and the night began.

The taste of that first pint was beautiful. It was the greatest sip of beer of my life to date. It felt like silk gently massaging my throat on the way down. I took my time to enjoy that first pint. I was pretty much the centre of attention. Question after question about what had happened on that night. The lads had noticed that Johnno and I had been beaten up. They noticed it plain as day while we were in the cookhouse, segregated from the rest of the troops. I told them about the back of the police van and how my hands were cuffed to the bar and how I just thought about protecting my balls. I told them about the 'when in Rome' comment made by the prick orderly officer. *I can't wait to see that silver-spooned bell end around battalion. I will figure out what to say to him when the opportunity arises.* They asked, obviously, about Stanley Prison. I tried my best to describe the conditions, the food, sleeping arrangements. They laughed about *Top Gun*. I shouldn't have told them that bit because all the dickheads did all night was make one-liners. 'I feel the need, the need for speed' or 'Tap on the brakes and they'll fly right by'. The list goes on. Two of the idiots stood at the bar and started singing *You've Lost That Loving Feeling* while serenading me. The final straw was calling me 'Maverick' for the rest of the night. I made it abundantly clear that I would let them get away with calling me it tonight, but from tomorrow it was 'Inni'.

I was enjoying myself, to be fair. I went to the toilet and came back to another pint provided by the lads. They just kindly kept bringing them to me when they noticed I was getting low. The beers were going down nicely. I got a little emotional at one point. I went outside, looked up to the sky to catch a glimpse of the moon. *I hope you're OK, Johnno mate? Keep pushing the time out. You will be home soon.* I did all I could to hold the tears back. I had to, I was out with a load of knuckleheads and I had new celebrity status. I was the lad who served some time, got home and did a little more and still it didn't break me. I knew I had their respect. The title of crow was going. I was the newish lad, but now I was identified as the alpha male. I was a leader. I once again returned to the lads sitting around two tables and, of course, yet another pint. The night went on. There were no dramas tonight though; everyone was well behaved and respectful to the locals. We had a good time. We had beer after beer, a couple of tequila chasers and then a few more pints. It was time to quit while we were ahead, call it a night and go back to camp. We all staggered to the nearest taxi rank and squared away our lift home. The fresh air hit me like one of those batons to the head. Luckily the lads took care of me and guided me into the back of the car. On arriving at Clive Barracks I stumbled out. I was like Bambi on ice; I could hardly stand up. The lads picked me up and I put my arms around their heads. We walked towards the guards and one of them checked our ID and the other laughed at the state we were in.

"Good night, lads?" I heard one of them say. We all made our way to the guardroom, where of course we had to sign back in. One at a time we went up, located our name and placed our signature to confirm we had returned. The lads still needed to guide me up. I got to the guardroom window and looked at the book. I couldn't see my name through the haze of the liqueur I had consumed, which had blatantly been too much. At this point the world dropped out of my arse. I didn't even feel it coming, but it did. Within a millisecond I had thrown up all over the booking in book and projectile vomited onto the guardroom floor. When I say sick, I mean sick. It was everywhere: down my shirt, over the book, the counter, the window frame, and onto the floor. I just froze. Then I heard a shout of "Get him in the back". This must have woken everyone in the guardroom, including my favourite Provost staff. The lads took me into the guardroom where I was made to stand to attention and got an absolute bollocking from the Provost Corporal who had only released me from the cells 5 hours earlier. Guess where I was going back?

"Get him in the cells," the Provost ordered. I was thrown back into the cell where I had spent the previous 5 nights and days. *Fuck it.* I lay on the bed and was thrown a blanket and pillow. The cell door was slammed shut and the keys turned to lock me in. This was a sound that was getting all too familiar. This was where I spent the remainder of the night.

The company had to be on parade for the nominal role every morning at 8am. We would march down from the lines of the platoon and gather as a formed up company. The COS would call the nominal role and report all present to the CSM, who would then brief us up on tasks or the training programme for the day. The nominal role was taking place and my name, Inman, got called. Obviously I wasn't there to answer my name. One of the lads, by all accounts, informed the COS that I was in the cells.

"No," the COS responded, "he got released yesterday at 5pm."

"No, Corporal. He got released and we all went out on the piss. When booking in, Inman threw up all over the guardroom. The Provost staff jailed him. He's still there now."

The COS's eyes widened by all accounts as if to say 'You are kidding. How much shit can this kid get into?' At this point the CSM made his way to the company and the COS informed him that yet again Inman was detained and of the reason why. The CSM asked the lads who I was out with what had happened. They informed him that we as a group had gone out, had a few beers. Inman drank too much and threw up on his return to book in. They admitted they should have taken better care of me seeing as I hadn't had a drink in 3 months. The CSM charged off towards his office. He must have telephoned the Provost Sergeant and told him to get me to him immediately. At this point I was awake. I had vomit down me, and had not shaven or cleaned my teeth.

"Get your shoes on, Inman. You're going to see your Sergeant Major." The Provost Sergeant took great pleasure in marching me double time – *left right left right* – in front of the eyes of the battalion up to my CSM to get another bollocking. I guarantee he thought I would be back with him in hours to do another stint inside. Sorry to disappoint you, bully fucker!

I was marched to the CSM's office and halted.

"Wait here, Inman." At that point, the Company Sergeant Major ordered the Provost into his office.

"Shut the door," my CSM shouted at him. For the next 5 minutes all I heard was an almighty roasting from my CSM. The Provost took a tirade of abuse. I heard the word REMF (rear-echelon motherfucker) called on numerous occasions. I also heard "Hasn't that lad been through enough?" and "You wouldn't have lasted a week in Hong Kong prison". To be fair, this was true. I would have loved to see how this bully would have lasted a night locked up. He would need his hot water bottle and favourite blanket, the bedwetter. The door opened. The Provost didn't look at me. He just scurried past and back to his little corner of power that is the guardroom. My day with him will come.

I stood to attention, smelling of sick and just generally feeling like death warmed up. I had the hangover from hell and was anticipating another jail stint for my actions.

"Come in, Inman," ordered the CSM. He closed the door behind me and asked me to sit down. He then proceeded to ask if I would like a tea or coffee. *Is this a trick question?* I thought. But he was genuine. I could tell by his demeanour.

"No thank you, sir."

"What I'm about to say must stay between these four walls." The CSM proceeded to show pity to me. "I'm glad you're back safe. Well done for getting through those few months. The CO has it in for you big time. He doesn't want you in his battalion. He should never have jailed you for five days in my eyes, completely out of order. Just be aware you are being monitored. If you fuck up again, they will get rid of you somehow." I appreciated his honesty and thanked him for it. He continued with words I will never forget. "Son, you've been through the mill. I wouldn't wish what you have been through for my worst enemy. And how old are you?"

"18," I replied.

"Use your experience and turn it into a positive. Do not dwell on it but accept it and let it create inner strength." At this point I could have burst into tears. I knew what he meant immediately. I was going to do just that. "Finally, son, I'm granting you a week's leave. Be back here on parade for next Monday morning. Get out of here, get home and see your family." I couldn't believe what I was hearing. I stood up, braced up and thanked him over and over. "Go," he ordered.

I marched out of his office and sprinted to 7 Platoon lines. I approached my Platoon Sergeant's office to inform him I had been granted leave, but he had already received the call from the CSM. I telephoned Vicki.

"Vic, I'm in Tern Hill, come and get me straight away." She screamed down the phone. She said she would be 45 minutes. I jumped in the shower, got into my Civvies.

"Stay out of trouble, Inman," said my Platoon Sergeant as he winked towards me. I smiled back as if to say, 'You know me. I will try, but don't bet on it with recent form.' I walked through the barracks, excited to find my true freedom. I had waited for this moment for months. I walked nonchalantly towards the guardroom. I popped my head through the window that only 12 hours earlier I was boffing my ring up over. I picked up the pen. Date, time, name, rank, number, destination: HOME.

I was stood across the road in a pub car park directly opposite to Clive Barracks, waiting for Vicki's little red Nissan Micra to appear. I could have waited in the pub, but that was probably not the best idea. She pulled in with a huge smile on her face. She jumped out and we embraced. She burst into tears. She had no idea. During the drive home I informed her that I had something to tell her. I didn't want to do it there and then but wanted to go out for a meal that night with a few friends and run through what had happened. On returning to Vicki's parents, we proceeded to phone around everyone: my best friend Neil, my sister and her boyfriend and a couple of close friends. We arranged everyone to meet at our local pub in Whittington, The Dog. I managed to book a table.

We all sat around the circular table and enjoyed our food. It was the best steak I had ever tasted. I took it easy on the ale. It was amazing to see everyone, all my close friends and my little sister. They too also seemed to be having a great time chatting between each other, laughing and joking. I almost didn't want to spoil the night by telling them the harrowing story which included their loved one. *Should I tell them after all? Or should I just lock what happened in a box, throw away the key and never mention it again?* I seriously considered it. Something told me deep inside that they needed to know. There may be repercussions if I didn't tell them. The meal was coming to an end. *Here we go.*

"OK everyone, I have to tell you something. I should have been home about six weeks ago but something happened to me out there." This is how I began. I told them everything from the start to how I ended up sitting with them at the table. Vicki, who was sat next to me, would often grab my right thigh and squeeze it. I couldn't look at her because I didn't want to see her tears but I knew they were there. I tried to fixate on my best friend Neil. Even his eyes were full of sadness. As for my sister – well, I was glad she had her boyfriend with her to comfort her. I went on to finish by saying, "I don't want pity. I just want and need you to know that I feel a little different now to before I left. I'm not the same person anymore. I finally feel that I have graduated from boy to man. I felt tough before I left, but this now is on a different scale. I have faced the worse that any 18-year-old can face and I beat it. No matter what life has to throw at me, from now on it doesn't matter. Nothing can ever be as bad as what I have just been through. I will go through my life remembering this. What has happened to me didn't break me, but it's going to make me. Make me into a stronger individual who believes in himself and knows he won't break. I truly feel amazing. I have been blessed with this experience. So please don't feel sad. However, I will finish by saying this: if I ever see those coppers again, the ones who took me for a spin in that wagon, I will kill them." And I was serious.

I went to bed that night but found it difficult to sleep. I was wondering how Johnno was and trying to image what he would be doing that very moment. Probably watching *Top Gun*.

A few days went by and life was slowly getting back to normal. I arranged to go out with Neil and have a few beers and chat, just him and me. We had a good night, had lots of laughs. At the end of the night, before we went our separate ways, he stopped me.

"I wish you had phoned me to let me know what you were going through." He assured me he would have flown out to Hong Kong. You know what? He is such a great friend; I have no doubt he would have.

I made my way up the hill from my local, which was 800 metres from my parents' house. Last orders had gone so by the time I got home I didn't expect anyone to be awake. I opened the back door and made my way into the living room. My father was sat on the sofa reading a newspaper. I sat down on the other side of the lounge and began to watch TV.

"You OK, Dad?"

"Yes mate. You had a good night?" he replied. The conversation went on. Out of nowhere it came.

"Dad, I have something to tell you." I intended never to

mention a word of what happened to my parents. I don't know why, but I continued. My father put his paper down and looked towards me. Over the next hour I went through the previous three months. He would often stop me and ask me a question and then I would continue. His eyes were transfixed. I have no idea how he must have felt as I told my story. I never will. We never spoke of the incident again. He probably put it in a box, locked it up and threw the key into the fucking ocean.

Vicki and I soon after split up and went our separate ways. I was to be introduced to Nicola by my best friend Neil. We spent a while getting to know each other and inevitably got together and started a new relationship.

4

NORTHERN IRELAND

I had been to Northern Ireland on numerous occasions as a private soldier. I had done my stint of being top cover in the Snatch vehicles (partially armoured, Land Rover-sized vehicles) and suffered the squeeze and the smells of being in the back of the Saxons (larger armoured vehicles). We as a company or battalion would usually find ourselves over the side of the water when marching season came along, around the 12th July. Nothing has divided Northern Ireland as much in recent years as the issue of the marches by what is known as the Loyal Orders. To Protestants, the parades are an expression of their heritage and culture; to Catholics, they are nothing but an exhibition of provocative sectarian triumphalism. We would often find ourselves stood at checkpoints during these marches being the buffer between the Orangemen and the local Catholics. It felt as though we were doing the same thing year after year and the politicians were getting nowhere.

I had just completed my NCO's cadre (promotion course) and been given my first tape (stripe). I was now a Lance Corporal. I was promoted in 1998, just before being deployed on a 6-month tour of Belfast. My job therefore would be to command a small team of four men. I had also moved platoons. I was now a member of 8 Platoon. You would often be moved around as you were promoted. This would help with the transition of becoming an NCO (Non-Commissioned Officer) and familiarity with your previous platoon and its private soldiers. The battalion was separated into four different areas of Belfast. C Company was located in North Belfast, specifically in an area called the New Lodge. This was the epicentre of terrorist activity in the north. The company were based in a small patrol base called Girdwood. This was supposed to be our home for the entire six months. Things didn't go to plan.

Our accommodation comprised of dark mortar-proof units that housed our platoon. We felt relatively safe. The patrol base had numerous sangars (guard observation points) around providing 24-hour protection. These sangars were manned by the private soldiers. As I was now a Lance Corporal, my guard duties meant managing the guardroom and making sure the private soldiers were administered and the guard rota (stag rota) was correct and managed fairly.

I shared a room with Lee, another Lance Corporal in the platoon, who was well experienced and a fine soldier who demanded and earnt his respect from the soldiers and ranks above. I also looked up to Lee. We got on very well and would become very close friends throughout the years, and are still in contact to this day.

Life in the patrol base was very simple. We would have company rotations. You would spend 2 weeks on guard duty, 2 weeks on QRF (Quick Reaction Force) or 2 weeks on patrols. QRF was great. You would spend your time with your kit and equipment next to you while in a rest room drinking brews, smoking your lungs away and watching never-ending episodes of *Jerry Springer*. Guard (duty) felt long and monotonous. You would spend 24 hours on duty followed by 24 hours off, usually in your pit (bed) recovering from the long shift.

Patrols were great. The patrol commander would brief us on a route around the New Lodge area. The patrol was broken down into 3 separate teams. We would move along the streets in what was called 'steers' (4-man teams), the patrol commander's team taking the central role with the two steers flanking him. We would not be in eye view of each other but would have continual comms (communications) through a secure network. This ensured that the locals could not listen in on our frequency and monitor our movements. I was in command of my steer, call sign W22 (Whisky22). I was a 19-year-old lad commanding a team on the streets of one of the most dangerous places on the planet. It was an absolute buzz.

The patrols would often get followed by younger upcoming terrorist wannabes. This process was called 'dicking or getting dicked'. They would be informing other terrorists of our location and our movements in order for others to go about their terrorist activity, knowing they could operate without fear or the element of surprise. They could be moving weapons or ammunition or preparing bombs. They could be doing countless things, but as long as the dicker was keeping them informed of our location, they could operate with no real threat of compromise. We could do nothing about the dickers. They would operate and observe us freely. We could do nothing about their presence. It was frustrating. The dickers would often entice the patrol. I would walk by, look and acknowledge them. 'Fucking scumbag' were the words that used to appear from my mouth towards their direction.

The New Lodge was dominated by what was known as the 'Big 3': three large high-rise civilian flats that overlooked the close vicinity. Dickers would often watch us from these vantage points and give running commentary of our movements to their scumbag terrorist mates. We also had an observation point in one of these towers. At the very top of one would be an observation unit who would gather intelligence on movements of known terrorists. Opposite one of the towers was a prominent crossroad that dissected the New Lodge. Right on the corner of this feature was a Sinn Féin office. We as a patrol would often be asked to steer away from the office as our presence could incite trouble due to the large gathering of known 'players' (terrorists).

During one patrol I received a radio message from the observation tower. "W22, there is a blue Vauxhall parked outside the Sein Féin office. The VRN (Vehicle Registration Number) is out of our view. Could you report? OVER." I responded and made my way with my team in tow towards the office to identify the vehicle. I could see the blue Vauxhall in question and quickly reported the VRN to the tower. As I continued around the corner away from the office, I was greeted by a very highly ranked player. He was seen very often by the side of Gerry Adams (the Sein Féin Leader) and had also escaped the Maze Prison with Adams years before. They were good friends, so I believe. For the purpose of this I will not name him but refer to him as Player X. Player X was in front of a camera being interviewed by a lady reporter, who was very smartly dressed. Simultaneously I received a radio message from the tower informing me to steer clear as the vehicle belonged to BBC Glasgow. *Fuck,* I thought, *let me just lead my patrol away.* This was not going to happen. As the team leader, I led the patrol from the front and dictated the direction the team travelled in. I turned away from the office to make my escape. After all, I did not want mine or any member of my team's face on camera; my team was my responsibility. As I attempted to lead W22 away, I heard Player X raise his voice towards me and the team.

"Look, this is all I get from the British Army. I get hounded and victimised constantly. They are always intimidating me. Why do they feel the need to bully me in this way?" As he shouted, I looked towards him. The cameraman controlling the large camera turned in my direction.

Immediately I shouted towards the cameraman, "Get that camera off my team." He failed to do so. I repeated my request. Again he failed to.

Player X went on to shout towards us, "I can't take a step around this area without being watched or followed by these people." I have to admit he used language and a tone becoming of a gentleman, this only because he was in the presence of a lady and being recorded by the BBC. I should have followed suit. For the first time my Maverick side appeared (*Top Gun*)! To be perfectly honest, I didn't really give a fuck, but I should have. I was still 19 years of age at the end of the day and had plenty to learn in life. I made a huge mistake. I was caught on camera shouting, "Go fuck yourself, you deserve everything you get!" The second I shouted it I knew I had fucked up big style. I had just given him the proof and ammunition he needed to back his story up to the reporter. Not only that, but my words were recorded for all to hear. Player X continued to question my team's presence in the area. Finally I buttoned it, kept my big gob shut and proceeded with the patrol route. During that patrol back to Girdwood I was wondering what the repercussions of my actions would be. It didn't take long to find out. Only the very next day my comment was broadcast on local news, together with a picture of myself gesturing towards Player X on the front of Sinn Féin Newspaper. It goes without saying that I was not flavour of the month with all the head shed. It was not the end of the world; however, at the time we were trying our best to work on what was called 'Heart & Minds'. This meant trying to come across as helpful, kind, all that bullshit, and I had just blown it.

Patrols continued. Thankfully there were no more camera crews to record my naivety. One afternoon my team was again deployed onto the ground. I recognised a dicker. *Nothing strange,*

I thought. I walked directly past him, expecting him to throw some obscenity in mine and the team's direction. He didn't. He waited for me to approach closer then, clear as day, said, "Lance Corporal Mark Inman". I was taken back. How the fuck did this bastard know my full name? Some of my colleagues didn't even know my first name was Mark. I was called 'Inni', that's what I was known by. It's not as though back then we had social media, Facebook or Instagram. I have no idea how he had got it but he had. It bothered me for a while, but again, looking back, that's all he had – my name.

Patrols were very eventful on the streets of Belfast. We would suffer abuse and were targeted with violence. I on one occasion walked alongside one of the Big 3 and had a full nappy of piss and shit land on my head, much to the delight of my team; they thought it hilarious. Dickers would often drive past and squirt piss out of bottles at us. I suppose in this day and age we were lucky as acid attacks had not been heard of.

I took my turn at guard duty and QRF but lived for the patrols. Getting out on the ground was what I joined the army for. The best times were in the marching season, where we would spend days on end manning baselines to keep the Protestants and Catholics apart. During the day, the different sides would form barricades in the streets from anything they could find, like cars, pallets and bins. Come evening time they would set them a light. We would park our Saxons in a line between the two sides, get our riot shields out and generally be a target for both sides to chuck bricks at all night long. When the pubs closed time, the youths would reinforce the barricades and we would bear the brunt. Every now and again the RUC would send a few baton rounds (plastic bullets) down range to keep them in their place. It was exciting stuff, but we were well trained and could handle it. One night I was chatting to the patrols commander, one of the better officers who looked out for the blokes, when we heard gun shots. One of Loyalists had decided to have a pop at us for preventing them getting to the Republicans/Catholics. I looked around. For a moment I thought one of the coppers had been hit. But I realised quickly that they had all hit the deck in case more shots came. I looked at my officer and he looked at me. We both said 'Fuck yeah!'. We had had our first contact. Okay, it wasn't much and we hadn't been able to fire back, but it was real. We were both incredibly calm. In fact, so calm, I had to remind the boss that he had better send a contact report to the ops room (Operations Room). It was the battalion's only shooting contact of the tour and the incident even made it onto the front page of the next day's Sun newspaper, with the headline 'Snipers Fire at Riot Cops'. The whole thing gave me a buzz and I wanted more of it.

I was preparing myself to go on R&R. I would get to go back home to the mainland for 9 days and go on a short holiday to Jersey with Nicola which we had planned. My bags were packed and I was excited to see her. I just needed to get through the next patrol and I would be leaving the following morning. I would be taken to Belfast City Airport in the middle of the night and catch a flight to Birmingham International. We would be taken at night when the streets of Belfast were at their quietest to avoid any unnecessary attention. This would also be the airports quietest time. We needed to stay as low profile as possible.

The next patrol was very eventful indeed. On 15th August, I took my patrol into the heart of the New Lodge. Things did not feel right that day. As soldiers on patrol we are taught to observe for 'absence of the normal and presence of the abnormal'. However, nothing seemed to stick out, if I recall. There was a strange vibe, something did not feel right. W22 must have been halfway through our patrol when I had a radio message from the ops room. I was told to make my way immediately to a prominent area by the name of Duncairn Gardens close by, where I would be joined by an RUC (Royal

Ulster Constabulary) unit. Duncairn Gardens linked together two busy A roads by the names of North Queen Street and Antrim Road. I consulted my map and took the team there by the quickest route. I felt the sense of urgency from the ops room. On arrival the team conducted their five metre – and twenty – metre checks and secured the area. Within minutes the RUC had arrived. We heard them before seeing them as they were sounding their alarms. An officer approached me and informed me that there had been a huge explosion in Omagh, and we were to set up a VCP (Vehicle Check Point) to identify any strange movement around Belfast.

The Omagh bombing was a car bombing that took place in Omagh, County Tyrone. It was carried out by a group calling themselves the Real Irish Republican Army, a Provisional Irish Republican Army (IRA) splinter group who opposed the IRA's ceasefire and the Good Friday Agreement. The bombing killed 29 people (including a woman pregnant with twins) and injured 220 others, a death toll even higher than that of any single incident during what were considered 'the troubles'. By all accounts, telephone warnings had been sent about 40 minutes beforehand but were claimed to be inaccurate, and police had inadvertently moved people towards the bomb.

We spent the next 12 hours at Duncairn Gardens, stopping random vehicles and supporting the RUC while they quickly asked questions to the drivers before letting them be on their way. Whoever was responsible for the bombing would have been long gone, an RUC officer informed me. They would have been in the south of the country within an hour. We had to be seen being proactive and showing a face and sign of strength.

I thought my R&R would have been cancelled. Luckily for me, I returned the patrol in time for my flight. It was a quick turnaround but I made it to the airport and caught my flight home.

Being home and walking freely without being in my uniform, holding a weapon or having another three lads watching my back felt strange initially. It took some getting used to, but after a few days I quickly forgot about Belfast and concentrated on enjoying myself in Jersey with Nicola. R&R came and went by too quickly. Within days, Nicola was driving me back to the airport to catch my last ever flight to Northern Ireland, as things were about to change dramatically.

On returning to Girdwood I was informed that C Company were packing up and moving. The Omagh bomb had caused there to be so much backlash for the so-called Real IRA. The Good Friday Agreement would be put into motion almost immediately. This meant we, as the British Army, were being removed from the streets of Northern Ireland for good. Patrols as we knew them were over.

We were not to be returned home to the mainland and Tern Hill though. The British Army needed to be ready to return to the streets and patrolling, should the Good Friday Agreement fail. Because of this we had to be moved to an area where we were away from the civilians but ready to return if need be at the drop of a hat. Our next stop would be the Maze Prison. This would be where we would stay for the next three months of the tour.

Her Majesty's Prison Maze (previously Long Kesh Detention Centre and known colloquially as the Maze Prison, The Maze, the H Blocks or Long Kesh) was a prison in Northern Ireland that was used to house paramilitary prisoners during the troubles from mid-1971 to mid-2000. It was situated at the former Royal Air Force station of Long Kesh, on the outskirts of Lisburn. This was in the townland of the Maze, about nine miles southwest of Belfast. The prison and its inmates were involved in such events as the 1981 hunger strike. The prison was closed in 2000 and demolition began in 2006, but on April 2013 it was announced by the

Northern Ireland Executive that the remaining buildings would be redeveloped into a peace centre.

The Maze was huge and our accommodation blocks would be on the outside of the prison but within the prison grounds. It was an eerie place. As part of the Good Friday Agreement, prisoners would slowly be released and integrated back into society. Some thought this was a huge gamble. Sentences were being ended and convicted terrorists, murderers, kidnappers and thugs were being released back onto the streets.

The only real task we had as a company was to guard the prison. This meant manning the guardroom of Long Kesh and providing over watch into the prison itself from the numerous sangars overlooking the H blocks. I mean, who was going to try to escape? The prisoners were being released anyway. All they had to do was sit tight and wait for their release date.

I used this opportunity to work hard and improve on my fitness levels. For the last three months, all I had been doing was living in a small patrol base, doing a bit of guard and patrolling. My fitness was the last thing on my mind at this point. I used the next three months to get back into good shape. I would run the perimeter of the prison countless times. During this stint of doing "fuck all" we were given some great news. Battalion was going on exercise in Kenya. We would return to mainland and start preparing for a live firing exercise.

Battalion left Belfast and Northern Ireland behind. That would be our last ever stint over there. Not only ours, but no other British Army regiment would return and patrol those streets or manage marching season again. Almost twenty years later, thankfully this is still the case.

5

KENYA

Before being deployed on a 6-week exercise to Kenya, the Battalion were gathered into Clive Barracks' huge theatre. We would spend the day being briefed on Kenya and what to expect. This included information about what we would be doing out there, areas we would be visiting, the locals (including the Maasai tribe) and general do's and don'ts. We were shown video clips of people with malaria and told how and when to take our anti-malaria medication. I remember us being distinctly warned about the local female population and how they take a liking to British soldiers, but how AIDS and syphilis were rife and not to interact sexually with anybody. Lee, who was sitting next to me, banged his knee on mine. I looked at him.

"Take note," he smiled.

"Fuck off, Lee. I'm going nowhere near."

"That will be a first," he whispered. With my pretty boy status and being renowned for being one for the ladies, the lads began a book on how long it would take me to buckle. If I remember correctly, most money was on 'within 7 days'.

After spending that day gathering information on Kenya,

we would all become rather excited about the prospect. Again, I was thinking about my 'rocking chair' – this is what I wanted, more life experience.

One of the section commanders became ill before we deployed to Kenya and could not travel. This meant that I, as Section 2IC, would have to move up and act as Section Commander. I would be in command of eight men. These men would become my responsibility for the duration of deployment. This was a good opportunity for me to express myself as a section commander and demonstrate I had the skills to do the job. Soon enough, there would be an opportunity to progress in the near future as places were coming up in the next six months to attend a promotion course. This, therefore, would be an opportunity to shine and show I was ready for the next step. All I had to do was deliver.

Battalion made its way to Brize Norton, an RAF base in Oxfordshire. This is where we would fly out to Nairobi, Kenya. We flew overnight. On landing and disembarking from the plane, the heat hit me immediately. It was about 4am and already the temperature was soaring. We collected our luggage from the terminal and were escorted to a series of minibuses. From here we would make the long journey to Mombasa, where we would spend the night before moving to battalion's base camp, called Nanyuki Show Ground.

This would be headquarters for the battalion and where we, as C Company, would be based for our adventure training part of the visit. Our first visit was to an area in Kenya called Dol Dol. On a map it looks like the middle of nowhere. As a company we jumped onto three 4-tonne vehicles and moved in convoy on a two-hour journey to the destination. The roads were bumpy and dangerous. They were not tarmacked but just dust track roads, which were used frequently as quickest routes. While trying to rest on the back of the 4-tonners we would often be thrown around. The journeys by road in Kenya were the most uncomfortable journeys by four wheels, of my life. During the journey we took on the views of the local area. Children would run alongside the vehicles with their hands outstretched, pleading for food or water. It was quite a sad sight to witness. I would go into my pocket and throw them anything that would hopefully make them smile. I had countless boiled sweets which I would throw. The children used to love BIC biro pens. We were told this on our brief day back at Tern Hill, so I made sure I stocked up before leaving the UK.

On finally arriving at Dol Dol, we had to make a base camp. First of all we needed to secure the area by rolling out barbed wire around the perimeter; this would be secured by stakes that we hammered into the ground. The ground was dry and dusty, so this was extremely time-consuming, not to say difficult. Once the perimeter was secure we erected our tents and made up our beds. They comprised of traditional camp beds which were clear of the floor. They had to be! As we finally completed our housing we discovered a hole on the outside of the tent. As darkness fell, this hole became the visible entrance and exit of a scorpion nest. There were hundreds. I recall the company store's CSgt pouring petrol down the hole and lighting it. This achieved nothing but just made the scorpions more aggressive. We made a fire in the centre of the camp and placed seats around the edge. This would be the area where we could gather together and enjoy a cigarette and brew (hot drink).

Over the next week we would conduct basic military training, go on patrols around the area and brush up on our map-reading and basic field craft skills. A far cry from the streets of Belfast only months before. We would go through section SOPs (Standard Operating Procedures). I got the section operating in the way I wanted them to. I chose who would be my 2IC, my LSW gunners and my grenade man. I was teaching my section ways and techniques that worked best.

They too were learning from my experience and my research into best techniques, hours of studying in my own time to make the perfect section. If my section performed well and were efficiently drilled, then my chance of being selected for promotion would be greater. I took this extremely seriously. Even though we had no physical enemy I treated it as if so. All our training would be for a purpose. I expected a high standard not only from my section but also myself.

The heat was a huge problem. Kenya is, after all, right on the equator, and with all the kit we would carry (which included our webbing, daysacks, helmets and weapons) it took a toll on the body. I had to ensure my soldiers were in the best condition possible. My main focus was to keep them hydrated. This was easier said than done. Instead of having to ingest our usual two litres of water a day, this became six litres due to the amount of sweating. This alone became a problem. Water was always readily available but the problem arose with the taste. The Royal Engineers on the ground would take care of the water by purifying it and making sure it was safe to drink. This meant the taste was horrid and of course the water would not be cold but warm. I began to notice my soldiers not drinking enough. I would therefore stop the section and get them to drink a full water bottle in front of me in order for me to know they were hydrated to a point. Over time, the platoon would not drink enough and on occasions we would have a casualty. I would instruct my section to observe the colour of their piss. If it was clear then fine, but the darker it went, the more dehydrated they were. On numerous occasions we would witness lads going into spasm. First of all you would see the hands go rigid and into contraction. This followed by the feet and then the head would go back with the teeth gritted. Almost as if they were having seizures. It was not a pretty sight. The casualty would be airlifted to the closest medical centre and immediately placed on a drip to rehydrate. They would then be reunited with the platoon as soon as it was safe to be. There were things we could do to help. On stopping we would put up ponchos to keep the sun off our heads, regular water stops go without saying, and keeping scarfs damp and place them around our necks. As the lads became more acclimatised, this happened less and less.

Our first week came to an end. We dismantled the base, making sure we left nothing behind, mounted the 4-tonners and made the long uncomfortable journey by dirt tracks back to Nanyuki Show Ground, where we would spend a couple of nights before commencing with another exercise under the canopy of the jungle. This gave us the opportunity to sample the local nightlife in Nanyuki. We were free to enjoy the local bars and nightclubs, which was exciting. There were two rules we had to adhere to. Firstly, we had to be back at camp by 23:59hrs (midnight). Secondly, we were to remain in groups and only go out in our tropical combat uniform. This let the locals know who we were. The local men were no trouble at all. We got on well with them and them us in return. There were a number of bars I recall. The Riverside was one, and the Sports Bar the other. Once we were in there it was hard to believe we were in Kenya. The establishments were reasonably modern. They had Western music, dartboards and pool tables. The beer was good too. We got to drink brands such as Tiger, Tusker and Cobra. The taste was good and beer always went down well with us lot, especially after spending a week dehydrated and drinking foul-tasting water. This would be a recipe for disaster, though, for some.

Women were plentiful. They would attempt to grab our attention and then come over to interact with us. For once in my life I wasn't interested. The lads' book completely went to pot. I knew I should have put a tenner on myself to last the distance. Lee and I kept ourselves to ourselves, favoured the local beer and enjoyed countless games of pool. With my experiences of being abroad, I thought I better keep a low profile, avoid too much beer and stay away from nightclubs. I used Lee as my protection. I wasn't going to get caught up in anything I shouldn't and land myself in the shit again. Twice would just be taking the piss.

Lee and I witnessed the lads engaging with the girls. They seemed to be having a good time. I kept my eye on them but they were free men, entitled to do what they wanted, within reason of course. Who was I to tell them to stay away from the girls? They were big boys and were told the risks. If they wanted to play Russian roulette, then let them. All too often they did. We would hear stories of the lads sleeping with the girls in a tent at the back of the pub. These tents were there just for that reason. Pay the girls and the girls would take them for thirty minutes into a dusty horrible tent where they would entertain the lads and the lads got a dose. Fucking crazy bastards.

23:59hrs was fast approaching. Lee and I were NCOs who needed to lead by example, so we made our way back to the Show Ground. We climbed into a local taxi. This taxi was infamous throughout the area. A local man, who drove a Volkswagen Beetle. He painted it up like Herbie from *The Love Bug* film. However, instead of its number being 53 he announced it to be 69! Not only that but Jiggy 69. He would ride around the area shouting, "Fucking Jiggy 69. Who want a ride in Jiggy 69?" Jiggy being the word for sex, of course, and the lads had only been getting loads of 'Jiggy' that night.

On returning to camp, just in time may I add, we needed to book in to the guardroom. The guard commander was a female Corporal who worked in administration under the cap badge of the Adjutants' General Corp. A fucking REMF (Rear-Echelon Mother Fucker), a term used by frontline soldiers, whom have little respect for those who don't want to get their hands dirty. Her name was Cpl Dobson. She was a pig. Had a sour face on her and believed she was more important than she was. I approached the guardroom to book in. I had evidently had a little too much to drink but I wasn't stumbling around. I just felt pissed. I was not wearing my beret as I placed my signature next to my name.

"Get your headdress on!" Cpl Dobson ordered. Bottom line, I'm an NCO in the Staffords and she's an REMF NCO – OK, she has one more tape than me, but we share the same Corporals' mess. Now remember I have a bit of a celebrity status in battalion due to my little escapade in Hong Kong. She was new to battalion and had just been posted in. She had no idea of who I was or my background.

"Who the fuck do you think you're talking to?" I angrily snapped.

"Lance Corporal, put your beret on," again she piped up.

I exploded, "Fucking make me, you petty bastard." With that she announced that her husband was a full screw (Corporal) in the regiment. She went on to inform me he was in A Company and "wait until he found out how I spoke to his wife".

"I will tell him his wife is a fucking bitch." I walked away knowing there would be repercussions, but I was not going to be spoken to like that by somebody who had just joined my beloved regiment.

That following morning Lee and myself were in the cookhouse. One of the A Company lads approached us and said that Ritchie Dobson had heard how I spoke to his wife and he wanted to give me a slap. *Oh, did he now?* I had never heard of this Ritchie Dobson. I did a little investigating and found out he was a full screw in A Company. Why had I not heard or known of him before? How did he not know me? I later found out that this was due to him only just joining the regiment a month before we deployed to Kenya. He had come from another regiment, the PWRR (Princess of Wales' Royal Regiment). He still wore their cap badge but was going through a transfer process and would soon be a Stafford. To transfer between two Infantry units is very strange. Usually there would be a background reason and that usually meant there was something to hide. If this fucker wanted to give me a slap it had better be good because I was prepared to go to war!

We left Nanyuki Show Ground that morning and made our way to do some jungle training. Again, this was another couple of hours by dirt track. Another uncomfortable journey being thrown around hitting every damn pothole. As a company we were scheduled to spend five days under the canopy of the jungle until returning to the Show Ground once more. For me this was not the case. During the day we were being shown how to build A Frames. The purpose of A Frames was to keep you off the jungle floor and have some protection overhead and an area to store your kit. After constructing the A Frames, which took hours, darkness fell. In the jungle, when it goes dark all movement stops. You jump into your A Frame until first light the next morning. The jungle came to life. You can barely get any rest as the noises are magnified by the darkness. *What the fuck is out there?* I thought. I hardly got any sleep that night. When I woke, I unzipped my gonk bag (sleeping bag) and placed my first foot towards the ground. That first night was non-tac (non-tactical) so we could remove our boots to sleep. As my foot touched the jungle floor I felt a prominent bite.

"Bastard," I shouted, and with that witnessed a black scorpion shuffle away. I had just been bitten by a scorpion on my right ankle. I informed the Platoon Sergeant immediately and got looked at by the platoon medic. You could easily see the strike mark from the little fucker. Within an hour I started to feel unwell. I began to feel nauseous and dizzy, almost as if I was suffering a bad hangover. I was casevaced (evacuated as a casualty) from the jungle that morning and sent back to Nanyuki. I was back at base camp in the presence of A Company and with C Company in the jungle. I was a sitting target.

I spent the next 24 hours bedded down in the medical centre recovering from my hangover. I was informed that I would not be returning to the jungle as they wanted to keep their eye on me – I could have some delayed reaction so it would not be in my best interest for me to return, and my immune system could be low and the jungle is not the cleanest place on the planet. I would be put at more risk of contracting something nasty. The following day I was released from the med centre and told to chill for the next few days until my company returned and I could continue soldiering. I went about my business freely. It didn't take long before NCOs from A Company were approaching me, telling me to keep my head down as Ritchie was after me.

"I'm doing nothing of the sort." They made Ritchie out to be fucking Godzilla or something to that effect. *Fucking bring him on.* That evening in the cookhouse, I was eating away and keeping myself to myself when I saw the pig of a wife with a geezer wearing a mustard-coloured beret. That must be him. You could see the blue and yellow stripes behind his cap badge, representing the fact he was a member of PWRR and not a Stafford. Not at this point anyway. The pig pointed at me and gestured to Cpl Dobson. He was nowhere near the Godzilla he was made out to be. He looked at me and made his way towards me. I stood to my feet, still feeling unwell.

"So you're the c**t who gobbed off at my wife?"

"Your wife was being a twat," I responded. I don't think he expected me to come back at him with that.

"Don't ever speak to her like that again."

"Or what?" again I responded.

"I will fucking knock you out!" he threatened. I was not having that.

"I don't think so," I replied, smiling at him with a grin from ear to ear. Things went back and forth but at this point a punch was not thrown. We were just feeling each other out. Plus, he could not be seen hitting me and be labelled a trouble-maker. He was, after all, going through the transfer process of becoming a Stafford, and an incident could have jeopardised this. He knew this, so had to box clever. We both went by our business but I knew this would not be the end of the matter.

That night I decided to go out to the Riverside Bar and have a couple of drinks with a few lads from HQ Company. I didn't want A Company to think I had no bottle and was staying in my accommodation waiting for my friends to return. I wanted to show them that I didn't give a fuck and if someone wanted to dance, then they better bring their dancing shoes because I had no fear! I was enjoying my evening when three NCOs from A Company approached me.

"Inni. If you carry on acting up you're going to get into trouble."

"Why are you fighting his battles? If he wants to fight, we can. There is no need for you to get involved. Anyway," I continued, "Who is this foreigner? I'm a Stafford, he's not. His wife fucking gobbed off and she got some back. Tell him to deal with it or fuck off." They went on their way. I had made my point. I was going nowhere and I had made it clear I was ready to fight if need be. They knew Ritchie didn't scare me. After all, last year I had spent some time banged up inside a Hong Kong prison. They had no idea what happened to me during those few months. They would certainly know that one man, Ritchie Dobson, wasn't going to cause me any lack of sleep. He wasn't in the same league. I do believe, though, that they thought I was getting a bit big for my boots. After all, I had this celebrity status of which they felt a little jealous. The army is full of alpha males' jealousy and the competition can be rife.

Not much happened over the next few days. I got the odd stare from Ritchie, the pig and some of A Company. A glare, which I precipitated, of course. C Company returned and after a while I told Lee and the NCOs in the Company what had happened in regards to Ritchie over the previous days. They also didn't know who this Dobson geezer was and believe me, it didn't go down well that some of the A Company NCOs took a foreigner's side and not a real Stafford's. The shit was about to hit the fan!

That night, C Company NCOs, including me, gathered into our mess. We got up to the normal stuff, taking the piss out of each other and having a few beers. Slowly we were joined by A Company. We usually all got on very well as we had been through quite a lot together, including tours away, external courses and growing through the ranks from private soldiers. Ritchie was not to be seen. As more beers started to flow, tensions started to rise. One of A Company NCOs, a Cpl Mutsinghani, piped up and again informed me that Ritchie was not happy.

"Yes, I gather so, but where is he tonight? Why is he not approaching me when my company are back?" This started a slanging match not only between me and Mutsinghani, but other NCOs. Bitching went back and forth and things started to get heated. A few of the lads started to square up to each other.

I raised my voice, "This is between me and Dobson; there's only one way to sort this. Go and get him and his fucking wife." I wanted her to witness what I was about to do. At the end of the day it was her fucking mouth that got these two companies at each other's throats. She was about to see her beloved husband suffer. I was completely wound up. My hands started shaking because I couldn't control my adrenaline. One of A Company's lot went to find my opponent. Within minutes he returned with Ritchie in tow. *Here we go,* I thought. *I have a large proportion of the battalion NCOs in the mess and I need to put up a good show.* As he walked into the mess, I ran towards him. I felt someone grab me around the waist whilst on my approach. This took me off my feet and I was swung around. Ritchie had obviously been taken back by my aggression. He started to buckle. He could see I was prepared to fight. He was not only in front of his own company's NCOs, but mine. He was the foreigner that wanted to join my regiment and theirs. He needed to tread carefully and make friends, not enemies.

I screamed, "Let me fucking at him." Ritchie made it perfectly clear that he didn't want to fight. He needed to win the mess over. He asked for calm. I kept my mouth shut, waiting for what he was going to say.

"I want to apologise for my wife. She can have a mouth on her at times. She needs to learn when to keep quiet."

"You wanted to fight me a few days ago. What's changed?" I shouted through gritted teeth.

"Inni, I'm sorry."

"You don't get out of it that easily." I pointed at him. "Why are you apologising? I want her here apologising."

"Inni," he continued, "she knows she fucked up. We are both apologising." With that I calmed down. I had made my point. I was not going to let anyone speak to me like I was a piece of shit. I'd had enough of that over the last few years. I'd also made it very clear that I was prepared to fight.

"OK, I'm happy with that." Ritchie approached me with his hand outstretched. We shook hands. That was the end of the matter. Ritchie stayed in the mess and had a drink. Both companies were back on talking terms.

Disputes in the regiment are never good. You have to find a resolution as quickly as possible. As a regiment, we have enough to fight against without fighting between ourselves. We need to stay tight and get on as a family.

Over the following years, Ritchie and I actually became quite good friends. We had gained mutual respect. He respected me for standing up to him and being prepared to go toe to toe. I in return respected him for having the balls to apologise in front of the mess. Ritchie's wife, in time, would also apologise, which of course I accepted.

This would not be the last time in Kenya I would be

prepared to fight another NCO. The next time, though, I would be fighting them!

C Company's next stop was a week's live firing. This is where the real hard work started. Live firing is the most dangerous part of our training. This goes without saying as we use live (real) ammunition. Any mistakes could be costly and life-threatening. During live firing, we would be shadowed by what's called an RST (Range Safety Team). The RST comprise of Corporals or Sergeants who follow your fire team, section or platoon while going through the attacks, ensuring safety and managing the range. Their job is to simply observe and control the safety of everyone going through the attacks, but not offer tactical advice or orchestrate section commanders' decisions.

The RST team were all Staffords apart from one Corporal who was attached to our unit. He came from the Royal Regiment of Fusiliers. I have racked my brain to try and remember his name, but I just can't recall it. His face I will never forget, but for the purpose of this we will refer to him as Corporal Tit, because that's exactly what the fucking prick was.

Every company went through the live firing stage of the exercise. Before my company deployed I was pre-warned about a member of the RST, a fusilier of Corporal rank that was a bit of a know-it-all. He spoke to the Lance Corporals and privates like pieces of shit. He was quickly gathering a reputation of being a bully and disrespectful to the lower ranks because he could hide behind his stripes and get away with it. Nobody liked him, not even other members of the RST, as I would later find out. He must have thought he was special and been a bit big for his boots. However, I would take him at face value. *He may be fine with me,* I thought. *I shouldn't judge people before I have met them.* I would make up my own mind on the Corporal in question. People often have personality clashes. Soldiers aren't going to get on 100% of the time. There are so many different personality traits to deal with. The general consensus was that he was getting a little bit too comfortable with being disrespectful of the regiment though. The regiment that was homing him! You don't walk into someone's home and disrespect them. This is exactly what he was doing, much to the disgust of many.

The platoon went through a process, beginning with Pairs Fire & Manoeuvre, Fireteam Fire & Manoeuvre and on to Section Attacks. On the final day all this would come together and we would go through a Platoon Attack. It was a long, hard demanding week, not just physically but mentally. On completion of each range activity we would be back-briefed individually by the RST who were following the attacks on how we performed and areas in which we could improve as individuals and as a team.

I had just commanded my section through a demanding attack which lasted almost thirty minutes. On initial contact from an enemy, which was actually targets rising from the ground controlled remotely by the RST who were following close behind, my section went straight into their SOPs. They returned contact, this being a couple of rounds in the general direction of the enemy, then zigzagged in a forward motion and hit the deck. After the enemy was identified, I, as section commander, gave my initial orders.

"Section, 400 metres, prominent bunker 12 o'clock, rapid fire!"

The section put a high rate of fire towards my indicated target. I went on to order my section 2IC to take over the fire control. I dressed myself back from the remainder of the section and came up with a plan of action to close with and destroy the enemy. I instructed my 2IC to remain in position with his fire team and put fire down while I led my fire team by right flanking into a gully approaching the said target. I dropped off a point of fire down into the gully and continued to attack the bunker with my grenade man at a ninety degree angle. I pointed the enemy position to my grenadier and we both crawled on our belt buckles towards the bunker. My grenadier posted a grenade in the bunker position. We both waited until the grenade detonated and then completed the attack by both firing bursts of automatic fire into the desired position, destroying the enemy and completing our mission with speed, aggression and decisive actions. I ordered my section to reorg (re-group) on the enemy location and went through our drills. The RST called a stop to the range. *Great job,* I thought. The attack went to plan. I couldn't be happier with my own performance and my soldiers.

We caught our breath, grabbed some much-needed water and waited for our attack debrief. My section was approached by Corporal Tit.

"How do you think it went? If you were to change anything, what would it be and why?" he said in a stern manner. Almost as if he didn't want to be there. I quickly got a negative vibe. I went on to say I thought the attack went well and as the commander, I was happy.

"Would I change anything? No," I responded. I was confident in my actions, my leadership and happy with my section's performance. The bullshit that came out of Cpl Tit's mouth was almost endless.

"Well, I would have done this. I would have done that. You didn't do this, you didn't do that." You get the drift here? He went on to say that my private soldiers were lazy and that the 2IC could have done better in his role.

"Have you got any positive feedback for me and my section?" I asked.

"You got through alive," was his response. Cpl Tit could see the dejection from the lads who had worked hard for me and themselves. He could also see the steam coming from my ears. I was clearly not happy with his feedback. I ordered my section to RV (rendezvous) in the safety holding area. I asked the 2IC to lead my section away. I stayed firm with Cpl Tit. As my section made themselves away, Cpl Tit shouted at them, "Fucking run away!"

Now, Corporal Tit is a rank above me and there is a chain of command and respect. He had none of mine. "Don't speak to my section like that. You know and I know they worked hard. The route I took to the enemy was the obvious one. The communication between the fireteams and my 2IC was excellent. The attack went perfectly." He began to raise his voice. "Fucking stop there," I said through gritted teeth. I started shouting and getting in his personal space. We were both quickly joined by another member of the RST who could see things were about to escalate.

"Inni, join your section," I was ordered. "Calm down, mate." As I walked away back to my section I pointed at him.

"I will see you soon."

"Fuck off," he muttered under his breath. I ran back towards him and threw my helmet to the ground and proceeded to remove my webbing (belt pack containing water and ammunition). We were face to face.

"All I have heard from others is how you think you are someone you're not. You're a fucking gobshite bully who has nothing good to say about anyone. I'm going to fucking drop you!" Again I was pushed away by the RST staff.

"Inni, join your section."

On returning to the safety area, I was asked by my Platoon Sergeant and NCOs what had gone on between me and the RST staff. I went on to tell them. They reported back to me that they had had similar despondent feedback from the prick. He had succeeded in getting on the wrong side of C Company's NCOs, as well as others in battalion. Cpl Tit became the topic of conversation over the next few hours. I decided at that point that he was not getting away with making my section feel low after all their good efforts. I was not going to let this bully speak badly of my colleagues. I would take matters into my own hands. His time would come!

Cpl Tit and I were kept apart for the remainder of the live firing exercise. He would look in my direction and I would mutter back, "Watch your step!" He would look away immediately. He had met his match; finally someone had stood up to him. I couldn't believe it had gone so long before someone had snapped. Just happens that it was me. I was extremely proud of my regiment and proud to be a Stafford. I was not having an outsider infiltrate us and gob off towards these fine soldiers. I was to become spokesperson.

C Company returned to Nanyuki Show Ground where we would take part in the last episode of our Kenyan experience. We were to be deployed on five days of R&R. The lads couldn't wait to spend more money on indulging with the ladies of the night. Risking getting a dose. Not for me. I managed to bag myself a slot in the jungle, housed in beautiful accommodation on the river's edge. This would be our base for white water rafting. What an experience. We would spend a day in the boat moving through the river and its exciting turns. An experience I will cherish forever. I felt so lucky. Another story for my rocking chair. We drank beer and had countless BBQs. Life felt good. During this week, Mike Tyson would fight Evander Holyfield in a heavyweight world title boxing match. We lads stayed up until 6am drinking beer, waiting in anticipation to watch the fight. It ended abruptly with Tyson taking a bite out of Holyfield's ear and spitting it on the canvas. Just another experience to look back on. I can say I was in Kenya white water rafting during that moment in sports history.

I returned once more to the Show Ground. Battalion were in the final stages of packing up and returning to the UK. It was only a matter of days before flying home and being once again reunited with Nicola. The NCOs decided to get away from the private soldiers for a while and go to the Corporals' mess. We interacted with each other well, stories were being told and the usual piss-take was going on. We were having a great night. Cpl Tit entered the mess. Either he was fucking hard or fucking stupid. The latter, I believe. This man had spent the last six weeks criticising at great length the NCOs in the room, and he had the nerve to walk in and drink in our company. Cpl Tit didn't see me at this point. I decided to bide my time. The NCOs in the mess looked at me, almost to gesture that he was here. Cpl Tit later on dug his own grave and made a stupid judgement call. He took it on himself to drink too much. He started to make his way through the lads again, criticising their efforts and calling them down. I couldn't believe the nerve of the man. He put the final nail in the coffin when he stood up proudly and, in a pissed-up action, proceeded to inform the Staffordshire Regiment that he thought "the Battalion is shit". That was it. I make it clear at this point that I am not a bully, but far from it. I also treat people how I expect to be treated myself. This fucker, though, was taking liberties.

"Get outside!" I shouted. The mess turned towards me, knowing what was about to happen. Cpl Tit looked at me. He must have drunk some hard juice because at that point he looked confident and motioned me towards him. This I obliged. I let him gracefully and kindly attempt the first punch. I pulled my body back as his right hook missed wildly. *That's it; it's all fair game now you have swung at me.* I proceeded to punch him square in his chest which took him back and he gasped for breath as I had just violently winded him. Two more punches picked with precision and he was down. Flat on his back in front of NCOs that he had abused for weeks. I peered over him and smiled.

"Can I have a debrief on that?" No response. The lads clapped and cheered. He made himself get to his feet. I waited to see if he fancied another go. He, of course, didn't. He scurried away into the safety of his accommodation, not to be seen again.

You will hear more about Corporal Tit. I come across him later on in my army career.

The regiment left Kenya and returned to Tern Hill. I have fond memories of the place. I saw wildlife that I never thought I would roam free. I visited a chimpanzee sanctuary, came across black rhinos, a family of hippopotamuses, zebras and much more. As for the scorpions, snakes and tarantulas, I wish I hadn't met those.

If I hadn't already had a name in battalion, then I had made it over these last six weeks. I was to become well respected within the Corporals' mess. What you saw was what you got. I was now a prominent figure in the mess. Other NCOs could see that I had an edge about me. I stuck up for my soldiers and defended them. I would not be spoken down to. I had earned my respect. I, in turn, would be respectful back. If I was crossed, then be prepared for the consequences. I will make it clear: I am not a bully but I defend those that are bullied. I have gone through life treating people how I expect to be treated myself. If you follow that simple rule, you will not go far wrong.

My father said to me once, "Mark, you make a great best friend, but if crossed you make the worst enemy." At the time I didn't think so. How my life evolves, I would have to agree.

I will finish this chapter by asking you to be kind to people. The world is full of hate. It's so easy to go through life being negative and down or judging people who are less fortunate than us. It's easy to follow others by bad-mouthing people and being disrespectful. Break the chain. Lead from the front. Good things happen to good people. Doing good things and making kind gestures on a daily basis is good for the soul. It makes you feel nice. On the other hand, if need be, you stick up for yourself and others who are not as strong as you. Protect the vulnerable. I had power but it was not abused. If you gain power, then use it in a positive manner. You will become respected. You will in turn be a leader, and more importantly, a good person.

6

THE ACCIDENT

I remember when I first joined battalion, I set myself a goal. When I was a private soldier I would strive to be the best in the regiment, and I achieved this. When I was a lance Corporal, again, I would work hard to become the finest, and again this happened. This was the attitude that drove me. I would not stop until my goal was achieved. I wanted to simply be the best. Be respected by my peers and be known as a formidable soldier. Similar to a professional footballer – they work to be the best, represent their country at the highest level and gain a reputation. I had the same desire. Whatever I did, I wanted to be the best at it. I wouldn't stop until I knew more than anyone else on any given subject. I would sit in my room of an evening and study pamphlets on field craft, weapon handling, tactics etc. I was a wealth of information. I wanted to walk into a room knowing that I knew more than any soldier in that vicinity. It was my life's mission. Nobody stood a chance against me. I had to be the ultimate soldier and not only that; I wanted everyone to know it. Being a soldier was not a job for me. I didn't do it for the money. I simply did it because I was a soldier through and through. I would have done it for the love, money aside. I had found who I was and who I was supposed to be. That is what I lived for. He was right, my grandfather was right.

Again, I achieved my target of becoming the best L/Cpl. My next target was to become a section commander. To achieve this I needed to be selected by battalion to go on Section Commanders' Battle Course (SCBC). This is a course conducted externally in the Brecon Beacons. Also known as Junior Brecon. I had to pass this to get my second tape (stripe).

Battalion held a pre-course for SCBC. Six of the best L/Cpls in Battalion at the time were brought together for a short course to see if we were ready for Junior Brecon and to find out who would become the top two candidates to be sent. I got a place along with a good friend known as Bill, or his nickname Funky. I was ready for my next stripe. I worked hard to prepare myself for the course. My fitness was excellent and I was extremely confident in my knowledge. I dedicated myself to mentally and physically preparing for this tough challenge.

Bill and I drove down to the Infantry Battle School, Dering Lines in the Brecon Beacons, South Wales together. We both knew that this was not going to be a cakewalk. The course was renowned for being tough. We would risk injury, suffer sleep deprivation, be cold, wet and hungry but still make command decisions and prove ourselves as leaders. However, we knew what the prize was at the end: a pay rise, our next tape and our own section in battalion.

The first part of the course would consist of learning to teach all the small arms weapon systems the infantry currently used. This included the 5.56mm rifle, LSW (light support weapon), 51mm mortar, 94mm LAW (light anti-tank weapon), GPMG (general purpose machine gun) and pistol. We were also to become range-qualified instructors. This meant we could manage the safety of live firing ranges and live firing exercises.

This part of the course was therefore mainly classroom-based. It lasted eight weeks and at the end, if we were up to standard, we would get our Small Arms Weapon Instructor's Qualification. I enjoyed this phase and passed with flying colours. It was Christmas time. We all packed up and went on annual leave. On returning two weeks later we would be on the tough phase of tactics. This would last ten weeks, most of it spent in the field (on the area of the Brecon Beacons).

I went home to Nicola, who at this time was six months pregnant. I was excited to become a father but nervous at the same time. The extra cash for passing SCBC would obviously come in useful at this time. This added an extra incentive, obviously, to passing the course. Over Christmas I would continue to keep my fitness up to its highest standard by going on daily runs, and also keep my head in tactics pamphlets to educate myself on areas which I was about to embark on.

Bill and I met up and made our way back to Dering Lines. It was a cold January, as you can imagine. Brecon is a different ball game! It was freezing. The first day back and we had to complete a simple military test. It's called the CFT (Combat Fitness Test): 8 miles with 45lb of kit and carrying your rifle. The march (tab) had to be completed in two hours to pass. If you failed then that was you finished. You would be RTU'd (returned to unit), sent back to your battalion in shame, may I add. Christmas told on some and they failed, not to be seen again. Bill and I passed with ease, and so we should. This would not have been a problem for us, as long as we stayed in shape over the Christmas period.

The first week was about to end. Friday morning came and we, as a course, had to parade on the square to have kit checks and ammunition divided up and be given command roles. I had the first section commander role. With this I was given a 349 radio. It was like having a brick on the left side of your chest and a jellyfish smacked on your ear. They were horrible things.

We were about to go onto the area and do some section attacks. Three 4-tonne vehicles were parked up on the square ready to take us that twenty minute journey from camp to hell (the area).

4-tonne vehicles are large trucks. They have a soft canopy overhead which can be removed. It offers little protection, only from elements such as wind and rain. They have pull-out wooden seats that run the length of the cab which you sit on with your backs against each other. The vehicle held sixteen of us in the back, all crammed up. I was positioned at the tailgate. I had a habit of always removing my helmet whenever I could. This was due to my having a tiny head; when I wore my helmet I looked a dick. I would look like a mushroom. On this occasion, for some strange reason that I will never know, I didn't. This would become costly.

The three vehicles moved in convoy throughout the journey. It was the 5th January and the weather was terrible. It was cold, wet and the mist was down. You could only observe approximately 100 metres from the back of the vehicle. I could just make out one of the other 4-tonners behind. We got onto the area and moved through the hilly terrain and down a re-entrant. The hill was quite steep and the roads were visibly icy. I distinctly remember thinking we were travelling far too quickly. As I thought this, I shouted as loud as I could, "Slow down!" I do not know if my demand was heard as the driver and the vehicle commander were in a compartment at the front which is separate and covered. Just then I felt the vehicle tip to the left-hand side. The wheels on the right of the vehicle cleared the road. *We're going to roll,* I thought. I was correct. The vehicle tipped further to the right until inevitably making it's first of three rolls.

Sixteen soldiers in the back of a 4-tonne vehicle beginning to roll is not a pretty sight or sound. Panic began. Lads started shouting in both fear and pain as the vehicle spun like we were in a washing machine. Legs and arms were broken, I later learned. Myself, however! Initially, I obviously displayed panic. Then two things amazingly came to me. The whole incident seemed to go into slow motion. The first thing to enter my mushroom head was, *Stay alive. Stay alive to see your daughter.* Now, at this point Nicola and I did not know what we were having. We decided to opt out of finding out what sex our baby was at our second scan, so to call the baby my daughter was weird. I knew, though, I could not leave my wife or baby girl. I had to fight to stay alive. Under no circumstances was my daughter going to grow up without a father. Secondly, I recalled a strange conversation that I must have heard years back and paid no real interest to. However, I recalled someone telling me of a car accident that they had heard of. Two young lads had died on impact but there was a young girl asleep on the back seats. She survived merely because she was asleep and in a relaxed state. There you go; there was my answer to survival. I closed my eyes and relaxed every muscle and joint in my body. I let the vehicle violently throw me around. I stayed true to my word and remained relaxed; I had to trust the story was correct. I recall being banged about but no real overwhelming pain during my spin dry.

The vehicle came to a stop. Chaos erupted. The lads in the vehicle were scrambling around to exit the vehicle at first opportunity. Not me. I was trapped. The first thing I thought, though, was *I've survived.* Little did I know things were about to become desperate. I found myself, having done numerous somersaults, landed in the corner of the vehicle on my back with my legs above my head. The position was extremely uncomfortable. I didn't scream, I tried to just wait patiently for the panic to die down. During this time I realised the removable wooden seats were bearing down on my legs, creating more pressure on my back and ribs. As the lads dismounted, selfishly they were crawling over the seats which were pinning me down. I felt my ribs crack distinctly as more pressure was forced onto the seats. Still I was not too frightened – I had survived and broken ribs were not going to kill me, after all. Then, to my horror, the chin strap of my helmet (the helmet that I usually removed, remember) slipped off my chin and into my neck. I was on my back pressed into the corner of the vehicle, legs over my head with the chairs on top of my legs. My arms were splayed at an angle in which it was impossible to release my chin strap. I began to choke. It was as though I had a rope wrapped around my neck cutting off my windpipe. I was fighting for a small amount of air. I became desperate. I attempted to move my arms in the direction of my chin strap but failed as my arms were pinned down by something heavy. Reality sank in. I had survived the crash itself but my fucking helmet was about to end my life. I became desperate. I started to fade and began to get tunnel vision due to the carotid arteries being crushed. I knew that if I didn't get oxygen into my lungs soon then my next attempt at breath would be my last. With one final burst of energy, I attempted to move my left arm. It didn't go far, but what it did do was grab the soldier next to me. I yanked my arm in the direction of my helmet as if to indicate where my problem was. Thankfully, he must have seen my situation. He leant over and opened up my chin strap. He had saved my life. My head fell back and I took a huge gasp of air.

"Thank you, thank you," I repeated over and over again. I never got to see who saved my life that day. I wish I could look into his eyes and thank him. At this point I knew I was going to be OK. Well, alive anyway, no matter what injuries I had.

One by one the lads escaped the vehicle. I was left remaining. All I could do was lie on my back and observe the roof. My instructor was laid next to me. He was reassuring me that things were going to be OK and that help was on its way, and to stay perfectly still. I remember hearing the screams from the lads resulting from the terrific pain they must have been in. I didn't feel too bad at this point. That's to say, my breathing was laboured and my chest felt tight due to the broken ribs. Then I realised. I couldn't feel my legs. Nothing, nothing at all! I began to panic.

"I can't feel my legs," I shouted.

"Relax," was the order I got back. I believed at that very moment in time I was paralysed. A moment of peace came over me. Think of the big picture I thought – even if I couldn't walk again, I would get to hold my daughter. Things could be worse. I began even at that early stage to accept that I was never going to walk again.

Approximately twenty minutes later I heard a familiar voice shouting, "Get back, you bastards." I wondered what was going on. I later learned that Sky News were at the scene. Imagine that! We were in the middle of a military training area and Sky News was there with their camera equipment, reporting. I then heard the propellers of a chopper. It was the air ambulance. It landed close by and a doctor came and introduced himself while I was lying underneath the wagon. The paramedics slid me onto a spinal board and secured me firmly to it. All I could say was, "I can't feel my legs". I was continually ignored. The paramedics obviously did not want to comment at this early stage. I remember being carried from my resting place in the vehicle out into the open of the cold air and towards the helicopter. I was loaded and within minutes I was in the air. I had an excellent view of the ceiling of the chopper about a metre above my head. A doctor would glance over towards my eye line on occasions and ask me questions. He told me that we were on our way to Nevill Hall Hospital in Abergavenny.

It was a fifteen-minute flight from the crash location to the hospital. During this time I still failed to feel anything in my legs. I felt lucky though. I kept thinking of how that damn chin strap had cut through my throat. Why did I not take my helmet off? It was something I never did, leave it on. I then began to think of my wife, Nicola. Being six months pregnant, I didn't want her to worry about what state I was in. Who was going to let her know?

We landed in what felt like a field very close to the hospital entrance. I was dismounted from the helicopter and placed onto a bed, still on the spinal board. I was wheeled in and informed that I was having an MRI scan immediately. I spent the next thirty minutes inside a tube with headphones on. Strangely enough, I began to drift into a sleep. The shock must have been wearing off after taking a toll on my body and emotions. When I came out of the scan I was wheeled into what I can only describe as a theatre. *What's going to happen to me?* I thought. A doctor piped up.

"Mark. I have some junior doctors with me here. I'm going to talk about your injuries." *Here we go!* The doctor proceeded to say, "As you can see, he has fractured his back in this location." He must have been looking at the MRI results. *That's it,* I thought, *I'm never going to walk again.* At the time I thought a broken back meant that. He continued to say that they needed to go through a meticulous order starting at the head. *You mean there is more?* I feared. The doctor went on to confirm that I had also fractured eight ribs. Everything else seemed at this stage to be OK. I did report that I had lost the feeling in my face on the left-hand side. This was trauma from that bastard 349 radio cracking me in the face as hard as a Mike Tyson punch. The feeling returned around six weeks later. The doctor confirmed to me that the loss of feeling in my legs was hopefully to recover within 48 hours. It was caused by inflammation around my spinal column and as the swelling went down, feeling would return. True to his word, it did. During all of this, I was dying for a piss. I kept telling the nurses that I needed to go.

"Just hold a little longer Mark." Holding it a little longer went on and on and on. I couldn't hold it anymore. *I warned you!* For the first time in probably twenty years I became a bedwetter.

I was taken to a ward within the hospital and settled in. I

still had my army clothing on (the bits that weren't cut off me anyway) and my face covered in cam cream (camouflage face paint). I lay there looking out of a nearby window, appreciating the value of life for the first time. *I almost died an hour ago.* I asked a nurse if she would telephone my wife. I warned the nurse that my wife was pregnant, so to tell her I was fine.

I could not move from my bed. My back began to throb. Morphine helped take me to my happy place. That evening I watched Sky News, wondering if the accident had made the TV. Bill (Funky) had come to visit me. I was so happy to see him. We were really close friends as well as colleagues. He told me that the course was on lockdown and they had to spend the weekend in camp, just in case any injuries came to light and to keep the newspapers and cameras away from Dering Lines. The accident had made the screen; a detailed report on the incident. The cameras showed the state the vehicle was in. It was completely destroyed. I remember thinking, *How has anyone survived, let alone all of us?* Then I saw a weapon on the ground. The yellow BFA (Blank Firing Attachment) was completely intact but the remainder of the weapon was completely flat. *Wow,* I thought. *That could have been one of us.* To this day, I can't believe how lucky we were.

So I told you earlier that I had pissed the bed that afternoon! Well, as time went on I was dying for a shit. "Bill, mate, I need a shit but I can't move my arms to wipe my arse." A nurse had brought me a bed pan earlier that day, but I couldn't position myself to go. I mean, have you ever tried to shit while lying flat on your back? It's fucking near impossible. I was so desperate that I achieved it. Bill helped pull my hospital gown up and slid the pan to my side. I tilted my body onto my left, giving Bill full view of my spotty arse. Pure relief! Bless my dear friend. He went on to remove the pan and wipe my arse as if I was a baby. Only a close friend could do that, hey?

The next day, Nicola and my parents came to visit. I was not well at this point. I suppose the adrenaline had left my body. I felt very weak and was suffering with nausea and vomiting. I was in considerable pain with my back and ribs and I felt I couldn't talk properly due to the punch delivered from my 349 into my chops. The Sergeants' mess very kindly offered to put Nicola up for as long as I was in hospital. She declined the offer and returned home to the Midlands to the comfort of our own home.

I was to spend four weeks in Nevill Hall Hospital. I had intense physiotherapy and was a regular user of the hydrotherapy pool. I was determined to leave as soon as possible. Bill would often visit me when he could, between exercises. He was doing well on the course and looked as though he was going to pass. I have to say, I was jealous. I wanted to get the course completed and in the bag. For me to pass, I knew I would have to return and complete the tactics phase. My day came to leave. I walked out of the hospital on crutches and returned to Dering Lines. A duty driver was provided to take me home to the Midlands to be reunited with Nicola.

I spent a further six weeks at home slowly recovering from my fractured back. I had one thing in mind and that was to get fit, return to Brecon and complete the course. I returned to work and quickly set on my task of achieving this goal.

In the meantime, my baby came along. I was right – it was a girl. My premonition was correct. We were to name her Bethan. I would call her my angel – I never told her why. My angel would be sure to visit me again in the future and, I believe, save my life yet again!

After three months of being back in battalion, a place came up on SCBC. I made sure it was mine. I was not fully fit but believed that my grit, determination and never-say-die attitude would serve me well and get me through. I arrived at Dering Lines and made myself quickly at home. I was placed in a section where I would have the same instructor as before: CSgt

Mendrowski, a Para who had definitely taken a liking to me. On returning he pulled me aside and asked if I was OK, and had I come back too early?

"No," I responded. I was eager to get this course cracked just as Bill had done months earlier. Bill had since been promoted and had been lined up to be posted out of battalion as an instructor at ITC Catterick. This is what I wanted more than anything.

Day 1 came and it was time to complete the CFT (eight-miler). We all paraded on the square and I looked at the three 4-tonne vehicles lined up to take us onto the area. I stared at them for a minute. I was going to have to get back in one. This was something I had not done since that day and not even thought about until now. Fear came over me. *I don't know if I can do it,* I thought.

"Get on the vehicles," I heard shouted. I made my way towards my vehicle. The lads got on one by one. I was the last. I threw my kit on, placed my foot onto the tailgate and offered my hand to the next man to pull me up. I sat on the tailgate. CSgt Mendrowski lifted the tailgate up and looked at me. He must have sensed some trepidation. *You ok, Inman?* He mouthed without making a sound. I nodded back towards him, terrified. I removed my helmet and we set off.

Being a passenger of a 4-tonne vehicle would never be the same for me again. I always had some fear every time I had to go on one. I suppose this is only natural. We arrived on the area safely this time, dismounted and prepared ourselves for the tab ahead, knowing we must pass this march otherwise we would be RTU'd. The march began at a good pace and I felt OK. I was clearly nowhere near the fitness level I had expected of myself or had been previously, but I was still confident that I could get through the next eight miles. Mile after mile went and my back became increasingly painful. Reality soon hit. I should not be here. I was halfway through the course and at the bottom of

Dixies Corner (a prominent landmark on Sennybridge area). I had a steep hill to climb for approximately 800 metres. The gradient increased along the way. The 45lb of weight in my Bergen (rucksack) began to take its toll on the base of my back and the pain increased step by step. I started to fall away from the main pack. Mendrowski noticed I was falling away and joined me.

"Fucking get up there," he ordered. He wanted me to pass this CFT; he knew how much it meant to me and admired the fact that I had returned quickly when others would have milked the injury and used it as an excuse not to return. He did his best to motivate me. I couldn't look up. My head was down, staring towards my feet, watching them take step by step. I would stop momentarily and bend forward, taking the pressure from the weight of the Bergen off my back for a split second. I glanced up towards the pack, witnessing them pulling further and further way. A safety vehicle was hovering behind, picking up casualties along the route. I was not going to get on the 'Jack wagon' (Jack-it-in wagon or quit wagon). Nobody wanted to get on that unless it was a genuine injury; even then you were looked upon as a bottler, and that wasn't me. I had gone through hell. I wanted to complete this course so bad I was prepared to crawl. It was not my decision to make, though.

"Stop, Inman," I was ordered.

"No, Colour. I can't quit."

"I'm telling you it's over before you make your injury worse." Mendrowski ordered me to stop. I dropped my Bergen and felt instant pain relief. "Throw your kit on the safety vehicle." I became a passenger of the Jack wagon, to my shame.

On returning to Dering Lines I showered and got into my working dress. I was sent to the medical centre where I was told I was being RTU'd. I was heartbroken. I genuinely thought my military career was over. I wanted to get out of Brecon as quickly as I could and be consoled by Nicola who, as well as Bethan, I thought I had let down. Looking in hindsight, I should never have gone back so soon. I could have messed up my one and only opportunity of returning to SCBC as most soldiers only get two attempts, the accident being my first and my stubbornness to return quickly my second. I was to return to battalion with the news of my failure.

I reported to my CSM (Company Sergeant Major) who placed me in front of my OC (Officer Commanding). I stood to attention before his desk as he made me feel a failure. Major Summers, a complete fucking prick. He didn't look at it as though I was brave for attempting to go back so soon. He looked at it as if I quit at the first hurdle. He went on to tell me how I wasted his time and efforts and that I would never go back for another attempt. So that was it. My dream of becoming a section commander was over.

I refused to let that cocksucker tell me I wasn't going back. I would give battalion no option but to send me. I became even more fixated with getting on SCBC and completing the course. It became at that point my life's mission and I was not going to let this knob call me a failure or a waste of time. I will show the pissant. And I did.

Over the next twelve months I worked tirelessly to get back to my best. I would push my body to places it had never been before. At this stage of my career, battalion were posted at Moor Barracks near Salisbury Plain, Wiltshire. Nicola and I had moved from the Midlands and into a pads house (army accommodation) in order to stay together as a family. At weekends I would put on my boots and run up and down the Seven Sisters (seven steep 100–150 metre hills) to work on my cardiovascular and leg strength while testing my back's resistance. I would load up my Bergen with more than 50lb in weight and tab miles and miles. I can honestly say I felt like a machine. Nobody in the platoon or company could compete with me. I was unbelievably fit. I felt ready.

I asked to go on Commanding Officer's Interviews, where I put a case over to him that he should send me one final time to Brecon to finish what I had started. I promised him I would pass. My Platoon Commander expressed to him how fit I had become and how I wanted nothing more than to right the wrong. I finished by saying after everything I had been through with this course, I felt I deserved one final attempt. I was granted my wish.

I returned to Dering Lines in the January after the Christmas break. Exactly one year since the accident. I had a new instructor. I believe he had got wind of what happened to me the previous year. He was a good instructor. A guardsman who pulled no punches! Exercise after exercise went by. I would often find myself in a command role, either section commander or 2IC (second in command). I knew I was doing well. The feedback I was getting after each command task was excellent. We had numerous fitness tests during the course; I smashed every one of them, and my back felt fine. Final exercise came. I was on the home straight, a two-week exercise on the area. I found myself being increasingly pushed, not only by my instructor but others in the company. This could only be a good thing. I was regularly put into Platoon Sergeant role. This role was only given to the soldiers who were performing well and needed to be tested that little bit further.

As I was running up and down the platoon line while on an extraction exercise, one of the instructors approached me. "Inman, You see that flag? That's endex [end of exercise]." I thought he was joking as we had only been in the field for 5 days. It was supposed to be a 14-day exercise. On reaching the flag we were met by the CSM.

"Lads, we need to leave the area immediately and return to camp. There has been a national outbreak of foot and mouth and we have no option but to leave the area. The exercise is over." I thought all my Christmases had come at once. I had completed SCBC. I'd done it. I knew I had passed, that went without saying. At that point I didn't care what grade I got. I was just happy that I had got through the course injury-free and excelled while achieving this year-long goal.

On returning to camp and cleaning all our kit and equipment and administrating ourselves, we were called one by one into our instructor's room to be debriefed and informed if we had passed or failed and given our final grade. Lads came out of the room with a smile on their face ("passed C grade", "passed B grade"). It was my turn. I was the last to go in. My instructor gave me a detailed debrief on how I performed week by week. He finished by announcing I had achieved a distinction. I could not believe what I was hearing. Nobody in the history of my regiment had ever been awarded a distinction. My thoughts went straight to that motherfucker Major Summers. *Wait until that bellend finds out my result. He'll be eating his words.* I couldn't wait to look him in the face. I thanked my instructor for all his efforts in guiding me and teaching me my new skills. He wished me luck and shook my hand.

The camp commander was also a Stafford. He had asked the CSM to send for me. I walked into the office and he could not stop congratulating me. "You are the first Stafford to ever receive a distinction on this course. Usually this accolade would go to a member of the Parachute Regiment, so you have broken the chain there. Not only that, there is a further surprise for you." I wondered what this would be. He shook my hand and again congratulated me on my achievements.

That evening I visited the cookhouse to get my evening meal. As I was sat eating, I noticed CSgt Mendrowski approach my table. "Can I join you?" he asked. He sat next to me and congratulated me on completing the course, coming back after all the odds were stacked against me and finally, achieving my distinction. He also shook my hand and continued, "I'm really happy for you." I'm sure he was true to his word. I bet he was pleased I never gave up. That's me, though. I never ever quit.

The following morning the course assembled at the theatre where we'd often have lectures and tests. We had our debrief and were congratulated on completing the course by the OC and CO. The Commanding Officer was handed a picture frame. Inside the frame was a bayonet. "I award this to the top student on the course." I knew I was in the running, but a Stafford would not win this, surely? "I take great pleasure in awarding this to L/Cpl Inman." I got out of my chair to applause from the other 150 soldiers and marched to the CO. I saluted and gathered my award. It was beautiful. Out of those 150 excellent soldiers who had just achieved section commander status, it was me who came top. What a privilege that I hold dear still to this day.

What I had been through that year demonstrates my never-say-die attitude. I wanted to be a section commander more than anything in the world. I could not give up on my dream. No matter what hurdles were placed in my way along that journey, I faced them and overcame them. Many would have quit and given excuses to why their dream had not been achieved. I strongly believe if you fail to achieve your dream then you have failed yourself and only have yourself to blame. Fight hard for what you want and never let anyone take your dreams from you. If you fight through adversity then it makes achieving your dream even sweeter.

7

PROMOTION

I returned home from Brecon and spent the weekend with Nicola and Bethan. Nicola and I celebrated my result with a movie and a bottle of wine or two. I spent that weekend relaxing and taking in my achievement. Already I was plotting my next move. In the back of my head I kept mulling over whether it was the right time in my career to attempt SAS (Special Air Service/Special Forces) selection. It had always been an ambition of mine since I first read *Bravo Two Zero* by Andy McNab. It was such an inspiring book. After my stint in Stanley Prison, I sourced a copy. I tore out the last page and kept it with me in my wallet for years. If you ever read the book and you get to the last page, you will understand why.

I knew that new doors were going to open for me. I could push to go onto Senior Brecon – Platoon Sergeants' Battle Course (PSBC) – straight away, but this would mean returning to Brecon over the next year, something I was unsure about at that particular time. I knew a posting out of battalion would also be an option. Bill (Funky) was in ITC (Infantry Training Centre) Catterick and was enjoying it. Maybe this could be up

103

my street? Or I could knuckle down and purely focus on my ultimate goal of becoming an SAS trooper.

Monday morning quickly came. I paraded with the remainder of Dragon Company. I had been transferred from C Company pre-SCBC and become a team commander of Recce Platoon (Reconnaissance Platoon). Recce Platoon is a much sought-after platoon within the regiment. They are called the eyes and ears for the Commanding Officer. The platoon would deploy in advance before the remainder of the battalion in order to gather intelligence of enemy movement. The platoon would often have the best soldiers in battalion as its members. Everyone in Recce Platoon knew this and had some swagger about them. It was a privilege to be a member of Recce for each and every soldier, no matter the rank. Being a part of Recce would also be a good stepping stone for SAS.

D Company, which was later renamed Dragon Company after recognition of the Hong Kong tour, comprised of four platoons – ourselves (Recce), but also Mortars, Milan (anti-tank) and the Pioneers. There was much inter-company competition between us all, which made for great banter.

Dragon Company was commanded by our OC, Major Grilsby, a great OC who I personally had much respect for. That made a change. Usually officers and I didn't have the best of relationships. The CSM (Company Sergeant Major) had a Mortars background and was not a big fan of Recce Platoon. He went by the name of Ted Cook.

While on parade, Major Grilsby spotted me. "Well, L/Cpl Inman, you had better come and see me." He and the rest of battalion had already got wind of my distinction result. My celebrity status had just gone up from C class to A. Initially I waited outside the CSM's office. He called me in and went through the motions of welcoming me back to 'his' company. At no point did he acknowledge my achievement. I could clearly see he had some sort of problem with me. It's not as though I had an ego, but I knew what I was capable of and I believe this made him uneasy. He was Mortars through and through and didn't give much to the other platoons, especially Recce. Ted Cook had always gone through the back door while climbing the ranks. He did it the easy way. He didn't complete SCBC or PSBC, but qualified through the ranks by doing Mortars qualifications. In my eyes he was a REMF, and REMFs don't go down well with me.

CSM Cook marched me into the OC's office where he remained while Major Grilsby rose from behind his desk and shook my hand. "What an achievement. Not only to get your Distinction but to come back after the year you had." I thanked Major Grilsby for his welcoming and kind words. He continued. "I only respect two kinds of people in this world, international rugby players and members of the SAS. You're not a rugby player, are you Inman?" I understood what he was getting at. Major Grilsby wanted me to go on selection. To hear it from him, though, was encouraging.

There had been two previous Staffords who had been successful in going through the selection process and being badged SAS. Many of the Regiment would not apply as they had a fear of embarrassment for attempting and an even greater fear of what others would say if they failed. I had just returned from SCBC with a distinction and 'Top Student', there was no doubt in the regiment's eyes that I should go for it. The general consensus was that I would go on selection and not return to battalion but be successfully badged.

I asked Major Grilsby if he knew how long it would take for me to be promoted to Corporal (Cpl). He went on to say that it would be in the near future. The Commanding Officer could have promoted me as a 'local' or 'acting' Corporal but he wasn't going to do this. After all, only a while back he had wanted to find a reason to kick me out, never mind promote me. The fucking prick, after all I had been through he still had it in for me.

I informed Major Grilsby that I would take serious consideration before applying for selection. I wanted to make sure I was ready.

Over the next few months I would settle back into battalion life nicely. There was still no sign of my second stripe which I found fucking annoying, especially when I would find out that others who had passed SCBC with me had been made up (promoted) within their regiments. It just went to show that my CO still had some resent towards me.

A battalion exercise was fast approaching. The regiment was preparing to go to BATUS (British Army Training Unit Suffield), Canada for three months. *This is great,* I thought. *Another one for the rocking chair.*

Battalion would have a bit of down time before this, however. It had been arranged for us to have some inter-company football. I was a bit tasty in midfield and the company knew this. On parade one Wednesday afternoon, known as Sports Afternoon, one of the Sergeants from Mortar Platoon was trying to get a team together. His name was Sgt Smith, another REMF.

"L/Cpl Inman, can you play?" he asked.

"Sorry, Sarge, I have an injury," I responded. I genuinely did have too – something I had picked up while running up and down those Seven Sisters on the back area. I had twisted my ankle and it felt sore. I wanted to protect it for the upcoming tour of Canada and not risk it becoming worse by kicking a fucking football around.

With that I walked away, only to hear Sgt Smith say, "It's because of wankers like this that company never wins anything."

"What did you just fucking say?" I bellowed towards his direction. The company froze. "Say it again. Say it to my fucking face, you REMF." A Lance Corporal gobbing off towards a Platoon Sergeant is not the done thing. However, by now you know I will not be spoken to with disrespect, especially in front of the company and definitely not by a fat REMF. Sgt Smith fancied himself a little. He thought he had some fight in him, so he too couldn't back down in view of his platoon and company. One of the lads held me back from approaching him closer. He knew from my reputation that I would not have him speak to me like that. All of a sudden I heard a familiar voice. "Lance Corporal Inman, get out of here, get to the platoon lines." It was my platoon 2IC, Colour Sergeant (CSgt) Torrance. Toz and I were also good friends, despite the difference in rank. Toz Torrance had taken me through my SCBC pre-course and took some credit for my distinction. He respected me and I, in turn, respected him. I proceeded to the platoon lines where I ran a bath. I wanted to bathe my ankle and at the same time keep a low profile. I got into the bath and started to relax. I was rudely interrupted by a knock on the door.

"Inni."

"Who is it?" The door opened and it was Sgt Smith. "You are fucking joking me!" I said as I rose to my feet naked with dick dangling. "You want to come and fight me while I'm naked to give yourself a chance?" I was furious and Sgt Smith must have seen this. "You're taking fucking liberties," I went on to say. Now, I was more than happy to fight if that's what he wanted, but come on, let's have a level playing field. Surely this was an unfair advantage. After all, I'm sure Sgt Smith would not want me mounted on top of him choking him out while I was naked. Live that one down!

"Inni, I have come to apologise. I shouldn't have said that in front of the company. I'm here to apologise to you." *Fair enough, Sarge.* He went on to tell me that CSM Ted Cook had observed the whole incident and that he wasn't happy with me.

"OK, thanks for giving me the heads up, Sarge." The

incident between Sgt Smith and I was closed. I got out of the bath quickly, expecting to be summoned to Cook's office. Within minutes, CSgt Toz Torrance entered the platoon lines.

"Fair play to you, Inni. I witnessed the whole thing. However, if you ever speak to me like that I will knock you out!" We both smiled at each other. I think Toz saw a lot of himself in me. He went on to say that the CSM wanted to see me immediately.

I got into my working dress, polished my boots and rubbed my beret down of any dust or fluff. I made myself look presentable and made my way to the CSM's office. *Get ready for a bollocking,* I thought.

"Get in my office, Inman." I marched in front of his desk and halted. I had given Sergeant Major Cook the excuse he was looking for to come down on me. "Who the fuck do you think you are?" I gave my side of the story and informed Cook that Sgt Smith had approached me to apologise. He didn't give a shit. I had just played into Cook's hands. I had given him the ammunition he needed to make an example of me. It must have given him great joy that the lad who had just returned with distinction, top student from SCBC – a course he never did – and was contemplating SAS selection – something he would never have the balls to attempt – would be on the other side of a dressing down. It became about him and his power. He could go back to the Sergeants' mess and tell all his mates he had bollocked Inman. I suppose he had to be seen doing something about my insubordination but the matter was sorted between Sgt Smith and me. He showed a lack of professionalism by calling me down in front of the company. CSM Cook went to town on me. He gave me a real roasting. I let him also. I stood there and took all he had to throw at me until he shouted at the top of his voice, "You think you're something else. You're SHIT!" With that I smirked. *Shit,* I thought. *You know and I know I am far from it.* "What are you smirking at?" I didn't respond.

He knew what I thought of that comment, and he knew I was on a different level to him. He was sat in the room with my OC, Major Grilsby, when he was encouraging me to go on SAS selection. Would you really want to send a 'SHIT' soldier on that course? The bloke was a fucking idiot. Zero respect for you, bedwetter!

This started a very rocky relationship between Cook and me. I found myself subject to his petty form of trying to piss me off and fuck me about. When Dragon Company would be on guard duty, he would place me as guard 2IC on weekends. He would also take great delight in putting me on duty over the weekend as COS (Company Orderly Sergeant). This was usually a task for new Lance Corporals, not the more senior ones like me. I knew his game. I would not let this go on for long. Whenever there was a shit job that needed supervision of an NCO, you could guarantee he would place me with the task.

The final weekend was fast approaching before leaving for Canada that Monday morning. I was looking forward to spending some quality time with Bethan and Nicola. It was Friday afternoon. I was in the platoon lines when I was summoned by the duty runner to report to the Sergeant Major's office. *What does the prick want now?* I thought.

"Lance Corporal Inman, you have been promoted to Corporal with immediate effect." There were no congratulations or shake of the hand. This is news he must have been dreading giving me. He must have hated every second of it. He just tossed me a rank slide displaying my second tape. I had worked fucking hard for this stripe and this was the best the motherfucker could say? What must have lightened his mood was, "Unfortunately, Corporal Inman, I have to place you on COS on Sunday." I could not believe it. I had just been promoted and the next thing, I was being placed on weekend duty. Remember, this was a job of the junior Lance Corporals, not a fucking Corporal. I didn't say a word. I wasn't going to give this tosser the satisfaction. He must have had this planned. *Let's fuck up Inman's last weekend with his family.* I turned away and left his office.

I removed my Lance Corporal rank slide and replaced it with my new one. I then immediately made my way to Battalion HQ. This is where all the admin is conducted and home for the CO and RSM. I entered the administration office and called over to Sgt Dobson, Ritchie's wife.

"I've come to sign off [hand in my 1-year notice]."

To leave the army you have to place a 1-year notice in. Sgt Dobson looked at me in shock. "You've just been promoted."

"Yes, I've achieved my goal, it's time to leave. Please can I have my papers?" Sgt Dobson didn't know what to do. She went into her superior's office and spoke to an officer of the Adjutants' General Corp. He came out to me.

"Corporal Inman, what are you doing?"

"Sir, please can I have my papers?" After some to and froing, my papers were placed in front of me. I signed them and returned to the platoon lines, informing nobody of what I had just done. Within 30 minutes, I was paraded in front of the OC Major Grilsby by Cook himself.

"Corporal Inman, firstly congratulations on your promotion – it's well-deserved."

"Thank you, sir."

He continued, "Why the hell have you just signed off?" CSM Cook must have known that this was a knee-jerk reaction to the fact that he had just placed me onto COS yet again.

"Sir, over the last six weeks I have done more weekend duties than any NCO in this battalion. I believe I am being punished for something. I have a young family at home wanting me to spend time with them before leaving for 3 months. My daughter is a baby and my wife has followed me down to Salisbury to support me. They do not deserve to see so little of me." Grilsby glanced towards Cook.

"Is this correct, Sergeant Major?" asked the OC. Cook responded with some bullshit about how I had just been unlucky and it had not been intentional. Cook must have been squirming in his boots. Major Grilsby read between the lines. He knew the reason why.

"I want Corporal Inman relieving of duty this weekend. Get one of the newly promoted Lance Corporals to cover COS." I had achieved what I set out for. I had belittled Cook and got my final weekend off with my family. *CSM Cook must fucking hate me.*

Major Grilsby went on. "You can get back to HQ and sign back on."

"No, sir. I have decided to leave."

8

CANADA

I had a lovely weekend with my girls that weekend. We had some quality family time together, courtesy of CSM Cook. The time went too quickly and before I knew it, I was saying goodbye to Nicola and Bethan. Bethan was too young at this stage of her life to appreciate her dad going away for three months. I felt sorry for Nicola. I was leaving her behind to cope with a baby and its demanding needs while I was playing soldiers on the other side of the world.

After a very long, tiresome journey we reached Canada and BATUS. I distinctly remember how hot it was. It felt so much hotter than Kenya had. It was the summertime and one of the hottest temperatures ever recorded in BATUS in history. Battalion went through a welcoming package which consisted of what we would be doing in Canada. Ranging from the exercises – both live firing and dry (blank) – the R&R package and what the army's expectations of us were in the local town. After this we were shown our accommodation and we settled in.

Our first week in BATUS comprised of acclimatisation.

This meant working on the vehicles we would be using during the two exercises. As a Recce team commander, I would command a small armoured vehicle called a Scimitar, a very small and agile armoured vehicle. It could fire 50mm calibre ammunition for longer range and 7.62mm for close-quarter battle. I had a private soldier as my driver and vehicle maintenance and a Lance Corporal as my gunner. I'm sure my Scimitar was jinxed; it would be forever breaking down and causing us problems. I fucking despised the thing. All in all I did not enjoy the mechanised (armoured) side to soldiering. I preferred to be on my feet in more of a light role. This led me to believe my future would lie in Special Forces (SAS) and not in continuing within the Staffords. That's if I was to remain in the military, of course. During this first week we were free to spend our evenings how we wanted. We would often go down into town and take in the local life. The lads used to descend on an establishment by the name of The Dolls House, a classy establishment popular with units before and after us. It was the most popular joint in town; popular because it would house the most beautiful girls who kindly stripped for a living. The girls had some dignity and didn't undress completely. I can't express how, but the place was really nice. It wasn't dingy like we would expect in this country. In Canada it is almost the norm. We would often visit, drink the beer and enjoy the views. We would play pool and just socialise with the locals and the girls. My platoon would visit regularly, and obviously I had to go to make sure the lads were behaving themselves and not getting up to mischief. I purely went to make sure my soldiers were acting accordingly, of course – this goes without saying! The girls began to become familiar with us lads. We respected them and treated them how ladies should be treated. The atmosphere was nice, friendly and relaxed. It was a good spot to enjoy our time off in. As a young, hot-blooded 24-year-old, I couldn't help but admire the girls and be in awe of some of the positions they could envelop into. I have previously mentioned that I was a bit of a pretty boy. I didn't have a lack of attention from girls either growing up as a young teenager and up until my late thirties. How things have changed! One of the girls began to take a liking towards me. She would often buy me a drink and encourage me to take her home. The lads thought it was great. I couldn't take the young lady up on her generous offer. I was a happily married man with a beautiful daughter at home. I would not want to disrespect them. Others would have easily buckled. I am proud to say "not me". I am not going to lie, I enjoyed her attention and it made some of the lads very envious indeed. I suppose it just helped with my ever-developing ego and notoriety throughout battalion.

It was time for the hard work to begin. We spent the day before deploying for exercise packing up our kit, sorting out our ammunition and housing it safely in the vehicles, preparing our rations and making sure our BVs (kettles) were working properly. These BVs were our lifeline. How could we, as soldiers, cope without our endless supply of coffee? I distinctly remember the date of this pre-exercise administration. I had my little silver portable radio on listening to England play Germany in Munich. The 1st September 2001 and Michael Owen scored a hat-trick to help beat the old enemy 5–1, a result which will forever be remembered. A shame we couldn't watch it, but the army and its admin comes first. I have a picture of me listening to that little radio still, a picture taken when an even more prominent event was listened to a matter of days later. This event would change my life forever.

Battalion deployed on exercise that following day. We went through the normal motions of closing with and gathering information on the enemy and reporting it up. The rifle companies would then attack positions previously identified by Recce Platoon. On completion we would go through debriefs of each mission, followed by regrouping and having fresh orders from the Platoon Commander. Day by day went by. It was a good soldiering experience and I learnt much throughout the exercise.

During this exercise, we had a break in which we harboured up the vehicles and administered ourselves as a platoon. We cleaned our weapons, made sure the vehicle was serviced, ate and, of course, got some sleep – all this before starting a fresh mission. Morning arose. My gunner L/Cpl Matts (Matty) made the crew some breakfast. I liked my boil-in-the-bag sausage and beans followed by a milky coffee. While sitting and eating, I turned on my little silver radio. The date was September 11th 2001.

My radio informed me that 2 United Airlines commercial jets had hit the Twin Towers of the World Trade Centre. I of course had no television, just my little radio to create the picture for me and the listeners. I (and others) naively had no idea what the World Trade Centre looked like. We later learned that a further plane had struck the Pentagon, the HQ of the United States' Department of Defence. Another had fallen out of the sky and crashed into a field. This was a coordinated terrorist attack by the Islamic group al-Qaeda. Militants associated with the group had hijacked the planes and gone on suicide missions, devastating the United States and the New York skyline. The Twin Towers would, after an hour and forty-two minutes, collapse in a heap. The death toll was in the region of 3000 innocent people, and 6000 were left injured. It also caused $10 billion worth of infrastructure and property damage. This act of terror would become known as 9/11. 9/11 was the single deadliest incident for firefighters and law enforcement in the history of the United States, with 343 and 72 killed respectively. Immediately the name Osama bin Laden was associated with the attacks. He was the founder of al-Qaeda and had been responsible for numerous other mass-casualty attacks worldwide. After establishing a base in Afghanistan, he declared war against the United States. Bin Laden was on the FBI's list of most-wanted fugitives in the world.

Things for us had just got real. This training in Canada had all of a sudden become very important. We weren't just training for the prospect of war. We would be going to war.

That night the regiment RV'd and paraded as complete battalion. The Commanding Officer addressed us by confirming what he knew of the situation and what he had been briefed to inform us. I remember him using the words, "Your training has never become so important. It is inevitable that as allies of the United States, we, as the British Army, will soon be at war." This is probably the wrong word to use – especially after 3000 people had just died – but I couldn't help feel excited. I wanted to help give that country some support. I wanted to help them give some pay back. If this meant me going to fight on foreign soil, then count me in. I would not hesitate.

Imagine spending your army career having trained and trained, doing countless exercises preparing for war which would not happen. You would almost feel cheated. You would feel like a professional footballer practising for a football match but never putting on the shirt and walking out to Wembley Stadium to win the FA Cup. That's how the army felt. This was my time, my war. I had to be a part of it.

The following exercise went by. We heard the word 'endex' come over the radio. We made our way back to camp and went through the monotonous post-exercise crap, cleaning the vehicles and servicing them then sorting ourselves out. We went to the cookhouse to get a decent meal and replenish ourselves. Our thoughts were on going straight back to The Dolls House to have a few beers and admire the girls. Word had got about that our flights back to the UK had been postponed. Due to 9/11, all flights out of America including Canada were ceased due to an ongoing threat. As a unit, we were to remain in BATUS with nothing to do. Battalion managed to pull some strings, to their credit, and arranged for numerous adventure training exercises. I was called to the CSM's office, Ted 'The Bellend' Cook.

"Cpl Inman, I want you to take nine private soldiers to a skydive centre in Calgary, Alberta. I have laid on a minibus for you. Ask for volunteers. You leave tomorrow. By the way, this has cost a lot of money for battalion, so make sure you complete ALL the jumps." Was this another attempt to piss me off? Little did Cook know that I had parachuting on my bucket list, so if it was an attempt to get one over on me, *you failed, motherfucker.*

I selected nine lads who I believed had worked well during the exercises and deserved the opportunity. All nine of them were well up for the experience and so was I. I did try to hide my excitement in front of the others as I wanted Cook to think he had one on me. The duty driver picked the ten of us up and off we went, a long 4-hour journey to Alberta. It gave us the opportunity to take in some of the sights, and at least we were away from battalion life and the bullshit that would often go with it.

On arrival at the skydive centre, I couldn't believe what I initially saw. On what I later discovered was the DZ (drop zone) was an ambulance picking up a parachutist who had landed on his back, breaking his coccyx. "Are you fucking kidding me?" I muttered. What the fuck was I letting myself in for? We dismounted from the vehicle and were escorted to our accommodation, wooden shacks that housed four per room. As the senior amongst us I had best pick of bed space. That went without saying. We had a recce of the area. There was a large hangar with parachutes laid on the ground, numerous fixed-wing planes jotted around and a training centre. The ten of us made our way into the centre where we were played a videotape that lasted twenty minutes. It was basically saying that should we have an accident, it was not the responsibility of the skydive centre. On completion of the video we had to sign waivers to this effect. For the remainder of the morning we were instructed on static line parachuting. This means you do not pull the cord to the parachute but the parachute has a long line that is attached to the plane. As you jump out of the plane and get a certain distance away, then the parachute is pulled and you glide down all nicely nicely. We then went on to be taught that when our chute opens it may 'flare', best described like a candle flame. If the chute has not opened and collected air like it should, then the chute flares and you make your way quickly towards the ground. In this frightening scenario, we were taught to place our hands into the ropes and attempt to vigorously pull them apart, hopefully encouraging more air into the chute and opening up fully. Should this fail, we would have a reserve chute. We would pull a handle on the right side of our chest, which in turn would release the original chute, which is flaring. After one second we would then pull a handle on the left side of our chest which should release a smaller chute which is secondary, our reserve.

As I looked at the lads' faces I began to see an element of fear. During the time we were at the centre we would have the opportunity to jump six times, weather (wind) dependent. Our first jump quickly approached. I had to lead, obviously. Four of us at a time mounted the plane. The plane took off and circled above until it hit the right altitude. I was to leave the plane first. However, it was not a case of just having the door opened then jumping. That would be too easy. I had to put my hands onto the struts of the plane wing. Once I was ready, I stepped out. This left me flying like bastard Superman, holding on to the strut of a plane with my feet trailing behind.

The instructor shouted, "Look at the dot." This was a prominent dot on the wing at eye level. I looked at it. "Release," the instructor shouted. I did so. I fell towards the ground with terminal velocity, with my legs kicking as if to find the floor which was 1500 feet below me. To my relief, my chute opened. I looked up towards it. I then tore off some handles that were Velcroed to the lines. This would help me control the direction the chute was travelling in. If I pulled down right, then I would turn right and left, vice versa. There was a one-way radio on the chute. An instructor on the DZ would instruct which direction to pull in order for you to hit the DZ, otherwise you would end up miles away in some farmer's field and not on the intended target area. As I glided safely towards the ground I started to feel some fear. If I was to look down, I could see my feet and the parachute harness digging into my crotch area. I thought to myself, *Is this harness strong enough?* I took in the views, which were pretty amazing. *Yes, another rocking chair moment,* I thought. *I have parachuted in Canada. Put that down on my list.* I was receiving instructions from the ground by radio. As I reached the ground with such pace, I was ordered to "flare". This means pull on both handles simultaneously. This in turn acts as a brake. I would then step out of the air and walk onto the DZ.

I looked up and witnessed another two lads making their way safely out of the sky towards the drop zone. *One missing,* I thought. I observed the plane that took us up land. One of the private soldiers had got out. He had bottled it. "There was no chance I was jumping," he announced. He, of course, had the piss taken out of him by the remainder of us. Now, the instructors said the second jump is your worst. The first time, when you are a virgin, you don't know what to expect, so you just do it. The second time is a different matter. You know exactly what to expect. They went on to say, though, that with every jump it becomes easier. We collected up our chutes and made our way into a large hangar. The purpose of this hangar was to re-pack the chute. The chutes were not our own. There must have been hundreds of chutes at the centre and although you re-packed a chute, you would not necessarily jump with the one you packed. This meant your life was in someone else's hands. If someone fucked up packing a chute then some poor bastard may flare or, even worse, pull the reserve. I found this very unnerving. We were taught how to pack the chutes and an instructor would always be present. He would talk us through the process, like making a bed, I suppose. Each chute would have a checklist which needed to be signed. At certain points of the pack you would have to stop. This was called a stop check. The instructor would check the chute at a stop check and sign the card and you would continue to the next stop check. This would continue until the chute was finally packed and ready to go.

Each evening we would eat a BBQ supplied by the centre and drink beer around a log fire. We all had a good time. Unfortunately, we still didn't have access to a television so were still unaware visually of what 9/11 meant. I had my little radio and would listen to updates. It appeared that the United States' military was about to embark on a huge mission to Afghanistan. They would be patrolling the mountainous areas in an attempt to find a needle in a huge haystack. That needle being Bin Laden.

Time went by on the skydive ranch. The lads began to bottle the jumps. One by one, they would approach me and say they didn't want to jump. Who was I to tell them they had to? They were here for some down time after working hard. It was supposed to be a bit of fun. The last thing I was going to do was abuse my power and rank by forcing them into doing something they didn't want to do. I was not a bully. Military training was different. If I asked them to do something, then they better damn well do it. This, though, was adventure training, not life or death.

I knew I personally had to complete my six jumps. Not just because that prick Cook told me to, but for me. If I say I'm going to do something, then I see it through. Anyway, if I was going to attempt to join the SAS I had better get used to jumping out of planes. They can jump from 15,000ft using a technique called HALO (high altitude – low opening), done with oxygen assistance due to the lack of air at that height, and all this to avoid radar. Not my poxy little 1500ft jump. I was taken up for the last time. There was just the instructor and myself. I went through the normal motions of holding the strut with both hands, releasing my feet, flying like Superman and finally look at the dot waiting, for the order to release. On releasing for my final time, I rolled backwards. I had not done this before. I then felt a thud. I struck the back of the plane for some unknown reason. It didn't hurt but I felt the force of the strike. I recall observing the plane from my back. My chute opened, I checked it immediately and to my horror it began to flare. I yanked the ropes as hard as I could but this failed to work. I panicked. From 1500ft it would only take 12 seconds to hit the ground travelling at terminal velocity. I had to act quickly. I pulled the ropes one final time and gave the chute the opportunity to open. It didn't. I had no choice; I had to do what I was taught to do on that first day. I reached for the right side of my chest and located the large loop handle, and pulled it away in a punching motion and with that force. I watched my chute disengage and felt a tug from my harness. I then pulled the smaller handle on my left in the same way I had just done on the right. The reserve opened. I glided down to the DZ with my heart pounding. I reached the floor and lay on my back thanking my lucky stars. The instructor on the ground ran over to me and checked I was OK. I didn't want to move. I was in shock. Once the shock wore off, a strange feeling of adrenaline came over me. I was on a huge high. I had just cheated death again. That feeling of the intense adrenaline rush would later in life become all too familiar and addictive.

Our time at the ranch ended and we made our way back to BATUS. On returning I was informed that flights out of Canada had recommenced and to pack our kit, as we were heading home in a couple of days. I telephoned Nicola and informed her I would soon be home. I made my way to my accommodation to start to pack up my belongings when I crossed paths with CSM Cook and Major Grilsby. I braced up to show my respect to the ranks.

"Corporal Inman, will you go to my office. I have something I need to speak to you about," said the OC. I made my way to his office and waited for him to return.

CSM Cook marched me in before Major Grilsby. My OC went on to inform me that battalion had received a posting order for me. I had been offered a posting to ITC (Infantry Training Centre) Catterick as a section commander for the duration of 2 years. I would be returning to Vimy Barracks, where only a few years before I was attending my Phase 2 training. This time I would be returning as an instructor of recruits. The other option would be placing in my application for SAS selection; at this moment in time, though, I had been signed off for the last three months. In nine months' time I would be discharged from the army and return to Civvy Street. I personally had no intention of leaving but I wanted to push them as hard as I could and make life uncomfortable for Cook. After all, he was the reason I signed off in the first place before leaving for Canada. I wanted to show that battalion were losing their prized Corporal due to the fact CSM Cook had bullied me. Surely questions were going to be asked sooner or later. *Why is Corporal Inman really leaving?* I could have made life very awkward for Cook and I think he began to realise this.

"Sorry, sir. I would like to kindly decline the opportunity of both. I have nine more months to push and I will be leaving the regiment." Grilsby looked shocked and Cook's arse must have been twitching. The shit was going to hit the fan for him. I was playing the system a treat. I, a Corporal, all of a sudden had a CSM in my pocket. Major Grilsby went on to say that both these options would be on the table for one week; if I returned to him a week later and still thought the same, then he would accept my decision. This gave me a week to let CSM Cook sweat. On leaving the OC's office, CSM asked me to go into his office.

"Corporal Inman, what a great opportunity for you. You need to be 100% sure before letting this opportunity slip by."

"I am 100% sure, sir. I was pushed into this decision, sir, and I will see it through." Cook went on by asking if there was anything he could do to help change my mind?

"Not at this moment in time, sir, no." With that, I left his office knowing I would not be getting fucked about in the very near future.

Battalion had packed up and we were ready to leave BATUS and make our way to Calgary Airport. On arriving at the airport, it finally dawned on me what 9/11 had consisted of. In the departure lounge was a newsagents. I could see countless magazines with images of the Twin Towers. I scrapped together enough dollars to buy myself a TIME Magazine. I spent the flight home reading in detail about the terrible events of that day.

To this day, I have not visited New York. It is a place I must go. I am drawn to Ground Zero as I must pay my respects. I know I will find the pilgrimage emotional. I still find it hard to contemplate what happened on that day. My heart goes out to the victims and families of all that lost those innocent people in those towers going about their normal daily business, the passengers on all four planes who must have been petrified, and those brave New York firemen and police officers. You all have my utmost respect.

9/11 also changed my life dramatically, as later in this book you will see. Everything I did from this point on was because of this day.

9

CATTERICK

My first job on returning to Mooltan Barracks was to inform Major Grilsby of my decision. I had spoken to Nicola about my options. Did I go on SAS selection now while my fitness was good and my confidence was at a high or did I pass on my knowledge to young recruits? I could shape them to be 'mini-me's; after all, the British Army was on the verge of war – any recruits I would be training could be joining their respective regiments and getting deployed immediately to Iraq. Nicola was very supportive. She informed me that should I take the posting to Catterick, then she and Bethan would move up with me. This would give us two years of stability. Knowing what I was doing for the next two years sounded nice. Bethan was still very young and it gave me the opportunity to bond with her and enjoy being a father. I was still young, I was 26. I could return from Catterick and go on selection after that. Decision made. I would accept the posting.

Within six weeks I was a new instructor at ITC Catterick, Vimy Barracks. Only years before, I had walked through the same gates as a recruit myself. Things had changed slightly from my day. Instead of breaking the training down into two phases like I had done, with my ten weeks basic training in Whittington followed by twelve weeks infantry training at Catterick, the whole of the recruits' training would be done in one location and in one complete course. I would receive recruits as Day 1 civvies and turn them into fully trained soldiers within the time period of six months.

I had received a telephone call prior to arriving at Catterick. It was Bill (Funky). "Inni, you're only fucking joining my platoon. I have just found out." This was great news. Bill and I had always been very close so to be posted out of battalion in such an important role with one of my best friends was music to my ears. This made the whole experience even more exciting.

On arriving at ITC, I was introduced to my new CSM and OC. They seemed OK. "We have heard great things about you, Cpl Inman," the OC announced. "I hope you thrive in this role and produce some excellent soldiers."

"I intend to, Sir," I responded. I was shown my platoon lines and was greeted by Bill. We embraced as if we were long-lost brothers. Bill went on to introduce me to the rest of the training team (platoon staff). Lieutenant Woodhouse, Platoon Commander from the Royal Welsh Fusiliers (RWF). A young lad who often fucked up! I liked him as he would often come to me for advice. I would also tell him straight what I thought about different topics. He let me manage my soldiers my way also. He rarely got involved and I respected this. I was not about to become micro-managed by anybody. My job was to produce soldiers and I was not going to have anyone tell me how to do it. Our relationship was good. Sgt Jones, Platoon Sergeant, another member of RWF. A great bloke and very funny; we too had a great working relationship. He lived on the 'pads estate' (army housing) close to Nicola and I. We would socialise a lot with him and his wife. The drinking sessions were immense. Sgt Jones was one of the finest Platoon Sergeants I ever had the privilege of working with. The section commanders comprised Cpl Wade 'Conrad' (RWF) – Jesus, he was one funny motherfucker – and finally, Cpl Saunders of the Royal Regiment of Wales (RRW). We didn't get on all too well. He had no real passion for producing good soldiers. He was just there for the easy ride. If he could back out of something he would. He would do the bare minimum to get through and this would tell in the quality of soldier he produced. He and I would clash quite regularly. He knew his place though and knew when to back down if things became a little heated. The training team was completed by Bill and me. All in all, we were a good team.

My first cohort of recruits came. I had made up my section room (their accommodation) with posters, educational military training information and motivational quotes. This room would be the recruits' home for the next six months. They must take pride in it and keep it tidy at all times. When I (or any member of the training team) should enter the room, then my recruits must immediately stand to attention in order to show respect to my rank and my status as their instructor. I was about to teach them everything from weapon handling, field craft, basic tactics, NBC (nuclear, biological and chemical warfare) and drill.

I expected high standards from myself, so in turn I expected high standards of my recruits. I could quickly see who the hard workers were who wanted to do well and the lads who just wanted to get by. I didn't have time for that. My soldiers were to be the best in the platoon. If this meant me spending longer with them in the evenings and re-teaching, than that's how it would be.

I had a reputation for being 'firm, fair but friendly'. This wasn't a game. I understood that I was producing soldiers who would be joining regiments and, in some cases, going to war immediately.

The British Army had just invaded Iraq. The Prime

Minister, Tony Blair, had sold the fact to parliament and the British public that he had strong evidence that Saddam Hussein had been harbouring weapons of mass destruction (WMDs) and that he needed to be overthrown for the threat to be eradicated. I wasn't too happy that I was in the UK training snotty nosed recruits when ideally I wanted to be in the Middle East getting involved. I had to look at the bigger picture. I was responsible partly for training these lads up and preparing them for war. I had to get through to them that this was not a game and in six months' time they could be face to face with the enemy.

My first cohort was going well and my soldiers were coming on nicely. They were already looking to be the best section within the platoon. I took great pride in this. It just spurred me on further. I wanted everyone to see that my boys were the best. They were the best because of me, my diligence and enthusiasm. I was making them into little Inmans.

The recruits had spent their first six weeks training and they were granted a long weekend off. They could return home with a travel pass (rail warrant/free travel by train) and have some down time. Before they left I very kindly informed them that they could bring back a duvet to sleep in. Until now they had been sleeping in army issue blankets and sheets. The blankets were horrid. I remember spending my training in them. They were known as 'itchy blankets' due to the hard-wearing fabric that was used to make them. My section at this time was mainly Welsh lads who intended to join either the RRW or RWFs. I did have a couple of Staffords and, of course, I made things a little harder for them. After all, I was sending them to my regiment. I couldn't be sending them any shit. The lads must have got their heads together as when they returned from their long weekend off, I was to walk into the section room to be greeted by ten Welsh flag duvets as bed covers.

"Are you fuckers taking the piss?" I shouted. "This is my

room and I'm English. Are you bastards doing this to wind me up?" With that, I ordered them to remove the duvet covers. "Make your beds back up with itchy blankets, you tossers."

The following morning, the platoon lines were being inspected by the CSM and OC. I was stood outside my section room and as the two of them approached, I stood the room/ section to attention. The OC walked around each recruit inspecting their attire, locker layout and general room tidiness. The OC noticed my recruits had army issue blankets on their beds and not their own duvets.

"Where's your duvet?" he asked a recruit.

"On top of my locker, sir," he responded. *Oh shit,* I thought, *the bastards have dropped me right in it.*

"Are all of your duvets on top of your lockers?" he asked the room.

"Yes, sir."

On leaving the room the OC looked at me. "My office, Corporal Inman."

I made my way down to the CSM's office. "Corporal Inman, why does your section not have duvets on their beds? Is it because they are Welsh flags? Do you have a problem with the Welsh?" *Think quickly,* I thought.

"Not at all, sir," I said with pure confidence. "The duvets were filthy, Sir. I was disgusted with the state of them, especially as you were about to inspect my room. With that, I ordered them to go back to army issue. May I add, Sir, that I did not appreciate you summoning me to your office as if I have done something wrong in front of my men." *Now I'm going too far, I'm taking this piss now,* I thought.

"That's a fair point, Corporal Inman. I apologise for that. Fall Out." With that, I left his office. *That was close.* I made my way back up to the lines to see the recruits proudly putting their bed covers back on.

"What the fuck do you think you're doing? Get those dirty

duvets off and get those blankets on." My recruits quickly knew they would never get the better of me.

I had always wanted a dog of my own. While I was settled at Catterick for two years, I thought it would be the perfect time to get one. I had come across an advertisement in the paper for a litter of Labradors. *This will be perfect,* I thought. *A little Andrex puppy will be an ideal family pet.* I telephoned the breeder who did not live far away and he invited me to his home that evening. On arriving at his home, he guided me into the back of his house where I saw a litter of ten beautiful puppies, five black and five golden. I knew that I would like a golden one, but which one would I choose? I sat on the floor staring at them. All of a sudden, a small, very cute head arose. The little puppy made eye contact, got up and walked gingerly towards me. He had chosen me. I picked him up and fell in love with him immediately. I think the breeder could see by my face how excited I was.

"Can I come back next week and collect him?"

"You can take him now if you want." I handed over £250 and left with Cassius in a small box. I called him Cassius (or Cass for short) after my idol Muhammad Ali. It had to be Cassius as I didn't see myself shouting Muhammad at the top of my voice down the platoon lines. I arrived home late that night. I was desperate for Bethan to meet Cassius. I went upstairs to her room and woke her gently.

"Come and see what I've brought home." I carried little Bethan downstairs. She stood staring at the puppy. She didn't move towards him to stroke or cuddle him but just stared. Maybe I shouldn't have woken her?

Wherever I went, Cassius would follow. He became my best friend and also the platoon mascot. As a puppy I would put him into my rucksack and run the 1-mile journey to Vimy Barracks from home, his cute little head popping out of the top. Once at my feet he would never leave me. He came to the lessons I taught, and as he got older he would come on the platoon runs and tabs with us – often showing his face to me before running off and enjoying the countryside. I had him trained on a whistle from a very young age so he responded well and I never worried about losing my friend. When I would take the platoon on the drill square he also came. As a drill instructor I had a pace stick. This would measure a full 30-inch pace that a soldier must stride while on drill. I would hold the pace stick in my right hand and Cassius would march proudly at my side on the left. If I moved my pace stick to my left hand, he would manoeuvre behind me to my right. We were incredibly in sync with each other; it was as if he could read my mind. Cassius would often come on exercise with me if it was only one night in the field. He would spend the night cuddled up to me in my sleeping bag, often making me sweat. He was my companion during long nights on guard also, staying at my feet under the guardroom desk. I decided to make him a bandana out of DPM (disruptive pattern material) so we matched. I also sourced a collar with a Stafford Knot on it. I adored him and so did Bethan. He completed our family.

Time was going by very quickly at ITC Catterick. I was enjoying the experience. I took great pride in seeing each cohort (platoon) pass out. I knew I had produced some very good soldiers. One thing I was noticing was my fitness levels dropping slightly. The only fitness training I was doing was with the platoon. I was not doing any extra. I would go on the odd run with Cassius but I was not up to my usual standards.

We would often get together as a regiment for some bonding. All the Stafford instructors and the Stafford recruits would gather in the NAAFI and get to know each other. It was usually hosted by one of the CSMs who had travelled from Mooltan Barracks in Salisbury. I quite enjoyed these meetings. It would give us a chance as NCOs to have some banter and a good drink together. We would often end up pissed and moving onto a local bar by the name of Jokers. It was a good opportunity to have some down time and get away from the pressure of being an instructor. I recall that for one of these meetings I didn't feel very well. My eyes felt sore and I kept rubbing them. My eyes felt heavy and I became increasingly tired. I just thought I needed a good rest so intended to wrap things up early and go home. As I contemplated leaving, I noticed that a good friend of mine, Conor Stalker – another Corporal instructor who had recently been posted into ITC – entered the NAAFI. I was always happy to see Conor. We got on really well and often took the piss out of each other. Conor, though, had a guest – to my absolute disgust, in walked Cpl Tit.

"Get that fucker out of here. How fucking dare you show your face at a Staffords' meeting after your gobbing off routine?" I was furious. Cpl Tit looked at me in pure horror. Conor asked me to calm down and let the past go. "Fuck off, Conor. Show some loyalty." I looked at Cpl Tit and ordered him out. He left immediately.

I made friends with another Royal Regiment of Fusiliers instructor while at Catterick. I asked if he knew Cpl Tit. I went on to tell him how Tit had spoken to NCOs and private soldiers in Kenya while he was attached to us. This Corporal went on to inform me that Cpl Tit had failed SCBC a record seven times. He was known as a 'Mong' in his battalion and not well liked at all. So this Corporal who had made out he was the dog's bollocks and was the big I am in Kenya had actually failed SCBC seven times and was regarded as a dickhead. This made matters even worse. He had made himself out to be this brilliant soldier but in fact was a deadbeat. I couldn't wait to have a face to face with him and let everyone know he had failed to be a section commander that many times. How the hell he got a posting to ITC I will never know. Getting this posting was for the cream of the crop instructors, not ones who had failed to this extent. It must have been an excuse for his battalion to post him out, to get him out from under their feet.

I would often see Tit marching his section around the barracks. I would belittle him in front of them: "What the fuck are you looking at?" or "How many times did you fail Junior Brecon?" He would never say anything back. He knew that if he did, I would be up to his platoon lines and bang him out again, but this time in front of his recruits. I have no doubt he treated those recruits of his disgustingly, especially judging how he spoke to us in Kenya.

I left the meeting with Cassius in toe that night. Cass jumped into the boot of the car and settled down for the short drive home to Nicola and Bethan. I told Nicola that I didn't feel well. She kindly ran me a bath. I had a soak and made my way to bed. I woke the following morning still feeling rough. My eyes were still bad and my chest felt rather tight. I opened my front door and noticed some snow on the ground.

"Come on, Cass." We ran into work together. I felt terrible even after 500 metres. My breathing appeared shallow and my legs felt heavy. It was the hardest mile run I had ever completed. Cass and I entered Vimy Barracks. My vision started to blur. I managed with great effort to get to the medical centre. I tied Cassius up to the bench outside and attempted to walk through the entrance to the centre. That's all I remember. The next thing, I woke in hospital hours later.

I felt terrible. The first thing I asked was, "Where's my dog?" A nurse came to me.

"Hello, Corporal Inman, you're in DKMH (Duchess of Kent Military Hospital). Your wife is on her way."

"Where's my dog?"

"Sorry, I can't answer that I'm afraid."

I had no idea what had happened to me or what was wrong with me, but all I wanted to know was that Cass was OK. The last thing I remembered was him being tied up and I had no idea how long ago that was. I lay in that hospital bed worrying and feeling shocking at the same time. Nicola walked in. Bill (Funky) had taken Cassius home and told Nicola that I had collapsed in the medical centre an hour ago, and had been taken to the military hospital around the corner from Vimy Barracks.

A doctor approached my bed. He took my blood pressure and listened to my chest. I was sent for an x-ray on my chest and had some blood taken for testing. After an hour, the same doctor informed me that I had pneumonia. The chest x-ray showed a dark mass on both lungs. I was to remain in hospital for a few days to be monitored and pumped with antibiotics.

After a couple of days I was released from hospital. This was only because Nicola reassured the doctors that she would monitor me and I would not be left alone. I was glad to get home. Cass was overjoyed to see me. That following week I hardly recall. I slept for approximately twenty hours a day for the next seven days. I slept on the sofa downstairs, as I had literally no energy to even get up those thirteen stairs and into my bed. I received visits from Bill, of course, and all the training team. The OC even visited me. He was to inform me that I was not to rush back to work.

It took three months to recover completely from my illness. I can't express to you how poorly I was. I understand completely how pneumonia is a killer. I was young, fit and strong but the illness took me completely off my feet, and three months off work demonstrates how nasty this illness is.

On fully returning to work I noticed a huge dip in my fitness levels. On subsequent outpatient appointments I was informed by the doctor that I had some scarring on both lungs. This scarring would be permanent. I asked if my fitness would return back to how it was before. The doctor went on to say that it should do; however, it could be hard going and not to expect results immediately – it could take a couple of years to get back properly. I didn't have two years. I would be returning to battalion within the next six months and this meant going on SAS selection, for which my fitness had to be at its finest. I began to worry.

Every year, reports were made about us instructors. The reports began with comments from our Platoon Commanders, up to the Officer Commanding and finally the Commanding Officer. It was time to receive my report. I went in front of the OC who praised me hugely on my professionalism and dedication in wanting to produce the best recruits. The OC went on to say that the Commanding Officer wanted to see me. I waited to be called by the RSM who marched me into the CO's office. You would only ever see the CO if you had done something out of the ordinary or you were in serious shit. On this occasion, it was the former. I spent twenty minutes having smoke blown up my arse by the CO. I won't go into detail but my praise was intense. He strongly recommended that my next move be the SAS. He thanked me for my efforts and finished the conversation by saying I was the best instructor in ITC and I deserved the accolade. There were three hundred instructors throughout ITC. The CO had just announced I was the best. This felt amazing. I knew many of the instructors and they were all excellent (well, most of them, hey, CPL Tit?). I would leave Catterick with a great report and my reputation as a second-to-none section commander.

I can honestly say my time as an instructor at ITC was the fondest of my army career. I had the privilege of working with some brilliant officers, SNCOs and NCOs. Each and every soldier I produced, I was proud of. If a recruit passed out with my name as their instructor then they deserved it, as I would push them harder and further than others. I hope my methods of teaching and the type of soldier I was rubbed off on my boys. I wanted the best for them. One day I would like to think that they would aspire to be in my shoes, passing on my teaching to their soldiers. I wanted to be their role model. I wanted them to be like me, my own 'mini-me's.

It was time to leave Catterick and return to my unit. I didn't want to leave. I didn't want to return to battalion. This left me one choice. Selection it was.

10

SELECTION

I returned to battalion and immediately fell back into the mundane day-to-day activities of mechanised infantry duties. I despised it. I had put my application in for selection on my first day back. I needed to get out of here. I would find myself on parade with Dragon Company looking around the lads and recognising numerous that I had trained at ITC. Two years had gone by since I last stood as part of this company and I could see changes that I didn't like. Many of my friends had decided to leave and I hardly recognised any of the private soldiers. The army had become far too politically correct in my opinion. I even had to justify swearing at a private soldier. This was supposed to be the toughest, hardest, most resilient army in the world but all I saw was standards that were falling by the wayside. This was not the army that I had joined eight years before. Lads who I had trained and who had called me by my rank were now stood at my shoulder referring to me as 'Inni'. Like I was their fucking mate. "Who are you speaking to? You refer to me as Corporal until I say you can call me Inni." I would never have dreamed of referring to a section or team commander by their name unless invited to. Maybe I had matured, but I found myself surrounded by boys who didn't take soldiering seriously. I didn't belong here any longer. I needed to find my way out. Selection could not come quick enough.

Over the next three months I worked hard on trying to recover my fitness levels. I used to spend hours of my own time training. You would find me in the afternoons on the back area, running, sprinting and setting up circuits for myself in order to train my upper body strength as well as my cardiovascular endurance. I was becoming more and more concerned. Something did not feel right after my pneumonia; it was as if I would hit a brick wall where usually I could plough through it. This must have been down to what the doctors had said about the scarring on my lungs. All I could do was continue working hard and pushing, hoping that my endurance would reappear.

I travelled back to the Brecon Beacons and reported to Sennybridge Camp. I had been here many times. It is a small camp originally designed to administer yourself from while on exercise on the area. It's small but can house a few hundred soldiers comfortably. Soldiers from lots of regiments and corps were in attendance, not just infantry. We had signallers, engineers, REME (Royal Electrical and Mechanical Engineers); the list went on. The Parachute Regiment had a strong contingent. I would find myself the only Stafford. The course went through a series of briefings about what was going to go on over the next three weeks. This part of selection is fondly known as the 'hills phase'. It is purely there to test the levels of fitness, both physically and, more importantly, mentally. I was taught by a very wise soldier that your brain wants to give up at only 45%. Your body can deliver the other 55%. This phase therefore is to test your guts and determination, pushing the body to places you have not been before. I felt unbelievably nervous for some reason. Maybe it was because I was about to embark on my life's goal. Every night we would have a briefing from the DS (directing staff) about what the tab (tactical advance to battle/march) would be the following morning. Our first briefing informed us that we would be completing a CFT (8-mile combat fitness test) – the same as I did on SCBC and many other times. The course congregated on the square, ready to go on the area. Firstly, our kit, which comprised of webbing and daysack, was weighed to ensure we had the correct weight limit. You would always have to carry heavier to compensate for the water that you would consume during the tab. For this short 8-miler I gave myself five pounds of excess.

I had never seen so many 4-tonne vehicles parked up ready to take so many of us onto the area. On that very first tab there was in excess of three-hundred, all of us with the same goal: to get through the hills phase and progress onto the jungle. Firstly, we had to get through Week 1, Day 1 – the CFT. I managed this with ease and so did the majority of the intake. There were a number, however, that failed. On failing a tab you would automatically be RTU'd, no questions asked, no matter what the reason for failing, be it injury, fitness level or lack of guts. Only one thing was happening: your kit was being packed and you were going home. That night we were again briefed on the next day's tab. We discovered we would be in 8-man teams, navigating between us from point to point (similar to orienteering over the area – a distance of ten miles) with an increased amount of weight on our backs. I was confident and familiar with this area of the Brecon Beacons as I had spent many days here while on SCBC. Again, the 4-tonne vehicles greeted us for the day's activity, another tab in the books. On completion we returned to Sennybridge and ate a good meal to get our energy levels up; get as much carbohydrate in us as possible and during the remainder of the evening, continually drink water. I got up about three times during the night because my poor bladder couldn't take the strain.

Over the following weeks, the marches would become progressively more difficult. We would operate in 4-man teams, then pairs, and then by the end of Week 1 we were on our own. I was navigating over the area in different locations, carrying increasingly more weight, and the distance was becoming greater. We had the odd night march thrown in also. This meant that time would be compromised due to the lack of light and trying to become more tactical with the use of our torches. During each march we would be given locations we had to get to. A member of the training team would be at a certain location. On reaching him, he would weigh our kit to see if we had the correct amount and make sure we were not dropping it. He would then give us a new grid reference. I would plot it on my map and decide the best and quickest route and then make my way to the next checkpoint, and continue this process until each tab was complete. With each tab completed I would feel a sense of achievement and always think to myself that that was another one out of the way. Lads were starting to pick up the odd injury here and there. You could visibly see the disappointment each soldier would have on nursing an injury that would wipe them off selection, along with the dreaded feeling of inevitable RTU. In my head I would have three missions throughout the day, to complete the tab, to stay injury free, and to go on to the next. With every day that went by I would feel a sense of accomplishment, as each day lads were dropping out either by injury or failure. The morning parade numbers were quickly dwindling away and less and less 4-tonne vehicles were parking up for that early morning journey to the area. The feeling that the hills phase was almost complete was getting closer and closer.

I knew it was getting closer as my body was beginning to tell me so. I'm aware that I am quite small in stature and when you think of an SAS trooper, you often find people imagining a 6ft 7inch bloke with bulging muscles and a black stripe running over his eyes disguising him from the world. Take it from me, this is not the case. They are just average men who have a bigger heart and brain than ego and muscles. However, because of my small frame and low body fat percentage, it was taking my body longer to recover from each and every tab. I started to feel tired in the mornings. My legs started to have DOMS (delayed onset muscle soreness) set in. My body was beginning to compromise.

I had made it to the last week. Just 5 more days until the end! It was a tough week. The distance was getting bigger, the weight getting heavier and now we had time limits imposed on us also. Our map-reading needed to be impeccable. If I picked one bad route or didn't read the map correctly it would cost me precious time, time which was sparse. On reaching each check post we were not informed if we had made it in our allocated time. We would only find out on completion of the tab.

The week was going reasonably well for me. I was getting through the tabs, with difficulty, but I was getting through them. The final tab was quickly approaching. Get through this next one and I was on the plane to phase 2, 'the jungle' – Belize. The evening brief came from the DS. We were about to embark on a 24-hour point-to-point tab over the infamous Pen y Fan, this being the highest peak in the Brecon Beacons at 2,907ft above sea level. As a course, we would make our way to the start point of Storey Arms. We would be set off individually and make our way over the next 24 hours from point to point, having our kit weighed and our new destination given. We would plot it on our maps and continue this until reaching our final RV and finding out if we had passed the hills/endurance phase. I made my way to my bed knowing it would be my final night in Sennybridge. I wanted an early night. I needed every minute I could grab in order to rest my body.

I slept like a baby that night. I slept, in fact, too well. My alarm went off and I could hear the lads rising from their pits. "Get out of bed, Mark." "For one last time, get out of bed." My bed felt nice and warm. I could hear the rain on the roof of my accommodation. For the first time in my life, I quit. I picked the comfort of a fucking piss-stained mattress over fulfilling my dream. It leaves an absolutely bitter taste in my mouth to admit this on paper and it has taken me years to admit to people and myself that "I QUIT". I have to accept what I did. I'm not going to lie and say I got injured or that I felt unwell because I didn't. I did feel exhausted, but I know that if I had got out of bed that miserable morning, I would have found the inner strength to pass the final tab. I have gone back to that day and that decision so many times. I put myself back in that bed. What was so attractive that I couldn't get my foot to the floor and push myself off that pillow?

I had never quit anything in my life. The first thing I quit on is my dream. I cheated myself out of fulfilling my potential. I cheated myself out of finishing my military career in the finest regiment on the planet. I cheated myself out of holding my head up high and being able to call myself one of the finest soldiers in the world. I can't say that now, because "I QUIT". I had dedicated my life to being simply the best, the best private soldier, best Lance Corporal, best Corporal, and for what? To fail at the very last hurdle. A hurdle being a bed! I had returned from a foreign prison, I had returned from a broken back. I am still to this day beating myself up. To come so close and work so hard for three weeks, for what? To pronounce to the DS that I was a quitter and I didn't deserve to wear that sandy-coloured beret and that winged daggered cap badge. I was RTU'd.

If I could go back in time, I know things would be different. This, to date, is the biggest regret of my life. What hurts the most is that maybe I wasn't the best after all. Maybe I was just another wannabe. I didn't have the guts or balls.

Don't make the same mistake I made. That decision haunts me. Never give up. Never give up the fight. You will without doubt regret it for the remainder of your days. I wish I could have looked my children in the eyes and told them that their father was SAS. I can't. I can show them how to quit. I hope, though, that I can show them how giving up hurts, not just in that moment of madness, but how the decision can have repercussions that will always hurt. It hurts me more than anybody else and to anyone else it doesn't matter. It matters to me.

11

TIME FOR CHANGE

After spending the subsequent weekend wallowing in self-pity and regret, Monday morning came by. I sat at the edge of the bed and looked at my uniform and boots. For the first time in my career, I didn't want to put them on. I felt disgusted in myself. I was dreading doing the walk of shame through the gates of Mooltan Barracks and hearing comments such as "Inni's back" or "Inni failed selection". After all, I was supposed to be the dead cert for getting badged SAS. I looked over at Nicola and delivered her the news, "I'm getting out!" I paraded in front of Major Grilsby and presented him with the news that "Sir, I didn't get out of bed". Luckily for me, CSM Ted Cook had since retired after his 22 years' service; at least I didn't have that prick rubbing it in. I went on to inform Major Grilsby that once again I would be signing off and serving my one year's notice. There was no way I would be changing my mind. I had failed selection and battalion and the army's standards were drifting. I no longer wanted to be associated with either organisation.

Over the following year, I would be offered teasers to remain in the army. I recall being offered a Platoon Sergeant posting at Whittington Barracks. I had just completed a 2-year posting with recruits. The last thing I wanted was to go back to another training depot, especially a non-infantry establishment. All attempts to persuade me to stay failed. I would be sent to the regiment's training wing as an instructor for my final few months. My job was to instruct private soldiers on NCO's cadres to help them get their first stripe, and also to prepare the Lance Corporals on the SCBC pre-course, getting them ready for Junior Brecon, the course I had made my name on.

During those twelve months I needed to consider my employment options. Iraq had been going through a stabilised period and was attempting to rebuild the country after the capture, court case and subsequent death penalty of Saddam Hussein, the country's dictator and tyrant. I got wind of a number of very senior ranked soldiers leaving the armed forces and going to Iraq as 'private security consultants'. Many people were calling them mercenaries. However you looked at it, these soldiers were leaving the forces and earning a huge amount of money working for private security firms. They were earning their money, by all accounts. They would find themselves in countless contacts (firefights). This sounded right up my street. I could continue soldiering in some capacity with senior soldiers that had much experience. I would also be getting my hands dirty and testing my skills, which up until now had not been tested under real contact scenarios. I looked into this option in much more detail and the more I discovered about the job, the more I wanted a piece of it. I knew this was the employment option for me. The money earned would quickly mount up, ensuring the deposit for a civilian house for Nicola, Bethan, Cassius and I.

On serving more than five years in the military, you are entitled to what's called a resettlement course. The course's fundamental purpose is to re-qualify you or teach you a new trade to help you gain the qualifications needed for employment in different sectors such as plumbing, electrics, gaining different driving licences, anything you can think of. You have up to the value of £2500 to retrain. I looked into a course that would prepare me and qualify me for 'close protection' (body guarding). This would give me what I would need to go to a private security firm and apply for a position in Iraq. I found a course called Phoenix, a 4-week residential course in Hereford delivered by ex-SAS officers and troopers. It was popular with the private security firms as it produced good 'close protection operatives'. On successful completion of the course, the top students to pass would be presented to companies and offered interviews for employment. This, therefore, would be the course I would attend. I enrolled on the course and waited for my joining instructions. Battalion agreed to give me time off to attend Phoenix.

Phoenix comprised an experienced training team in a beautiful location in Hereford. The accommodation and course headquarters were of a stately home appearance and quality. All the course instruction would be held here, apart from a week at a medical training establishment in Hereford centre, this part of the course being called 'MED-EX' – an intense 1-week course designed at training us all to be first responder qualified. Phoenix was intense and demanding. We would also spend a week learning new and aggressive driving techniques using two vehicle movements. We would learn all the Hollywood stunts such as handbrake and J turns. This week was a simple pass/fail. If you failed your driving week, then you would not be successful in gaining the CP (close protection) Qualification or your SIA (Security Industry Authority) Licence, and your £2500 would be wasted. CP and driving come hand in hand. Your vehicle and the way you drive it is so important. The clients need to feel safe while in your protection. If they don't feel safe as passengers, they probably would not be confident in other aspects of your protection.

Each morning before breakfast, as a course we would get our PT (Physical Training) kit on and make our way into Hereford for 06:00hrs. We would assemble at a mixed martial arts gym. Here we would learn hand-to-hand combat techniques. We were trained to be aggressive and use our fighting skills as our last resort of close protection. I would leave the gym with new bruises or slight concussion on a daily basis. It was a tough hour of combat training but enjoyable. The final week of the course was test week. We were given scenarios and clients to protect. We were given information by our client on where they would like to go and what they intended to do. The team then had half an hour to plan a journey using a pre-planned route, and back-up should we be compromised. Part of the team did a recce. They secured and familiarised themselves with the venue then briefed the bodyguard of what they knew, this included locations of safe rooms, entrances and exits, toilets etcetera, before the CP team escorted their client to his or her desired destination. The bodyguard would then go through his personal protection phase, ensuring the client's needs were catered for while continually keeping the remainder of the team updated on his location and planned tasks. The initial recce team would then be given orders for the client's next location and they would deploy and start the process again. It is surprising how much goes into close protection. You need to be on your toes. It's as if you're not only there to provide the client security but also act as a PA (personal assistant). You need to be aware of the locations of hospitals in the area, police stations, the best restaurants and safe houses. The list goes on. The planning and preparation that goes into a single client move is phenomenal.

I enjoyed the course even though I felt the pressure of knowing I had to pass and what was at stake. I wanted to chase the money. I wanted to be able to provide financially for my family but at the same time do a job which interested me and once more excited me.

The course had twenty eight students. We all completed the course but ten failed. I worked hard and showed the same professionalism that I prided my military career on, showing willingness to learn, diligence, enthusiasm and a good work ethic. I also conducted my body guarding role in a confident way while leading my team in my usual leadership manner. I had passed and finished the course as one of the top five students. That very afternoon, I was interviewed by a number of private security companies, which included RISK Management, Olive and Black Water. I was also interviewed by a lady who recruited for Action Group. She interviewed me with a very different approach. Instead of telling me where I would be deployed and what I would be doing, she asked more about me, what I wanted from a security firm and what I saw myself doing. This interviewing technique impressed me. It was different than the others. I felt comfortable talking with her and I began to feel that this was the company for me. The lady offered me a contract at the end of the interview. She informed me that the majority of recruiting she did was for contracts in Iraq. She was to offer me something different. She said that she liked my character and that the report I had from Phoenix was impressive. She was also familiar with my military record and because of this, she offered me a unique opportunity.

"I would like to offer you a contract in Kabul, Afghanistan." She went on to say that this contract was Action Group's most lucrative contract to date, a new contract that had only been signed off four weeks beforehand. It would be providing close protection to members of HMRC (Her Majesty's Revenue & Customs).

I was overjoyed. I accepted the contract and quickly signed the paperwork the moment she placed it in front of me. I couldn't wait to get home to tell Nicola that I had been successful in not only passing the course but securing employment. I had been offered a rolling contract. Working eight weeks in country and then four weeks' leave (home). I would also be paid for my month's leave, my salary – £6000 a month. This would be tax-free as long as I registered myself with an accountant and put in for ex-pat status. I also couldn't spend longer that ninety-one days in the UK per year otherwise I would be taxed. I thought I had won the lottery. I was going to work abroad as a close protection officer earning good money. I believed I had made the correct choice in deciding to leave my regiment.

I returned to my battalion and quickly asked for an early release due to having gained employment. Soldiers would often ask for early release and nine times out of ten it would be granted. Not for me. The head shed of the regiment were still bitter that I was leaving so intended to keep me as theirs until the very last minute. It became public knowledge throughout battalion that I had just been awarded a contract in Afghanistan. I was asked about it constantly. "When are you going?" "What weapons will you have?" "What are you doing out there?" "How much are you getting paid?" Lads were genuinely interested and some, you could see, very envious. The regiment was about to leave for Basra, Iraq, earning pittance and being governed by utter bullshit. I was going to Afghanistan, earning big bucks with the best weapon systems, vehicles and communications, as a civilian and, more importantly, with no fucking army BULLSHIT!

I completed my duties one particular day and was making my way to the cookhouse to get some scoff (food). I noticed the Commanding Officer walking swiftly towards me. He usually would be escorted by the RSM but oddly not on this occasion. The CO had always recognised my achievements and gave me excellent yearly reports which, of course, were the highest grade you could be given. Due, however, to my decision to move onto bigger and better things and, in his and others' eyes, leaving battalion in their time of need (i.e. an Iraq tour of six months), he, like others, resented my future employment option. As the distance between us closed, I braced up and saluted him, remaining professional to the end and placing my personal feelings to the side. The Commanding Officer decided to blatantly ignore me as he continued past. *Fuck you,* I thought, and with this I turned around.

"I was saluting your rank, not you as a person. I expect you to return the salute." He turned immediately and glared in my direction. We locked eyes. I could see he was raging inside by the colour change in his face. I stood firm. *He must have a comeback for me, surely?* I waited. He also must have decided to stay professional. He turned 180 degrees and continued on his route. I made my point clear.

My final day of serving in the British Army came. I handed all my kit and uniform in. I was wandering around camp in civilian clothing grabbing signatures from the head shed such as the QM, CQMS, Adjutant, MTO etcetera, confirming that I had nothing left to hand in or do. I was being wished all the best and having my hand shaken by JNCOs, SNCOs and even some of the officers. The last thing that I needed to do was go on Commanding Officer's Interviews, this being a formality for every soldier leaving the regiment, no matter what rank. *I'm not going to give him my time of day.* I got in my car and drove past Battalion HQ where he would have been sitting behind his desk waiting for me. As I moved slowly past BHQ, I honked my horn as loud and as aggressively as it could go, wound the window down and gave his office window the finger. "Fuck you!" I shouted. The guard saw me approach the barrier gate. The gate rose and I left the hospitality of the 1st Battalion, the Staffordshire Regiment, for the last time.

I loved the Staffordshire Regiment dearly, and am proud to say I served them to the best of my ability. I still hold my time serving close to my heart. We were a family, a band of brothers.

May I take this opportunity to thank my fellow warriors? It was a privilege being in the company of so many of you. As for some of the officers who look down on the working class, thinking they are superior due to their education and background, and those who only join to get Daddy's inheritance – go fuck yourselves!

This is a picture I have of my Grandfather "Charlie" in his RAF Uniform.
My inspiration and reason I joined the military.

This is my portrait which was taken at Whittington barracks
before my Passing Out parade. See how similar we look.

Myself in front of a Kenyan Landrover.

Myself at dusk.

On patrol in North Belfast.

On a VCP (Vehicle Check Point) On the day of the Omagh Bombing.

On exercise in BATUS.

One of my parachute jumps.

My broken down Scimitar.

Instructor pose.

A young me, live firing in Hong Kong.

Close Protection drills.

On duty in Kabul.

Donna & CJ (Charlie-Jack).

Bethan with Cassius.

Cassius in his final years.

Bethan today.

Donna & I.

12

DUBAI

On leaving the army, Nicola, Bethan and I moved in with Nicola's father. It was a stopgap until I earnt enough money and spent three months in my new employment in order to qualify for a mortgage. We could then settle down as a family and start a new chapter in our lives.

I received a phone call a couple of days after leaving. It was head office of Action Group. I was informed that I needed to report to London, Buckingham Gate, this being head office of the company, in the next couple of days. Here I would meet up with my new team members and collect our plane tickets to Dubai. From Dubai we would charter a civilian plane to Kabul.

I attempted to talk to my 4-year-old daughter and explain to her that Daddy was going away for a while and that she must be good for Mummy. I looked into her innocent eyes. She had no idea where I was going or what I would be doing. She only understood that she would not see me every night and that I wouldn't be putting her to bed and reading her a story for a bit. Nicola also appeared down but she understood why I had chosen this route. She knew it would make me happy and in

151

turn provide us with our first proper family home. I was picked up a few days later by my friend, who had volunteered to drive me to London. He collected me; I put my bags into the boot of his car and sat in the passenger seat. Bethan came to the front door and waved me goodbye. I can clearly see this image as I write this. It was a 'lump in throat' moment. My friend took one look at Bethan and said, "I can't take that myself, and we need to get out of here." I waved her goodbye.

"Goodbye, angel."

I got to Buckingham Gate and entered the office. I was led to a meeting room. I sat at a large wooden table. One by one, somebody else would join the table and take a seat. Nobody made a sound. No one wanted to make the first move in talking. Eight of us completed HMRC Team 1. We were the first close protection team to enter Kabul and reside as Action Group employees at the British Embassy. We all looked around the table, weighing each other up. All of a sudden a scouse bloke popped up.

"Well, I will be the first to talk then. I'm sure we are all going to get to know each other in time." His name was Mike. He had just completed his 22 years as a Colour Sergeant in the King's Regiment. Nice geezer but typical scouse. He broke the ice and we all started to engage in conversation.

The lady that had interviewed me a few weeks earlier entered the conference room. She gave us a PowerPoint presentation which lasted an hour. Here she gave us details of what we would be doing in Kabul and who we were contracted to protect. Our mission was to provide protection for members of HMRC. They were conducting a government mission in trying to eradicate our country's heroin at source. Ninety-five percent of the UK's heroin comes from Afghanistan and its poppy. The conditions in Afghanistan are perfect for the production of the poppy and therefore heroin. Farmers would use their fields to harvest the poppy and sell it to the local drug barons, who would employ locals on minimum wage to produce heroin from the flower. It was big business for all concerned. The drug baron got paid from dealers throughout Europe, the barons paid the farmers for their fields of poppies and the farmers hired the locals to farm the poppy into heroin. The locals would therefore depend on the heroin trade also to feed their families. The penny then dropped! HMRC wanted to eradicate the poppy and we were there to protect them. We were definitely not going to be flavour of the month with the locals, farmers and drug barons. We were about to destroy their way of life, take money from their pockets and food from their tables and children's mouths. I was beginning to see how this was going to go down. The government were using taxpayers' money to see heroin off the streets of the UK, and this was the best, most efficient way of doing it: HMRC take away the poppy fields by educating farmers into growing other resources and paying them to do so, and burning existing stocks of poppy and farmed heroin itself. This was without doubt going to cause a shitstorm.

HMRC Team 1 (the name of the newly formed team) was presented with our plane tickets to Dubai. We would fly out of Heathrow that day. On arriving in Dubai, we would be put up for the night in a hotel called the Millennium Airport Hotel. The following morning we'd report to the check-in desk at Dubai International Airport and charter a civilian Ariana flight to Kabul. It would be a 2-day trip before reaching our destination. Well, that was the plan.

As a team, we took off on a long 8-hour flight with Emirates Airlines. As planned, we arrived in Dubai. What a place. The first thing I felt was the heat. I was then taken aback by how beautifully clean the place was. Dubai always seemed to be under construction. During the night hours you would hear building work going on. Low-paid workers imported from Pakistan and Afghanistan would build at night because it was far too hot in the day to work. You could see that Dubai's intention was to make this area a massive attraction for tourists. By all accounts, the oil in the region was running low, and this was their main source of income. Due to amounts running low they needed to hit the tourist market, which in turn would create another money-spinning back-up to boost the economy and create work. I would honestly describe Dubai as the capital of the planet, an absolutely stunning part of the world.

We booked into the hotel and made our way to our rooms. We partnered up and shared the rooms. The room was huge, though; it could have homed a family. My partner was a Scottish lad by the name of Tim. I had recognised Tim back in London while sat around the briefing table. He in turn recognised me. We had only served as instructors at ITC Catterick together and had been involved in a number of piss-ups in the Corporals' mess. The team met up later on in the hotel restaurant where we sat at a table together and ate. We unanimously decided to go and recce a local bar with the intention of having a couple of drinks and returning to the hotel in order to get some rest before making our way to Dubai International for the next leg of our journey. We started to bond as a team from this point forward.

As agreed, we had a few beers and got some sleep. Morning quickly came. We jumped in taxis and got to the airport check-in. We discovered on arrival that all flights into Kabul had been suspended for one week, due to Ariana Airlines' employees striking. How dare they? One of the lads contacted Buckingham Gate, HQ, and informed them of our situation. We were told to go back to the hotel and enjoy a week at the pleasure of Action Group, keeping expenses down to a minimum, of course. Team bonding was about to begin.

We had the most amazing week. We all got to know each other well. More importantly, we all gelled. The team consisted of a couple of older lads by the names of Mark and Vince. One was an ex-marine, the other a Para. Good lads, down to earth, and you could see they were wise. We had Richard and Mike who joined forces as they were scousers. Dan was an ex-CSM Green Jacket, another older bloke who kept himself to himself but was such a gentleman that we all looked up to him as a kind of father figure. If Dan asked you to do something, you did it, because he in return would do anything for you. Then there was Jack, Tim and I, the three younger lads. Me, of course, being the wild and youngest one. The mixture of experience, age and background made the team fantastic to work in. We all brought something to the table. I quickly became fond of the lads.

During that week we would surround the swimming pool and throw crates of beer in to keep the cans as cool as possible. It was if we were on a stag do enjoying the Dubai sun, drinking beer, and topping up our tans while getting paid. This had to be a rocking chair moment. It was a perfect way to bond and get to know each other before reaching Kabul. We did everything together. We sat at lunches and evening meals together, went to the gym, did some shopping and, of course, consumed so much beer that we almost drank the hotel dry. I believe that that experience made our team as tight as any team I have ever worked in. We worked hard for each other, trusted each other and respected each other. Time would tell, but when we hit the ground we would work like a well-oiled machine. The team was simply the best. After ten years I still fondly remember each and every member. I think about some more than others at times, as not all the time we had together was fun. We also had bad times and lost a few on the way.

The last night in Dubai we spent, of course, together in the hotel bar. I sat with Tim minding our own business when a young girl approached me and asked if she could join me. She pulled up a stool and we began talking. I don't think she was trying to hit on me and I certainly was not her, but as always female company can be nice. We spent half an hour or so chatting. She went on to tell me that she came from England somewhere and had been holidaying over the last two weeks. She excused herself and said she would be back shortly. As she did, an Arab dressed in traditional white robe and red headscarf approached me. He was of large stature but appeared to be no threat to me at the time. He started at me, asking why I was bothering the 'white girl', and went on to say that her mother had recently passed away and the last thing she wanted was for me to be pestering her. I very naively erupted, "Who the fuck are you barking at?" I went on to say that the young girl approached me and asked if she could join me, and what the fuck did it have to do with him anyway? I noticed the team positioning themselves around the local. I caught their eyes. "You will be fucking mad to try anything in here."

He told me that he was going to leave and that he would be returning with a knife.

"If you return with a knife then I will use it to cut out your fucking Adam's apple and then take a bite out of it." Not a nice image I know, but I was not the person he should be messing with and I wanted him to know. Secondly, if he was brave enough to pull a blade on me, he was going to be the one being stuck with it. The Arab glared at me. I could see he was weighing me up. He knew I wasn't frightened, so with that he left the venue. The young girl in the meantime had returned to the bar and I shortly joined her once more. We continued drinking and talking for what felt like an hour or so. At no point did I notice the Arab return, but he had. I was tapped on the shoulder by a middle-aged American gentleman.

"Sir," he looked at me with concern, "I need to tell you that that gentleman over there says he has a knife on him and that he is going to stab you. I just needed to let you know." The kind American gestured in the direction of the Arab. The lads in the team were aware of the situation and could see I had a problem on my hands.

"Lads, leave this to me!" I often use the tactic that the best form of defence is attack. I needed to take control of this situation and not let him dictate when or where his attack would come from. He was in my world now. He had better be prepared for the consequences. I made my way towards the local; we made eye contact.

"Get outside," I instructed him. I made my way immediately to the glass double doors and turned, waiting for him to join me. I gave him the opportunity. "Get it out then, show me the blade, but get ready to fucking eat it!" I was angry on a scale that I have not seen myself before. I was ready to fight and, truth be told, I was ready to stick him (stab him). If he had the nerve to do this to me, then I was going to finish him. He could see I was prepared and ready.

"You are crazy," he replied. "I have never come across anyone as crazy as you in all my time. I don't have a knife, I assure you that." He had de-escalated the situation; he was no longer threatening or aggressive. I had him surrendering at that very moment in time. "Please, mister, let me buy you a drink." With this, he placed his hand out to shake mine. I shook his hand. He led me back inside and to the bar. He must have been a frequent drinker at the hotel as he ushered the bartender and ordered me a drink. He asked me to enjoy and left me be. Tim and Jack knew what was going on and that the Arab had just bottled it. They joined me at the bar. Over the next hour, the Arab would continue to buy me drinks. I didn't put my hand in my pocket again that evening.

Once more I was lucky. Not because the Arab decided against taking me on, but because of the fact that the law enforcement in Dubai is on another scale. Somebody witnessing the incident could have called the police and it would have been the Arab's word they would have taken, not that of the young white British lad getting pissed up. There have been numerous incidents where British citizens have landed themselves in a cell in Dubai for absolutely tiny misdemeanours such as sexual intercourse out of wedlock or sexual activity on a beach. Recently, a young British lad spent two weeks in a cell for simply touching an Arab's waist while manoeuvring past him in a bar. As you can see, dickhead here was naive and lucky not to be banged up abroad once more.

The following morning came. I woke with an obvious headache from the amount of alcohol consumed courtesy of my local Arab friend. We made our way into the hotel lobby where we regrouped as a team. Three taxis were waiting to escort us to the airport where we would finally be saying goodbye to Dubai for the time being and moving forward to Kabul.

13

KABUL

We all got onto the plane courtesy of Ariana Airlines. As we walked towards the plane, we looked at each other with fear. *Are we really going to get on this plane?* It looked as though it was going to fall out of the sky at any moment. It looked like the fucking Millennium Falcon out of Star Wars, a right lump of flying shit. We were the only Westerners on the flight. It was full of local Afghans and they were smoking away. I couldn't believe what I was seeing. The interior looked like a throwback from the 1970s; not only that, but the plane absolutely stunk. We would later find out that in 2001 there had been seven separate incidents of Ariana plane crashes in Kabul alone, and in 1998, one of its planes crashed in bad weather into mountainous terrain on approach to Kabul Airport. It killed all forty-five passengers. The plane looked like something that Indiana Jones found himself jumping out of in a rubber dingy. It was a fucking death trap. This would be the last time we would fly Ariana. We as a team refused to fly with them again. The British Embassy from here on supplied us a UN plane, which would ferry us from Kabul to Dubai and vice versa.

We landed in Kabul. The airport was tiny. We walked off the Millennium Falcon and onto the runway, which was barely secure. We made our way into the terminal where our bags would be located. Of course, Westerners' luggage looks so much different from Afghan locals'. Once all the luggage had been collected by the flight you would make your way out into the open and exit the airport. No customs and excise. My bag did not show. The airport staff tried to make out that it must not have been on the flight. *Yes, OK,* I thought. I peered through a hole where the luggage was loaded onto the tiny carousel. The staff tried to prevent me from doing so. I saw my bag. I tried in vain to grab my bag but was stopped. "That's my bag," I shouted. I got back "No, no". I had been in the country for 5 minutes and the bastards were trying to rob me already. I got to my bag and unzipped it. I knew I could prove it to be mine as I had photographs of the girls – Nicola and Bethan – and I was obviously on those pictures. I got my album out and showed the staff. They had no choice but to concede. The cheeky bastards went on to ask me for money as a way of rewarding them for reuniting me with my belongings.

"Go fuck yourselves, you robbing bastards." Of course, their intention would have been to rifle my bag, take what they wanted and probably sell what they didn't. These locals had just got off to a bad start with me.

On exiting the airport we felt vulnerable. We had no weapons and we were gathered together in a huddle. The flight must have got in earlier than expected as we were briefed that the British Embassy RMP (Royal Military Police) would be picking us up. Our escorts finally arrived and we mounted the vehicles. We made our way to the British Embassy, a short drive away. I was looking through the window attempting to take it all in. I initially noticed that all the cars were Toyota Corollas which were painted either yellow or yellow and white. They had hand-painted the word 'Taxi' in black on them. The cars were so beat up and dented that they could not be road safe. They would not be passing an MOT in the UK. I was to later find out that the Taliban had banned all ownership of cars. The only vehicles that were allowed were the taxis. What the local car owners would do would be to decorate their own vehicles up as taxis.

The Taliban had ruled Kabul with pure fear and had countless rules that needed to be imposed, such as a complete ban on women working and being educated. Women must wear a burka (a long blue dress covering the women from head to toe, not even seeing the eyes). If they didn't then they would be publicly whipped. If women were to engage in premarital sex then they would also be stoned to death. There was a ban on cosmetics. Women would have their fingers cut off should they be found wearing nail varnish. Women were not allowed to speak in public. No music was to be listened to. No watching television. Everyone was ordered to attend prayer five times a day. The list goes on and on.

We made our way to the embassy where we were briefed on the area. We were given maps and shown videos of prominent landmarks throughout Kabul. We were then shown the vehicles that we would be working with. They too were Toyota-made. They were large 4×4s that were B6 armoured. They would offer excellent protection from both small arms fire and also IEDs (improvised explosive devices/roadside bombs). These vehicles would have their durability tested over the following few years. They also had ECM (Electronic Counter Measure) protection. ECM provides an invisible bubble around the vehicle. It means that anything that needs a remote signal is prevented from working. For example, mobile phone signals. Often IEDs would have a mobile phone attached to some explosive. A terrorist (player) would wait for a vehicle to get in range of the IED then either call or text the phone attached to the device, in turn detonating it. The ECM would prevent the signal. We would often drive past locals going about their own business; they would be on their phones, talking away, and we would drive past. All of a sudden you would see them looking at their phones because the signal would have been lost, this all due to the ECM on our 4×4s. Our vehicles stood out like sore dicks on the streets of Kabul. The locals knew that it had to be Westerners inside. This alone would make us a target.

Two members, experienced employees of Action Group, were tasked in taking us through our weapon handling and familiarising us with the area. They also taught us some excellent techniques on the ranges that we would implement in our SOPs, such as vehicle crossover drills and weapon change drills. Our first week in country was intense but we had so much to learn before we met up with the clients we would be providing protection for.

The weapon systems we would be using were the finest in the world, a far cry from the weapons of the British Army. We were all given Glock 17 semi-automatic pistols – this was a beautifully reliable pistol – and HK G36 rifles. This weapon was by far the finest rifle in the world. I never once had a stoppage (failed to fire). The butt would fold away to make the weapon easier to transport. It was fed by a 30-round (bullet) magazine. The joy with this weapon, though, was that the magazine could be locked together. As soon as you fired 30 rounds, the magazine could be quickly changed in order to continue firing without a huge delay, something that later on I would find useful.

We spent long days getting orientated with Kabul. We needed to familiarise ourselves with safe houses, police stations and military camps, including HQ for ISAF (International Security Assistance Force). This was a combination of NATO forces, so the camps would have a mixture of different foreign armies, which included German, Dutch, Belgian, French etcetera. The team had to know Kabul like the back of our hands.

The team spent many hours on the live firing ranges. We drove onto the ranges that were used by the Afghan Army. On entering the range and driving through the miles of area, we would see all the destroyed tanks that the Russians had invaded with in the 1980s. There must have been hundreds.

I loved range days. Tim and I would pair up and work as a unit. We had such a close understanding of each other's movements that the rest of the team would comment on how smooth and in sync we were. I could feel it also. As I raised my weapon and fired towards the rising targets, I could see Tim doing so simultaneously; as my weapon came down, so did Tim's. We completely mirror-imaged each other. If Tim moved backwards, I would provide perfect cover and fire and likewise, Tim in return for me. There is nobody else that I would have wanted in a contact (firefight) next to me other than Tim.

The team's accommodation was a house off a main road two minutes from the embassy. The house was secured by local guards employed by AG. We had 24-hour protection comprising of four men armed with AK-47s. We also had our weapons that would be with us at all times. We would sleep with the pistols on our bedside tables and the rifles underneath our beds. We had two chefs who would prepare our lunches and evening meals – great food, to be honest. We had two female cleaners who worked really hard in making the house look clean. They would also kindly do our laundry for us if we threw them some extra US dollars. In the evenings we would congregate in the large comfortable living area, where we were provided with a huge television and DVD player. We had an excellent SKY TV package so we had all the sports channels and movies. If we wanted to exercise, we would jump in the wagons (4×4s) and either go to ISAF HQ and use their gym or a British Camp called Camp Souter up the road from us, just off a prominent road that linked Kabul to Jalalabad. This road was known as IED alley, a popular long strip of road in which IEDs would be placed or which suicide bombers would target.

HMRC also had their own C-130 Herc, a small military-style plane that would carry our clients, us and our vehicles from Kabul to anywhere in Afghanistan. We would report to Kabul Airport and get straight onto the runway. The C-130 would be waiting for us with the tailgate down. The vehicles would be driven onto the plane and secured. In time, we would fly all over to locations such as Kandahar, Jalalabad, Herat, Bagram, Samangan and Mazar-e Sharif. I personally hated flying. The lads picked up on the fact and would often take the piss: "Give him his milk", referring to B A Baracus from *The A-Team*. I couldn't wait for the plane to land and get off that fucking thing. I found the taking off and landing the worst. Once it was in the air it wasn't so bad. I would put my earphones in, listen to some music and attempt to get some sleep.

Our weapons would always be ready to go. As well as being fully loaded, we would make sure there was a round in the chamber. Should we come under contact at any point we could draw our weapons and immediately start engaging with the enemy. We would not have to go through the process of 'cocking' the weapons (placing a round from the magazine into the chamber). There, for me personally, was another reason why a round was permanently in the chamber of my pistol. I promised myself that should I find myself in a situation which was looking bad or in which we were overrun and faced capture, I would make the decision to take my own life. At no cost was I going to be taken hostage and have my face plastered all over the *News at Ten* while wearing an orange boiler suit. A gentleman by the name of Ken Bigley had been captured in Iraq a year or so before and subsequently been beheaded by his captors. This was not going to happen to me. Not only for my own sake, but also under no circumstances was my daughter ever going to see that image of her father in that position. My destiny was to lie in my hands. If it came to it, then I was more than prepared to pull the trigger. I stood by this rule until my final day in Afghanistan.

Our induction process was complete and we were now ready to meet with our clients. The clients of HMRC were housed in a beautiful mansion in a green zone area of Kabul. A green zone is supposed to be as secure as you can get. Their mansion had excellent protection including high walls surrounding it, CCTV and numerous armed guards courtesy of AG. It was a little fortress. It was stunning also. You would not think you were in Afghanistan. The floors were pure marble and the interior was made with the most beautiful wood. It was almost like a Beverly Hills mansion. As the contract was new and we were the first close protection team on the ground, only a few clients were in Kabul. Over the next month, more and more would be coming out to us. We therefore had to be ready to collect them from Kabul Airport on their arrival.

One thing I quickly noticed while looking out on to the streets was the amount of children with missing limbs, far too many of them. They would walk around with their tiny hands stretched out begging for a dollar, while propping themselves up with an old stick as a crutch. Children as young as four or five having to go through life with this huge undeserved, disadvantage. It would have happened by innocently playing in the streets, probably flying kites or chasing each other. With one dreadful step onto a landmine, things as they knew it would change. It was heart-breaking to witness. It showed the level of war that these children had grown up knowing.

The team had settled into Kabul nicely. We all got on well. We had the finest equipment including vehicles, weapons and radio communications. We were housed in good accommodation with our own chefs and cleaners. Kabul at this point was also quiet. There had been no significant terrorist incident over the last six months. I was working for a well-known and very professional company earning some serious money and had no army bullshit to contend with. This was just too good to be true. Or was it?

The team started a tradition. Whenever we used to go out on a job together as a complete team, be it visiting a checkpoint or flying over to the other side of the country, we would always get together before deploying, place our arms around each other and say the Serenity Prayer:

God grant me the serenity
To accept the things I cannot change;
Courage to change the things I can;
And wisdom to know the difference.

Now, I'm not religious by any stretch of the imagination, but I and the others found some sort of comfort from saying these words. I don't really know why we started to say it, but we did, and we would say it and it stuck. It has embedded so strongly with me that I now have it tattooed onto me as a reminder of the team and its strength, and in memory of what was about to happen in Afghanistan.

14

FIRST BLOOD

A couple of months had gone by. I had already returned home once and spent four weeks with Nicola and Bethan. It felt as though we had pure quality time together. Nicola had decided to stop work temporarily so she could spend more time with Bethan at such a young age. I was earning really good money so it wasn't as if she needed to work. We both therefore agreed that Bethan would come first.

Before leaving the girls and returning to Kabul via Dubai, I promised that next time I returned we would go on holiday somewhere and relax. After all, I was only allowed a limited amount of time in the UK because of tax purposes. Nicola agreed and started planning destinations. I said goodbye to Bethan. I started to talk to her gently about if something ever happened to Daddy. I made a promise to her that I would always be there in her heart, and that I would always be proud of her and that I loved her so much. I needed to hear Bethan say back to me that "Daddy would always be there". She repeated the words to me, unaware of the importance of their meaning. I made her say these special words every time I left home for Afghanistan. I needed her to understand that should the worst happen to me, then this is what I felt, and that somehow I would always be there looking over her.

Nicola drove me to Birmingham Airport and we said our goodbyes. "See you in eight weeks." We hugged and parted ways. Vince and I were on leave together at the same time. We flew by Emirates to Dubai, where once again we spent the night at the Millennium Hotel. We wandered down to a local bar called Jules Bar, downed a few beers and talked about what we had been up to. We both agreed that we missed the lads and that on our final week's leave we just wanted to return and get back to work. As promised, the British Embassy had arranged for us to passenger a UN flight into Kabul. This felt so much safer and more comfortable and the smell was vastly different. On arriving in Kabul we were collected by a vehicle from our own team. They took us straight back to the house where we were greeted by the lads. We made up our rooms, which would be home for the next eight weeks and collected our weapons. We were back!

The following weeks went without much to report. We did our daily tasks of moving clients of HMRC around Kabul. They were training the local police in stop and search techniques at various VCPs (vehicle checkpoints). They would observe the police to make sure they were going through the correct processes and ensure the sniffer dogs were reacting in the way they should be. We would often find ourselves providing protection on these VCPs for a couple of hours. We would then have to move the clients on as we could not be in one location for too long for safety reasons. Our job was to protect the clients and if we thought we were static for too long, we would instruct them to move. Often the clients didn't like us telling them to wrap up. Tough, we were there to protect them. This was not a game; we were in one of the most dangerous environments on earth. Sometimes the clients would act quite nonchalantly, thinking nothing would happen to them. It would take an incident for them to realise different.

I recall one morning the team moving in two vehicles; the front vehicle held the bodyguard and clients and the vehicle in support behind held the lads, all ready to rumble. It was called a PES (Personal Escort Service) vehicle – basically, we were the vehicle behind that carried the big guns. There would be four of us ready to jump out, all guns blazing, to put down a rate of fire so the client vehicle could get away. We were taking two HMRC clients to a VCP about an hour out of Kabul centre. The client vehicle led the way and we were in tow. We arrived at the checkpoint and the team got out. We secured the area before letting the clients out of their vehicle and into relative safety. The two clients observed the VCP for a short while. A civilian vehicle approached. It was not of yellow and white colour but brown. The vehicle was reported over our radios so we all had knowledge of it being parked up in our vicinity. Three men got out. They appeared well dressed for Afghans. They presented in suits and had some form of ID around their necks. They approached the two clients. I was protecting one at the time so my client was no further than a metre away from me. As the civilians approached I shouted, "Stop!" I raised my weapon slightly in order for them to obey my order but not frighten. The men asked if they could show us ID, which they did. Their ID claimed they were local police. They spoke very good English. They wanted to take our two clients to their local station to find out more about what their intentions were in the country and what they were doing on these checkpoints.

"I'm sorry, my clients are going nowhere," Mark, the team leader, informed the officers.

"They will be coming with us," one of the suited men responded. With that, he pulled his suit jacket to the side and showed his pistol. With this sign of aggression I lifted my weapon and shouted, "Don't move". With that, the other two officers pulled their pistols from their holsters and aimed in our direction. My trigger finger got itchy. Who was going to buckle first? *Stay calm,* I thought. Eight lads had weapons out and pointing towards the three; they in turn had pistols pointing in the direction of the clients. The clients froze and you could visibly see their concern. They were frightened. It was all real now. I found myself in the middle of a Mexican standoff. I quickly decided who I would be putting down first and in which order I would double tap (two rounds at each target). I went over the routine I would display in my mind, over and over. I was ready. I had nothing else running through my brain at that moment, just the order in which my weapon would operate its two rounds towards and then re-aim onto its next unlucky target. One of the officers had thought better of the situation. He slowly and purposefully returned his pistol to its holster. I remained in the alert position with the butt of my rifle firmly in my shoulder and glancing over my sights. The order of double tapping had just changed. I would take the one on the right first who was still showing his piece. The officer placed his left hand out to the side and tapped towards the ground, signalling his comrades to copy his very wise decision. They did so. They turned their back on us and made their way back towards their car without saying another word. As they drove away, we logged the vehicle plate and then quickly ushered the frightened pair of clients into the front vehicle and off we escaped back to the client's residence. On the way back we made contact with the ops room. We informed them what had happened. Later that day, we as a team were informed that the British Ambassador had personally got in touch with the police commandant, who assured him that none of his officers were in that area on that morning. This, therefore, had been an abduction attempt. Maybe now the clients would realise that this was no holiday destination, and from now on they never questioned our security decisions.

We were gathering more intelligence over the following weeks that the Taliban were going to make an attempt to return to Kabul and cause chaos. They could not just roll in as a unit, but our intelligence suggested that they would try to infiltrate bit by bit. We needed to remain alert on the VCPs as we often found ourselves sitting ducks at these locations. The VCPs would be located on prominent entry and exit points to the capital. If the Taliban were going to make an attempt to re-enter Kabul, they would be coming through one of these points.

On one occasion, the search team pulled a public bus off the road. All the occupants were instructed to dismount; they were all asked to identify their personal luggage and lay it out on the ground in front of them. The bus was searched by the police officers and their dogs. I noticed a small bearded man with a rotund stomach looking at me. He had a very stern expression on his face and I could immediately sense that he did not like me or the fact I was there. Could this be a member of the Taliban? He certainly had the appearance of a Taliban soldier. I decided I would closely watch him and attempt myself to see into his luggage. I witnessed a young Afghan police officer go through his holdall. It was full of police uniforms wrapped in clear packaging. The uniforms were new. Why would this man who was clearly not a police officer have a holdall full of police uniforms? The police officer searching the bag moved on to the next person. I couldn't believe that a police officer himself would not be questioning this man's reason for having so much police attire. I was not happy. Something was not right here. I took it upon myself to approach the man. I looked him square in the eyes. He started muttering something at me and glaring back at me. It was as though we were about to have a prize fight and the press were in attendance and wanted the pre-fight stand-off. The penny dropped. He was cursing me. I grabbed his bag and opened it. It was not my job to search these people, but it was my job to provide security and I knew this man had something to hide. I continued to take out the uniforms. There were twelve wrapped-up Afghan National Police uniforms. He had either stolen them or been given them by a corrupt police officer. They were being taken out of the capital and given to the Taliban in order for them to infiltrate Kabul. I shouted over to the senior officer and explained what I thought. He agreed and the man was quickly arrested and the uniforms confiscated. As the man was led into custody he looked at me. I could see the anger in his face. I decided to soften his distress and blew him a kiss. I later found out that the man in question was a member of the Taliban and my theory was correct.

Fridays in Kabul are the equivalent of our Sundays. This is Afghanistan's holy day. Prayers would happen in the afternoons at the local mosques and public prayer areas. Due to this, we decided that we would keep a low profile at this time of the day. Anything that needed to be done on a Friday would happen first thing in the morning, making sure we were off the streets at this time. This for two reasons; firstly, the traffic would be chaos and secondly, to show some respect to the locals and their religion.

A job came through for us. One vehicle was requested to take a female client from the client house to CNPA (Counter Narcotics Police of Afghanistan), a small police station on the outskirts of the city used to train the search teams and dogs. I volunteered for the job as bodyguard and Richard offered his services as my driver. Richard and I left our house and made our way on the 5-minute drive to the client's mansion. I met with the female HMRC officer. I went through the normal brief that I gave to all clients in my care. "Should an incident happen then stay close to me, listen to me and do what I say. If I need to manhandle you then don't fight against me."

Our 4×4's were left-hand drive; I always liked the client I was protecting to be sitting behind the driver. This meant that I could look behind and gain eye contact with them. Some of the lads didn't like their clients wearing seatbelts. This was because should an incident happen then the client had to press and release the belt, and under stress they might panic and waste valuable time in a contact situation. Personally, I always asked my clients to put them on. This was because I deemed at that moment in time that the biggest threat to the safety of the client was a road accident. The biggest SOP for a driver initially is to press the central lock button when all passengers are complete in the vehicle and are ready to move.

We left the mansion. Richard and I decided on the route beforehand that we would be taking to CNPA. We assessed that the journey should take no longer than twenty minutes. Richard pressed the lock button and we felt secure in our armoured vehicle. As we left the mansion I also placed on our ECM equipment. The vehicle would always carry a substantial first aid bag and breakdown kit. We carried water and food and pre-packaged 'grab bags'. These contained extra ammunition, smoke grenades, radios and other essentials in case we found ourselves having to dump the vehicle. My rifle would be hidden from public view between my legs but remain loaded with a round in the chamber. I sent a radio check from the vehicle-mounted radio, ensuring that I had good communication with the ops room in case an incident would occur and that the ops room would keep me updated with any information I would need while on the ground.

My female client had been in country for a while and was one of those who I considered did not take the security threat seriously enough. It felt as though it was almost a game to her. How her opinion and actions were about to change!

The journey took a little longer than the twenty minutes we planned. Kabul seemed to be really busy, busier than a usual Friday morning. There's no road etiquette on the roads of Kabul. The standards of driving are horrendous. You would see minor bumps and crashes frequently. I often witnessed cars driving down the road in the wrong direction, U-turns on a main road, driving around a roundabout the wrong way; just continual dangerous, erratic driving in an attempt to get to a destination quicker. To pass your driving test in Kabul constituted of driving up a road 500 metres, turning around and driving back down. No wonder the standards of driving are bad. I doubt very much that Afghanistan have their own version of *Top Gear*'s Stig.

We arrived at CNPA. I showed the guard my dip plates (diplomatic plates/red VRN plates which informed everyone that our vehicle was of diplomatic status), which were positioned by elastic bands on the other side of the sun visor. We entered the station, parked up and Richard released the central locking. I opened my door and made my way around the rear of the vehicle and opened my client's passenger door. Richard radioed the ops room, informing them that we had made our destination. CNPA was a safe and secure location; however, I stayed close by my client just in case – anything could happen. I was not just going to let her roam around not knowing her location. She was my responsibility. I would be her shadow for the duration she was away from her accommodation. I stayed in communication over the personal radios with Richard, who stayed with the vehicle.

My client completed the tasks she had gone to CNPA for and it was time to return. She jumped into the back of the wagon and placed her seatbelt on. I entered the vehicle and confirmed with Richard the route we would take back. This route always had to be different from the previous route, as we needed to keep changing in order not to create a routine. We needed to keep our choices different to help minimise the chance of ambush. If we took the same route there and back then we were opening ourselves up for a potential hit. I radioed to the ops room and placed on the ECM.

The streets were still busy, the afternoon was approaching and I wanted to get the client back quickly. As we got to the centre of Kabul the vehicle could barely move. The roads now were dominated by pedestrians and not the yellow taxis. I could hear the delivery of prayers over speakers which boomed over the town. Our vehicle began to move very slowly. I observed three young men walking with their backs towards us in the centre of the road. I was sure they were aware of our presence but just in case, I asked Richard to beep the horn. The three lads looked around and continued to walk at the same pace, almost as if to antagonise us. I wondered if they were doing this on purpose in order to set us up for an attack, but I had to doubt this as the area was heavily populated and any incident would also involve the locals. This had to be purely to piss us off, then.

"Let them know we are here, Richard." Richard, with this instruction, drove close up to the young men. Still they showed no sign of moving out of the way. I could see that this infuriated Richard. With that, he revved his engine in an aggressive manner. He was hoping that this would shock them into moving to the side of the road. They obliged and moved, two of them moving to the left and one to the right, opening the road up for us to continue forward. As they moved, Richard accelerated. He must have done this momentarily too soon. He had only run over the foot of one of the men. Not a good feeling, having a 3-tonne armoured 4×4 running over the metatarsals. This must have caused serious injury. I turned around to observe through the rear window to see the man in question on the floor, clutching his foot, screaming. His two friends started to run towards our wagon shouting in anger. This gained attention from the locals who in turn added their frustration to the fact we had injured somebody and were driving away. Our vehicle had stopped once more.

This gave opportunity for the locals to gather around our wagon, banging angrily on the outside. We found ourselves surrounded.

At this point I was not overly concerned; we were in our little protective bubble and secure in the comfort of the 4×4. I looked at the client who I could see was concerned. I made the decision to go into the glove box and take out a smoke grenade. I had the option of getting Richard to unlock the doors. I would open mine and throw the grenade underneath the wagon, and then Richard would press the accelerator which would help disperse smoke, getting the civilians to back off, giving us the chance to drive through. Before I had a chance to get Richard to ping the doors, the rear passenger door was opened. Richard had forgotten to lock the doors before leaving CNPA. I immediately glanced towards my client. I saw a set of hands attempt to pull her out of her seat and out of the wagon. The seatbelt, thankfully, had helped keep her inside the vehicle. Without hesitation or even thinking of my actions, I leant over and grabbed the bottom of her right leg. I was pulled in the general direction also but with this I reached with my right hand towards my pistol and removed it from its holster, and in one sweeping movement brought the pistol up and under facing the attacker. He looked at the pistol and froze. I didn't. I released two shots (double tap) into the area of the face. His body crumbled to the floor and with this violent action the population moved back, giving me the opportunity to scramble over to the back seat and pull the door shut. "Lock it," I shouted and Richard obliged.

The client was screaming. I have never heard a sound like it. Her terror was uncontrollable. She had no control of her emotions. I was on top of her with my pistol still in my hand. Immediately I noticed blood on her clothing and then as she brought her hands away from her face I could see it there also. I needed to be firm with her. "Calm down and be quiet." This barely helped; she continued screaming. Richard at this time had accelerated away from the situation; nobody now was going to get in the way. I leant over to the front and grabbed the radio. "Sierra Oscar this is Tango 1 2, contact shooting wait out." This gave the ops room initial information that we had been involved in a contact which comprised of a shooting.

Richard made our initial escape. I tried to remain calm myself. After I composed myself I got back on the radio and informed the ops room in more detail of the incident. We were told over the net to make our way directly through the green zone and into the back gates of the British Embassy. As we drove through with the client still screaming we stopped and the static guard conducted an initial underneath search of the wagon, walking around with mirrors to see if a device had been placed on the undercarriage of the vehicle.

"Fucking hurry up!" I shouted. Poor guard had no idea I had just been involved in a serious contact and there's me screaming at them for doing their job. They let us through and we parked outside the front entrance to the main embassy building within the grounds. I knew what was going to happen. We had been briefed that should an incident which involved the taking of life happen, then we would be arrested on suspicion of murder by the resident RMP team. This was just formality and at the end of the day, each and every one of the team had diplomatic immunity. This didn't mean we could walk around shooting folk freely with a licence to kill and we didn't have double 0 numbers. My client was escorted away to safety. I never saw her again. I'm not surprised; the trauma she went through that day would stay with her for the rest of her life, I am sure. It's not every day an Afghan local attempts to pull you out of a car. I had no choice in doing what I did and I have no regrets in doing it. If I hadn't acted accordingly, that young woman would more than certainly have been raped, beaten and probably killed. My actions that day saved her life; however, it was our lack of actions that put her in that position to begin with (i.e. not locking the vehicle doors). I hope this young lady has got on with her life and it has not had detrimental effects on her. I can't think about that too much because I will never know.

Richard and I were separated immediately, arrested and cautioned. We were led into the embassy and a room that I had never been in before. It was a large room that had a glass room inside it; a room inside a room. The glass room was designed to be soundproof to any outsider listening in – not only an outsider of the room, but an outsider of the whole building. With technology these days it is not surprising, the equipment available that has the ability to penetrate a building and listen into noise or conversation. This glass room was the most secure in the building.

I sat down at a large table and had two RMP officers flank me either side. I was about to be interviewed by a gentleman in a beautiful blue suit. I have no idea who he was and he didn't come forward with the information either. He must have been an employee of the embassy whose job it was to get us out of this shit and smooth things over. I looked down at my hands and noticed blood on the top of the left fingers. I was wearing a beige shirt which was open and not tucked into my brown combat pants. Not tucked in because it would cover my pistol and holster, which had now also been taken off me. Under the shirt I was wearing what used to be a white T-shirt, which now looked like I had spilled a bottle of Merlot down it. I saw the interviewing gentleman look at my face, not into my eyes but around my face. *What is he looking at?* I thought. I proceeded to touch my face and wiped downwards towards my chin. I looked at my hand and saw blood. How much more did I have on me? I wanted to get this blood off me immediately.

"Can I go for a wash first, please?"

"No," I was firmly told.

"Please, this feels terrible; I want it off my face."

"Not until we have done this," again I was told. I lost my temper.

"Well, I'm not saying a word until I get to wash this shit off." The well-dressed geezer attempted to interview me.

"What's your name, who do you work for and what's your job title?"

"I'm going to tell you one more time. I'm saying fucking nothing until I get to wash the shit off my face."

He attempted to ask me again. *Fuck you,* I thought. *I'm saying shit.* This went on for ten minutes until he conceded and asked the RMP to escort me to the washrooms. I looked at myself in the mirror. I was covered in blood. I started to rinse my hands and watched the blood trickle away over the white porcelain washbasin. Reality hit. I had just killed someone.

I remember spending my very first night in the army back at Whittington Barracks. I recall lying in my bed that very night and before I went to sleep something was bothering me. I had to question myself. *Could I kill another man?* I remember thinking maybe I would struggle in doing so. I thought about it for such a long time that night that I fell asleep thinking about it. Within weeks of army training, I never had to ask myself the question again.

How did I feel now? Truth be told, I didn't give a fuck. Fuck him. He shouldn't have done what he did. Actions have consequences. He must have known that we were armed in that vehicle. I continued to wash my hands and face. I also noticed bits of bone in my hair. All I could think about was getting this horrible shit off me.

I was escorted back to my interviewer. I answered all his questions truthfully; I had nothing to hide. Everything I said was both written down and tape-recorded. I wondered what Richard was saying. I just hoped he too was just telling it straight. The interviewer left the glass room and I must have waited for about an hour. On returning, he told me that he had been onto the head police commandant and that he would be instructing his officers to start an investigation the following morning. We were told to return to the house, clean ourselves up and pack our bags. We were being flown out of Kabul that evening on the nearest available UN flight, this being the reason why the investigation started the following morning. We were going to be in the safe location of Dubai. If anything was to come of our actions, we would obviously not be returning to Kabul again.

As promised, we were on the flight a matter of hours later. Mark and Vince took us to Kabul International Airport where we chartered our flight. We honestly didn't know if we would be returning. We were instructed to go to the Millennium Airport Hotel on arriving in Dubai and wait for a telephone call.

Two days later we were on our flight back to Kabul. No further action.

That had been my first taste of a drug that would become almost my downfall and my demon. Like a drug, I needed to chase the next fix and the more I had, the more I wanted. Not only that, but the impact of the drug would become less and less the more I had it, so I would have to have a greater dose. The drug was adrenaline.

15

CRUISE INTO KANDAHAR

The CP team had been on a number of flights all over Afghanistan in recent weeks with the HMRC clients. They were making sure that other search teams were up to standard and overlooking further training of the National Police. We would mount our C-130 Herc from Kabul International Airport with the two 4×4s and all our weapon systems. The flight crew would strap the vehicles down and we would leave our rifles in the wagons unloaded. We would keep our pistols on us; however, they would also be unloaded. The last thing you want is a round being discharged while in the air. Our seating comprised of four small rows positioned in front of our wagons. The back of the plane was just an open space. This part of the plane would have one small window on each side. We would often be allowed to leave our seated area and climb up to the cockpit and sit with the pilot and co-pilot. It was an amazing experience. I would sit in the small cockpit and take in the views of the terrain below me. The plane flew relatively low over Afghanistan's landscape, which consisted of rolling mountainous areas; now and again, I could identify small villages. I often wondered how these self-sufficient populations would cope. They clearly had no electric source and I had no idea what they did in regards to water. The mountains went on and on. How anything could survive outside a city, I would never know.

The previous evening we had received a set of orders for a complete eight-man team move to Kandahar, the second largest city in Afghanistan. It is located in the south of the country and is a major source of marijuana and hashish as well as, obviously, opium. On this occasion, we would not be carrying any clients. Our job was to simply fly to Kandahar, visit the local CNPA, provide protection for a burning (organised burning of drugs in order to destroy) and return to Kabul. A nice easy number! We organised our personal kit and packed up the wagons for the morning trip to Kabul International. First light came and we travelled in convoy, made our way onto the airfield and were greeted by the aircrew, which we were now becoming very familiar with. The crew organised the wagons, ensuring they were strapped down, and we made our way to the passenger seats. I prepared myself for the dreaded take-off. The plane rose into the air. As it was such a small plane in comparison to what I was used to, I could feel the turns and its manoeuvres with more distinction. The plane would circle Kabul city in order to get to the correct elevation to clear the surrounding mountains. Kabul, after all, is like a city within a bowl, the bowl being the mountains that dominate the city.

The flight to Kandahar took roughly ninety minutes. Kandahar Airport at the time was not particularly secure. It was fenced off to some extent but it didn't take much to compromise the area. The manned security was also minimal. The runway was very basic. There was one runway which was needed by aircrews for both take-offs and landings. It had one building adjacent which acted as check-in, departures and arrivals, but nothing special. No duty-free or bar to prepare yourself for your 18–30s holiday.

Our C-130 Herc approached the runway in its normal fashion. "Brace yourself for landing," one of the aircrew announced and of course I did. The wheels of the plane touched down and bounced a couple of times. All of a sudden there was an explosion that felt as though it came from underneath the belly of the plane. Then there was another. The plane's brakes were applied heavily by the pilot. My initial reaction was that we had crash-landed. Again, another explosion happened. This one felt louder; I knew at this point we were in trouble. I looked at Tim and Dan's faces.

"What the fuck is going on?" I shouted in fear. One of the crew popped his head from the cockpit. We needed to dismount immediately. The plane had come to a standstill, but its position was tilted to the right-hand side. I could smell smoke and began to panic. The door, which was small and only big enough for one person to exit at once, was opened. We all made our way to this point. The crew told us to jump from the door to the landing strip. This was a distance of eight foot due to the tilt of the plane. One by one we jumped out. When it was my turn I could feel flames from the undercarriage and smell burning rubber. I could see the lads that had disembarked the plane before me run away from the stationary vehicle. One by one we were following each other to a safe distance away from the Hurc. After jumping down I did not look back. I just wanted to get as far away from the plane as I could. I didn't know what had happened or the state the C-130 was in.

As we made it a safe distance from the plane, we all circled in 'all-round defence'. We were shoulder to shoulder together in a 360 degree circle facing outwards. There were eleven of us in this tight circle. We had all drawn our pistols, loaded and cocked them. The plane was probably 250 metres away. It was on fire. The flames had generated from the wheels upwards to the belly and out to the wings. Everything we had was on that plane; our vehicles and rifles. We found ourselves with our plane on fire with no kit but only our Glock pistols, which held 14 rounds in its magazine; we all had two mags each, these therefore totalled 308 bullets between us.

"What the hell happened?" one of the lads enquired. The pilot said he thought he had seen landmines on the runway. Insurgents had pierced the security of the airport. They must have waited to see our plane. They had made their way to the runway and placed landmines onto it. As we landed, the plane's wheels struck the mines, causing the landing gear to explode which ignited the plane. We estimated that we had nine seconds to get off the plane before it was completely destroyed with all our kit on it. We just watched the plane in disbelief as it was engulfed by flames in front of our very eyes. We had only been on that very plane seconds before. We were lucky to evacuate and make our way to safety. Or were we?

If the Taliban had planned this attack then we should be expecting a second wave. We were sitting ducks with only our pistols as immediate protection. The effective range of a Glock 17 is approximately 45 metres, but it can fire up to longer distances. This is substantially shorter than our rifles, which would by now have melted on the burning vessel. Should the Taliban mount a follow-up attack, we would not have much of a fighting chance. Should this happen, which to be honest we expected, I would need to count my rounds (count how many times I operated the trigger) in order to save the last bullet for me!

We waited, clutched closely together like a band of brothers. We had 360 degree coverage but could see nothing. We remained close-knit for ten minutes with, surprisingly, nothing happening. We started to hear sirens approach our location. Two sandy-coloured jeeps were making their way towards us. Immediately we recognised them as friendly. The

Afghan flag on the side of the jeeps' doors made that clear. The vehicles were open-backed with a driver compartment. We could just make out the driver and passenger was wearing some sort of headdress (military or police caps). The vehicles were Afghanistan National Police. What a relief. The rescuers pulled up alongside us.

"Come, come." The driver had wound his window down and ushered us towards him. We didn't hesitate; we split ourselves into two groups and made our way onto the back of the jeeps. The vehicles sped away, taking us away to the safety of the airport terminal. We all looked back in the direction of the plane, taking in the sight and realising once again how lucky we had been to escape the plane and not be involved in what could have been a murderous firefight.

The team stayed firm at the airport. We got the message to the ops room and the British Embassy of what had occurred that morning. We were instructed to hold tight, as a UN plane would be with us within twelve hours to collect the team and return us to Kabul.

That UN plane took almost 24 hours to get to us. We were held in a small room for security. We had very little food and water, and we took it in turns to get some sleep. During this time we would look out onto the runway to see the plane being removed. The airport still needed to operate and the C-130 was preventing this from happening. The plane was housed at the airport for the foreseeable future. We never found out what happened to it or the B6 vehicles.

16

7/7

I was supposed to be taking my four weeks' leave commencing the 5th July 2005. Vince and I would be taken to the airport by the lads and fly out of Kabul on a UN flight, arriving in Dubai mid-afternoon. Vince and I would always spend our first night's leave in Dubai, stopping in the hotel that we became familiar with, the Millennium Airport Hotel. We would get into our rooms, shit; shower and shave then head straight for Jules Bar. We would enjoy a good steak and drink beer. The taste of that first beer would be like velvet hitting the throat. It felt like our little bit of luxury between leaving Kabul and returning to the UK. However, at the last minute an important job came through which meant that our leave had been postponed for one week. Vince and I were furious. I couldn't stop bitching and whining. I felt so hard done by. I phoned Nicola, who was also not welcoming of the news.

I should have been reunited with Nicola on the 7th July after landing at Heathrow from Dubai, getting on the underground to Euston Station and then going on to Birmingham New Street Station by rail. That job that my leave got postponed for may have been a blessing in disguise, as on 7th July when I should have been in London and on the underground system, there was a series of coordinated terrorist suicide attacks targeting civilians travelling on the city's public transport system during morning rush hour. Four Islamic terrorists separately detonated three bombs in quick succession aboard London underground trains across the city, and later, a fourth on a double-decker bus in Tavistock Square. Fifty-two people, all UK residents but of eighteen different nationalities, were killed and more than seven hundred were injured in the attacks, making it Britain's deadliest terror incident since the 1988 bombing of Pan Am Flight 103 over Lockerbie, Scotland, as well as the country's first ever Islamic suicide attack.

How ironic if I had been caught up in this terrible incident having just flown back from Afghanistan, one of the most dangerous countries in the world. The team witnessed the horrific events unfold on our television set. A message had come through from the Embassy that we were to remain 'locked down' (not to leave the house under any circumstances). This made sense as tensions were getting increasingly high amongst the lads. The last thing we should have been doing was going on the streets of an Islamic country feeling as hot-headed as we did. We needed to remain professional. The best thing for everyone was to stay firm in the comforts of our accommodation.

That evening, the British Embassy as well as our location was bombarded with vehicle horns. The locals must have got wind of the attacks in London and a small minority of supporters were driving around with Afghanistan flags waving from the yellow vehicles and shouting "Allahu Akbar", meaning 'God is greater' in translation. They were celebrating what had occurred in London in front of our house and the embassy. You could only imagine the anger that was portrayed in the house during that evening. These disrespectful actions went on for a couple of hours.

That following week, we didn't have much work to do. Everything was kept very low-key; the clients of HMRC were also told to stay firm and let the dust settle for a few days. I was to go on leave with Vince the following Wednesday.

On arriving at Heathrow, Vince and I were to make our way by the underground to Euston Station. I looked around the passengers, who all looked very solemn. Many were wearing traditional black armbands around the left arm as a sign of respect. These very people themselves were probably on the underground only seven days beforehand. It was a very strange experience that day. Reality of the atrocity hit home. I was used to conflict and it was becoming second nature to me, but these poor people didn't deserve what had happened. The journey was quiet as if everyone was still in shock, and also as if they were continuing to contemplate what had happened only days ago and showing continued respect. It was to make what I was doing in Afghanistan more justified.

I would go home on that leave and begin to throw my money around. I decided to buy myself a brand new Audi TT. A beautiful black car with black leather interior, a motor I could have only dreamt about while in the army. Nicola and I had also secured a mortgage and brought our home, a large 3-bedroom house with a huge garden overlooking a cul-de-sac. Bethan's room was decorated in pink and Cassius loved the back garden. As a family, we also had a holiday in Cyprus where yet again we spent quality time together making memories. This was where my little girl learnt to swim. Life was good. My family were being rewarded financially for my hard work and the risks I was taking. It all felt worth it. I was doing an exciting job and the girls were beginning to see the benefits of the decision I had made to work in the close protection industry. I recall walking into my local pub and all my friends wanting to hear the stories of what I had been up to, buying them pint after pint. Money was not a problem, I had plenty of it, and while I was at home I was going to spend it on the people I loved and cared about.

I noticed a change in myself. It had become clear that I was very selfish. Not in regards to money, as the girls got everything they wanted. They came first. I noticed, however, that I was not concerned for my own life. This being very selfish! If I should die then my wife became a widow and my daughter had no father to guide and support her through life. At the time I didn't take this into consideration. It wouldn't happen to me! I justified it by claiming that if I cared and had a fear of dying then I would not be able to perform my job correctly. If I thought about being shot or blown up, then the element of fear would affect the decisions I would make and my performance in a firefight. I truly had no fear at the time. I was beginning to feel unstoppable and untouchable. I had been in a few contacts (firefights) at this point and had got out safely, with the bonus of an adrenaline rush. *Let's bring on the next one.* I wanted more. Why? I was tasting adrenaline and I needed more. Towards the end of my four weeks' leave I was having withdrawal symptoms; I needed to get back and taste some action. I could only manage being at home for about three weeks – after that, I needed to return. I could have been missing something; the lads could have needed me. I then realised that home was actually Kabul.

17

I'M SORRY

I returned home to Kabul, reunited with the team and got back into life as I knew it. On spending time out of country, we as individuals would like to reacquaint ourselves with a few things, such as the local area, the weapons and driving. I hated driving in Kabul – as previously mentioned, it is a bit of an all for one, with no particular rules or specific Highway Code. It was like a ride at the fair – dodgems. I didn't like the left-hand drive either. However, I had to pull my weight and do my share. I couldn't expect the lads to drive all of the time, that wouldn't be fair.

The first few days back and I reluctantly volunteered to drive as part of a recce of the city. We wanted to gather more information of possible routes and alternatives to keep our options open when planning journeys. I would be driving and I would have Mike, Tim and Vince with me. Vince would be in the passenger seat, with Tim and Mike seated behind. We left the embassy and made our way through the green zone. Traffic was really busy on this occasion. I made my way parallel to Kabul River, which was not really a river but a sewage pit or dumping ground for rubbish which was dried up in the summer. I came to a prominent roundabout, which had three exits. I was attempting to go straight over the island and over a bridge towards the Afghanistan Olympic Stadium. This stadium in the past had been used for countless public executions by the Taliban and was a symbol of fear. There were permanent bloodstains on the football pitch's centre circle due to this. I approached the roundabout with caution as you would often see cars travelling in the opposite direction heading straight for you. Due to this chaos, local police would often be positioned at these prominent decision points in order to maintain the flow of traffic and deter the locals from driving erratically.

I pulled onto the island and joined the middle lane of three. I, of course, was in a large Toyota jeep approximately seven foot high, the average width of a 4x4 but weighing 3 tonnes. Flanking me on either side were the decorated yellow and yellow and white taxis. As I manoeuvred around, I could see a police officer through my front windscreen. He was stood in the vehicle lanes for some strange reason, bang in the middle of the road. He was wearing the traditional police uniform of drab grey colour with a cap and holding an AK-47. He saw me approaching him. As he did he realised that he was not in a safe position. If he was to remain where he was, he would have been hit by me – well, that's if I hadn't applied the brakes and come to an immediate stop, or he could move to either side of my vehicle and risk being hit by a much smaller car, being a taxi. I witnessed the officer attempting to make up his mind. He took a step forward, changed his mind and moved back, then took another step forward. All this time, I was closely approaching him. He was trapped. He had to make a decision. Be hit by my B6 armoured brute of a vehicle or get a tap from a taxi? I was confident he would get out of the way and make the right decision, so was not overly concerned. Vince shouted and gestured, "Get out of the way." The officer looked straight into our cab and panicked. It was as though he had so many options running through his head that he just didn't know what to do. I had no reason to apply my brakes as I wasn't driving excessively or with any real speed and I was sure he would move in the end; he would be crazy to stay where he was. He unfortunately made the wrong decision. As my vehicle got close, he decided his best option would be to jump onto my bonnet while holding his AK-47 with both hands. He looked straight into my eyes; I will never forget his facial expression. I was in shock that he had made this decision and he was clearly terrified. I can't reiterate enough. It sounds as though I should have just applied my brakes, but all he had to do was take one step forward or back. Why he made this outlandish decision, I will never know. His jump didn't reach the required height for him to remain on my bonnet. Within the blink of an eye, he fell to the ground and underneath my rear left wheel. I had driven over the officer. I and the others felt the bump as I drove over him.

We were instructed from the first day on the job to never, under any circumstances, stop a vehicle. Should we find ourselves in an accident, we should make our way immediately to a safe location and report the incident immediately to the ops room. I knew, therefore, that even in this scenario I was forbidden to stop. I shouted in panic, "Is he dead?" I didn't want to look back or glance in my wing mirror. Mike and Tim were looking through the rear window.

Tim turned around and calmly announced, "Of course he's fucking dead." I then looked for myself in the wing mirror. I could see a lifeless body on the ground and beside him, I saw a mangled AK-47. I didn't want to see any more. *Look forward and get out of here,* I thought.

This would become easier said than done. The civilians in the area, both in their vehicles and on foot, had just witnessed me run over a police officer and attempt to drive away as if I didn't care for his life. I did care, but I could not stop the vehicle. After what had happened previously with the three young men on that Friday afternoon only months earlier and how that turned out, I was not prepared to be surrounded again. Cars attempted to block my position and I could see locals running towards us. I felt terrible but I needed to get the lads and myself away to safety. Vince got on the radio to the ops room and informed them of what had just happened. The two cars in front stopped. I had to keep moving. I didn't want to cause anyone any further injury.

"Drive through," one of the lads shouted. I put my foot on the accelerator and made gentle contact with the two cars to my front. I was not going to ram them out of the way like you would see on a Hollywood action movie, but I drove firmly, pushing them away from me. This also ensured that my vehicle would sustain very little damage. If I was to ram them with speed and force then I would be risking my wagon becoming immobilised, which would lead to greater problems and further risk. I had to get across the bridge. Once over the bridge, the road filtered into four lanes and I could make my escape. Once other locals started to see that I was not going to stop and I was damaging vehicles that were preventing me from my getaway, then they decided not to join the campaign in preventing me. They, after all, did not want their precious vehicles to be damaged by the Western bullies that thought they owned the roads.

We made our escape to a safe location on the outskirts of Kabul. We went directly to a police dog training facility where the dogs were cared for and trained. This would become our location of safety for the next eight hours until tensions on the street would calm and we could make our way back to the embassy where we would be interviewed separately.

The incident was put down to an accident, and that's what it truly was. I was led to believe the embassy had compensated the family of the officer financially. I hope the family received significant money. It's the least they deserve.

I am truly sorry for what happened to the officer that day. I am sorry for his family and friends. He was a young gentleman, probably in his late twenties or early thirties. He had a life to live and I took it away. I took many lives during my time in Kabul, but this was the only one I feel sorry about. I know I didn't intentionally cause his death, but I am still responsible. He, in turn, made a wrong decision that day to position himself in the middle of a busy road and decided foolishly to walk into my path. If I had thought for one minute that that was going to be his decision I would have braked sooner. I couldn't read his mind or second-guess his actions.

That was it though – from that moment, I decided to retire myself from driving. The lads were good and understood why.

Accidents happen in life. I could have beaten myself up about it and spent hours and hours going over what had happened. Should I have done this? Should I have done that? What if I didn't volunteer to drive that day? What if, what if, what if. The result doesn't change. The officer sadly died and I have to live with it, and I do. I cannot let an accident of such magnitude destroy my life also. One man lost his life that day. I can't let it ruin my life as well. Life must go on.

18

SUICIDE ATTACKS

The longer that went by and the more contacts I had been in and survived, the more risks I found myself taking. I started to go out on the ground at times not wearing my 50cal body armour (vest). I was chasing the adrenaline rush, getting every little bit I could. With every risk I was taking, the more I enjoyed that buzz and the feeling of the drug, the drug that I was wanting more and more of. I could see that this was becoming a problem. I was becoming addicted to the feeling. It was giving me a high. It started in my stomach like butterflies and rose up into my chest where I could feel my heart pumping and up into my jaw where I would grit my teeth and then smile. I had pure control of the emotion fear, but from fear you get adrenaline. This meant I had to take more risks. I needed to put myself in situations that others were afraid of, but I needed to be in. What's the worst that could happen? Come home in a coffin draped in a Union Flag having died a glorious death? Better than living a boring life, working a nine to five job, going through a mundane existence achieving nothing in life. I couldn't think of anything worse. If this meant dying rather than living a life like that, then so be it.

A couple of new lads had come into country. They needed to be trained up by the team. This included being orientated to the ground. One lad by the name of Rex spent some time with myself. He spent a few days with me. I showed him around Kabul and introduced him to places that he would be visiting. I assessed his driving (yes, funny that) and saw how confident he was before placing him with a client.

We were in the ops room when some intelligence came through of a possible suicide bomber in a red Toyota Corolla in and around the area of Jalalabad Road. I was just about to leave the embassy and show Rex where we got our vehicles serviced by a civilian contractor who operated under the name of No Melon. They were ex-British military REME lads who had set up a company in Kabul for all civilian contractors. No Melon was situated just off Jalalabad Road. We would have to travel approximately three miles down it then turn left into a quiet street to find the place.

"Fuck it, let's go." Rex had only been in country a few days and I didn't know how he would respond in a firefight or even if he had the minerals to knuckle down in one. Lots say they have the bollocks, but when it comes down to it, some bottle it. As we walked across the car park towards our wagon, which Rex would be driving, I could sense his trepidation at the prospect of going out with a possible suicide bomber riding around looking for a target.

We left the embassy and made our way past a prominent roundabout called Massoud Island, from that we continued towards IED Alley/Jalalabad Road. We drove past some apartments by the name of Russian Flats, where I noticed almost immediately some odd behaviour from a vehicle in my wing mirror. We were being sharked (vehicle moving in and out of lane to get a better view of what's in front). It was a red Toyota; was this the possible bomber? The chances were high as red cars are extremely rare in Kabul. I told Rex that there was a red Toyota behind us but to just continue forward, making no rash movements. Rex looked nervous. I started to feel my little adrenaline friend appearing. I observed as the red Toyota made its way towards us by overtaking cars behind. *Let it come closer,* I thought. I wanted to look inside the vehicle. The red car pulled alongside us, travelling at about 40 miles per hour. I was briefing Rex throughout, informing him what was happening and insisting he should stay calm. I peered down into the car from my elevated position. I couldn't make out the driver; it was only a right-hand vehicle drive. It was very strange. But what I did see was the passenger seat fully declined with a huge gas canister lying across the seat. I could also see wires in all different colours.

"This is it, Rex, this is the suicide bomber." We were without doubt his target.

Suicide bombers work in different ways. The bomber himself could drive up to us and detonate or he could be 'proxy' (taken against his will and his family held, then ordered to carry out the task or his family would be killed (blackmailed)). In this scenario, he himself could detonate the bomb or there may have been a follow-up vehicle following that detonated him when he became close. Either way, he was going up and so were we if we weren't going to act fast. Rex, to his credit, held his nerve; he could have panicked and put his foot down or turned away.

"Listen to me carefully," I instructed. "We are very near No Melon. It's a turning on the left in approximately eight hundred metres. When I say 'brake', hammer the brakes on and turn the wheel to the left, wait for a gap in the oncoming traffic then go." The driver must have been working alone, he was delaying the detonation. I felt no fear; I was soaking up the action, loving every minute of the adventure. "Get ready, Rex." Rex had no idea where he was going – he had to just trust my directions. This was the first time the poor fucker had been on the road, and I was introducing him to a suicide bomber.

"Wait, wait, wait, BRAKE, BRAKE!" Rex slammed on the anchors, the car proceeded forward. All those hours of watching *Top Gun* in Stanley Prison had paid off. Didn't Maverick say 'bang on the brakes and he will fly right by'? A gap in the oncoming traffic quickly appeared and Rex turned into it. At that very moment, before we even turned into the street, the fucker detonated. BOOOOMM! The suicide bomber must have panicked; he was obviously not expecting the immediate braking as we had acted naturally in the moments leading up to and before the manoeuvre. The explosion popped my ears and made the interior of our vehicle feel as though we were having the life sucked out of us, as though we were in a vacuum. We drove directly to No Melon knowing we had just escaped an attack. I was buzzing. I out-played, out-thought and out-manoeuvred the bastard. I had come up trumps again. I had a smile from ear to ear.

"Stick with me, Rex, and you will be fine." I have no idea what Rex must have thought of me. More than likely a fucking crazy bastard! One thing was for sure – he had to be impressed with my calmness and almost nonchalant attitude during the whole experience. Truth be told, I enjoyed the adrenaline, I got another kick and yet another fix. We were let into the gates of No Melon. Before dismounting the vehicle I got on the radio: "Contact bombing, wait out." Rex and I stood on the roof of No Melon where we were to witness the aftermath – police vehicles bellowing their sirens and the British military also attended. The bloom of smoke dominated the skyline and the smell of explosives was obvious.

I telephoned the ops room and briefed them up rather than sending a contact report over the radio. "Only you Inni, only you would have gone out on a routine task knowing there was a suicide bomber, and more than that, you get away scot-free," said the ops room operative. Rex and I remained at No Melon for a couple of hours. We talked about what had happened over and over again. I suppose, looking back at it, I broke Rex in well. Truth be told, I acted again in a selfish manner. OK, fine, if I wanted to chase bad guys and get in some dirty business then fine, it's my life and my decision. I shouldn't have put Rex in that predicament. I didn't give his feelings a second thought. I just wanted to get out there, get involved and get my fix. At the time I never thought about it, but looking back as I have matured, I realise how little I thought of Rex's life as well as my own.

On returning to the embassy later that day, we were informed that the suicide bomber had killed three innocent civilians going about their business. If I hadn't been so eager and gone out, they too would also probably be alive. Or would the bomber have found another target, causing even more devastation? I can't be held responsible for the three that sadly died. I didn't pack a gas canister full of explosives; I didn't decide to blow myself up, taking as many as I could with me. I have to, again, look at it as a misfortune. I didn't wake up that morning thinking *I'm going to kill 3 innocent civilians*. Just like the sad events of the police officer's death, I am not directly to blame. I cannot let those deaths haunt me.

Only three weeks after this event another suicide bomber would once more hit us. This time there was no avoiding it. Luckily, the armour of our B6 vehicle stood up to the pressure of a motorcyclist pulling up alongside us and detonating while in Kandahar. There were four of us in the vehicle and we all survived. This time we didn't see it coming. It all happened so quickly that I don't recall much. We were parked up outside a police station. We were waiting for the gate to be opened so we could enter; while we were waiting, the bomber pulled up and without hesitation detonated himself. Luckily for us, the bike was not stacked with enough explosives to completely destroy the wagon and its contents. The wagon would never be used again and it remains in some training location in Afghanistan as evidence of how protective the vehicles are and to show the damage a nutter can inflict. We were all obviously shook up. We had minor injuries such as cuts and bruises and some mild concussion but we lived to fight another day. It just made me feel even more untouchable. I had now survived a suicide bomber – add that to the collection – and of course, another dose of adrenaline for good measure. I have a problem with my hearing these days. I'm sure I'm going deaf in the right ear. I'm not surprised!

We didn't always get away unscathed. Not long after this, Mike and Richard were returning to the house from a small task with clients. It was late at night so visibility was poor. Kabul didn't have lampposts to help illuminate your path; this made road moves at night dangerous so it was something we would very rarely do. Richard was driving and Mike was in the passenger seat. The road was quiet, which was not unusual for this time of evening. An IED had been placed at the roadside; Richard and Mike had been the target. Once again, the bomb would not completely destroy the Toyota Land Cruiser, but it tipped it onto its right-hand side and into Kabul River, a landmark which the lads were paralleling. The jeep was hurtled to the right and into the water, which wasn't that deep but still significant. The wagon was on its roof submerged in the water, with only the wheels visible. Richard had managed in the chaos to find the central locking button and release the locks. He was not wearing his seatbelt. He managed to just about open his door by force of panic and make his escape to the surface of the river. Mike sadly never joined him. It appears as though Mike was wearing his seatbelt. We will never know if Mike had been knocked out in the blast and subsequent roll, or if he had fought to escape but failed. Either way, our dear friend drowned that evening in a dirty horrible river. Richard felt bad about the whole incident and that he lived and his friend died. He asked himself if he could have done more and if he would have changed anything. Richard began to suffer emotionally. He was sent on compassionate leave but never returned to the team. I hope my dear friend Richard is OK. I hope he has found some peace and has accepted that there was nothing he could have done.

Mike was adored in the team. He was a real character who made us smile when we were down and laugh when we were bored. He had real energy. Mike, if you recall, was the first of the team to speak when we all met that first day at Buckingham Gate in London. He always had something to say. He was a genuinely lovely man who I think of at times and smile. He left behind a wife and two teenage boys. Those boys would be very proud if they knew what a brave man their father was. Mike was the first death in the team, which was unbelievably close. It felt as though we had lost a brother. It hit us all hard. Sadly, we couldn't go to Mike's funeral – work commitments kept us all in Kabul. Would I have gone, given the chance? No. It made us realise we were not indestructible, we could be hurt and we did have emotions. I didn't want to believe that if I carried on in the reckless way I was continuing, that next time it could be me.

Mike was the first, but sadly he would not be the last of us. There was more pain to come in the following months.

19

HOTHEAD

Tempers were high after the locals' reaction to 7/7, the recent suicide bombing in Kandahar and, of course, the loss of Mike and resignation of Richard. They were replaced and we were joined by two new members of the team, Simon and Craig. Decent lads but they had big shoes to fill. I felt a little sorry for them as they were coming into a close-knit team that had been together for a while and gone through so much as a unit. They could see this and they partnered up quickly and became good friends.

I had been promoted to team 2IC. I felt ready for the position as my experience in country had outdone anyone else in the team. The extra £800 a month in my wage packet was an additional bonus. When Mark, the team leader, was on annual leave I would be in command of the team.

The team had been working hard orientating the new lads to the area and making sure they were trained on the team's SOPs. I received a message from the ops room saying that we were needed as a complete team to report to the client's home. We immediately set on our way. The team jumped into the two wagons and made haste towards the green zone. As team leader at the time, I commanded the front vehicle, with the other close behind. Tim on this occasion was my driver. This is a journey we completed almost on a daily basis so we all knew the drill. We made our way from our accommodation towards Massoud Island; here we would turn right around the island towards the US Embassy. We would approach the guard, who were all Westerners, and show two bits of ID. Firstly, I would drop my dip plates (diplomatic plates) and then show my British Embassy ID. The vehicle behind would mirror my actions and we would drive through and enter the green zone, and then go on to the client's mansion.

As my vehicle approached the guard, I showed my credentials. The guard holding an AK-47 waved the wagon through and we set on the 1-mile stretch to reach the green zone. As we had travelled approximately one kilometre, I received a radio message from Dan. "Inni, the guard won't let us through!"

"Why's that, Dan?" Dan continued to say that I hadn't told the guard that we were travelling in two vehicles. I went on to ask Dan if he dropped his dip plate and showed his ID? Dan confirmed to me that he had. "Then why the fuck is the prick not letting you through? I'm turning around." I instructed Tim to turn and go back to the guard. I was furious. I approached the guard and asked what his problem was.

"You never told me you were in two vehicles." He spoke in a South African accent.

"I don't need to. Both vehicles have diplomatic plates on show and we both had ID informing you we work for the British Embassy. What is the difference between my vehicle and this one?" I said, pointing to Dan's. The guard knew he had fucked up. That was all he had to do for a job – let diplomatic vehicles through and turn others away. How easy could he have it? "Let him through," I ordered. The guard couldn't backtrack; he couldn't admit to me that he had made an error in judgement. "Come on, tell me the difference between my vehicle and his? No difference, but you let me through and not him." He went on to say that he wasn't letting either of us through.

"Tim, pop the doors." I got out of the vehicle and went face to face with the guard. He took a step back and cocked his weapon and pointed it to my chest as if to frighten me and for me to back down. It would take more than this.

"Are you fucking stupid? Go on then, pull the trigger, pull the fucking trigger." All this as I walk towards the guard, showing no fear. I could see he was panicking as he didn't know what to do. His attempt to frighten me had failed dramatically, what else could he do? "Shoot me, I'm a British Embassy employee. Go on, pull the trigger and set off a shitstorm. You have just got yourself sacked."

I returned to my vehicle and could see the lads' expressions on their faces, as if to say "He's fucking lost it!" I got into the vehicle and got on the radio to the embassy's ops room. I needed to speak to the head of security operations. I was informed to report to him straight away. We drove to the embassy where I told him what had occurred at the US Embassy. The head of ops was furious. He jumped into my wagon and asked us to take him to the US site. A different guard was on. I showed my dip plates and ID, and we were waved through. The head of ops instructed Tim where to go. We pulled into the embassy and my man got out.

"Stay here, Inni, I won't be long." Only five minutes later he returned with a grin on his face. The South African guard had admitted in front of his guard commander and my head of ops that he had cocked his weapon at my chest and that he was not sure what to do. With that he was on the next flight out of Kabul, sacked.

What did I take away from this? Again I showed that I had no regard for my own life. I didn't know if the guard had an itchy trigger finger. He could have been a nutter given a gun and wanted some opportunity to use it. I didn't care. I walked him down while he was pointing a 7.62mm AK-47 at my chest. I looked into his eyes and he was more afraid of the situation than I was. Further to this, on this day I had opted out of wearing my 50cal vest. I had no protection, just my white T-shirt and my shirt over the top. My team remained in the two wagons, watching me from their security. They knew I didn't care.

I had been in Afghanistan for almost eighteen months and could see that I was becoming a different man. I felt aggressive, short-tempered and I didn't suffer fools lightly. Things had to be done my way, and if they weren't then you'd better have good justification as to why not. This was not the man that I wanted to be. I was never a bully, I was the one who always wanted to help people and stick up for people against the bully, and now I was becoming one. I could put it down to all the contacts I had been in and close shaves that I had found myself getting out of. I had to change; I had to start calming down otherwise I was going to get hurt. Maybe I needed some time off to re-evaluate life, work out what was important. The life I was living was not part of the real world. At the time, I thought what I was doing *was* the real world. Only now I look back and accept that it wasn't. Is it normal to wake up, every day, thinking, *could this be my last?* Is it normal to enjoy being in a firefight? Is it normal to have no fear while working in the most dangerous country in the world? Of course it's not. I realised that something had to change, but I just couldn't face returning home and accepting that maybe it was time to get 'a normal job'. This is what I despised the thought of. I was still young. I made myself a promise. *If I'm not dead in five years, I will quit.* I honestly and truly felt that death was my only route out.

20

WISHING WELL

I had a normal working day, nothing out of the ordinary had happened and I was going through a dry spell where I had not been in a contact for around four weeks. Kabul was relatively quiet. I was around four weeks into my eight week stint in country, so still had a few weeks before returning home to see the girls. I would often speak to them both over the telephone or Skype.

I went to bed after watching a film on my laptop and drifted off to sleep. I would be up early in the morning as the team would be deploying on a VCP in Bagram. I wanted to be fresh and ready for the morning's job. The team had gone through a set of orders that evening so we all knew what jobs we were assigned to do, what vehicles we would be manning, and what route the team would be taking. Mark gave the orders as he was in country, which meant I was back in my 2IC role.

I must have been in a deep sleep as I do not recall any tossing or turning, or getting up to go to the toilet in the middle of the night. However, I would start commencing with a dream. Not a dream, more a nightmare that was so real. I had never before had a nightmare so profound which left me in a state of terror. It has been almost ten years since I had this dream but it has only been over the last few months that I have been able to talk about it without having to fight my emotions and hold back tears. This is how powerful it was. Words will never be able to express its reality and how it left me feeling. It has to be one of the most significant happenings in my life, and I have lived through a lot.

It was a beautiful sunny summer's day. I didn't have a care in the world and life couldn't be better. I was sat on an old bricked well. I call it a wishing well. I could hear the birds singing and see butterflies in the distance. I was evidently at peace. This scene would stay present in my dream for a couple of minutes. All of a sudden, my peaceful scene turned to terror. I fell back into the wishing well and proceeded to fall into the darkness of the abandoned feature. The sun had now disappeared and all I was aware of was how dark, cold and damp my surroundings were. I needed to prevent myself from falling to my death or, even worse, reaching the bottom and never being rescued. I was, after all, in the middle of nowhere. I looked to the light and began to panic slightly as the light was fading as I was falling further down the well. Then I saw my angel. Bethan's face appeared over the wishing well. I could see her so clearly that it felt unbelievably real. She didn't say a word to me, she just watched as I fell away. My panic increased; I knew what this meant – I was losing her or, to be more accurate, she was losing me. I reached my right arm out to the side and stretched my fingers in an attempt to touch the side of the well. I felt my fingers scraping in my efforts. I tried the same with my left; I reached out in vain again. This time I felt my fingers touch the well but while doing so, my right hand came away and the scratching of the tips of my fingers disappeared. I strongly believe that during this experience I actually felt the sensation in my fingers. I felt the pain of my attempt. After failing at my first attempt I looked up at Bethan. Again, she didn't say a word, but she looked sad as if she knew she couldn't help her father's predicament. Her face this time looked smaller due to the distance; I was falling away from sight. I tried again, again and again to touch the sides, all this time my heart accelerating in beats and breaking as it did so. Bethan was still watching my plight. I knew what this meant; I had to accept what was happening to me. For a split second I found some peace. I looked at her beautiful blonde hair and innocent face. She looked motionless. I had five words for her. The words which I embedded into her from a young age, the words that I got her to repeat to me time after time: 'I Will Always Be There!' As I said those painful but promised words, I fell further and further until I couldn't see the light shining past her beautiful face. I had died.

I woke from my terror. This, ironically, was the most frightened I had been in years. This was fear and this feeling was alien to me. My pillow on which my head was resting was soaked; the sweat was significant. I immediately climbed out of bed and turned my room light on. This would be the last time I would sleep in the dark for probably two years. I had both my hands on my head walking around my room, going over and over the dream. *That's all it was, all it was, was a dream.* That's what I kept telling myself. My heartbeat was not only rapid in pace, but I could feel the intensity of each beat both in my chest and throat. My mind was working overtime. *What the fucking hell was that all about?* I started to fight back tears. I hadn't cried for as long as I could remember so this also felt a new experience for me. I had better get used to it as I would spend many a night crying myself to sleep in the foreseeable future. It was the middle of the night but I needed a shower. I would feel better once I woke completely and I needed to remove the sweat which covered my body from shin bone to the back of my neck. You would have thought I had just got out of a soak in the bath, judging how I looked. I got into the shower but couldn't get the image of Bethan's face out of my mind. I changed my bed sheets and attempted to go back to sleep. I decided to leave my bedroom light on which probably didn't help, but I failed to return to sleep that night.

I don't know what happened to me that night. Was it just a dream? I don't think so. I'm not religious and never have been. I had started to almost feel god-like myself with the amount I had survived and faced. I had finally been broken by something in Afghanistan, and that happened to be Bethan, my own daughter. Something happened that night. I don't know what. Maybe a premonition of some description! I now believe in the power of the brain. I say this because the next day I was shot on the VCP.

21

THE INEVITABLE HAPPENED

We ate breakfast as a team then RV'd at the vehicles. Mark commanded the lead vehicle and I brought the second Land Cruiser up from the rear. The first part of the tasking was to collect two clients from their mansion. We would then move on to Bagram to over watch a vehicle checkpoint being operated by the local police. This was a task we had completed over the years on countless occasions; we all knew our tasking and what to expect.

We travelled forty-five minutes to the VCP location. It was up and running by the time we arrived and seemed to be operating in good fashion. From the previous evening's orders, we knew our positions within the checkpoint. Craig would take the Minimi (5.56mm light machine gun, belt fed from a 200-round box) up onto high ground to provide over watch from a dominant position, the effective range of his weapon system being 300–400 metres. Mark would provide close protection for one client and I the other. The clients would stay very close to us as we were their immediate line of protection. Tim stayed close by, bouncing between Mark and me. The rest of the team would provide tactically what's called 'cut-offs', providing protection on the extremity of the VCP and from a distance. This should mean that the centre of the VCP, where the clients and searches were being conducted, was safe. Anyone with the intention of causing harm or destruction would have to go through the cut-offs first, this therefore giving us in the centre of the VCP time to react.

The clients went about their business chatting to the local police and asking questions. Cars were being selected by police officers in the area of the cut-offs for search. Once a search had been conducted, then another vehicle would be waiting to go through. All this time, vehicles that had not been selected for search would drive past, well away from the VCP. If any weapons, ammunition or drugs were found in the vehicle or in the possession of any individual, then they would be taken into custody and have their vehicle confiscated with the possibility of it being destroyed; this surely a huge deterrent for anyone thinking of carrying such contraband.

We would not spend long at a checkpoint. If we remained static for too long then word could get about that we were in the area and a quickly organised attack on our location could take place. The longer we were on a VCP, the increased risk. Our average time at a checkpoint would be approximately two hours. We would then instruct the clients that we would be collapsing the VCP and returning them to the safety of their home. Often they didn't like us dictating this to them, but tough; it was for their own safety, and ours for that matter. Two hours would be plenty on a VCP; what more would they get out of another thirty minutes?

It was a hot day and as we were static on a VCP I had opted to wear my 50cal vest. I attempted to keep myself cool by shoving bottles of cold water down the sides of my armour, lowering my body temperature. We often took small breaks, returning to the air-conditioned wagons for five minutes to cool ourselves off or have a cheeky fag. This was the purpose of having a floating man, in this case Tim. Mark went off to the jeep for his cigarette and swig of water and Tim took over body guarding duty of his client. Tim and I were roughly 20 metres apart.

I heard shouting from the right-hand cut-offs. I looked in their direction and could see from 50 metres away that a taxi had penetrated the VCP (failed to stop). The vehicle, of course a yellow taxi, was quickly approaching the VCP and had no intention of stopping. It was travelling at a good speed. I grabbed my client by his body armour strap and forced him to the ground. "Get down." As he went down towards the ground I placed my knee on his back, ensuring he was hitting the deck and not panicking and doing something stupid like running off, and stayed there. I could clearly see that the windows of the oncoming vehicle were down and that the car had a full capacity. I brought my rifle up into my right shoulder and pulled the safety catch down with my right thumb. I had the option to go to single fire or automatic. I chose automatic in order to get maximum rounds down and be as aggressive as possible. If it was to go down, I would be firing bursts of two to three rounds into the vehicle without hesitation. I had no idea what Tim was doing at the time but I'm sure he would be mirror imaging what I was doing as we always operated in sync. My eyes were fixed on the taxi, waiting for confirmation that this was an organised attack on our position. I realised it was when I saw the muzzles of two AK-47s appear from both the passenger and the rear passenger windows. I fired a burst in the direction of the windscreen; in return I received fire back. My memories of the incident are quite vague but what I can recall I will continue with.

I received what felt like a kick in the chest from a raging bull. It lifted me off my feet and drove me hard into the ground. I recall my breathing being affected. I had the wind completely taken out of me. I was physically fighting for my next intake of much-needed breath. Everything seemed to go in slow motion. While on my back I turned my head to the left. I could see the vehicle continue on its path through the VCP and saw the operatives of the checkpoint on the ground. I looked towards my dear friend Tim. He was dead! His eyes were open and looking straight at me. I could hear aggressive fire from the high ground. Craig would be putting fire down towards the taxi in an attempt to immobilise it.

At this moment I did something which, if I didn't have witnesses, I wouldn't believe would have been possible or happened. I remember peeling off my 50cal vest from its shoulder straps. As I did, it fell to the ground. My left arm felt heavy. I looked towards the taxi, which had stopped travelling, and noticed it had come to a complete standstill. I ran towards its parked position. I heard nothing in my ears apart from my heart beating loudly. It was the only sound I could hear, no shouting, no shooting, nothing. Only the heartbeat that was like a drum sounding off, *thud, thud, thud, thud.* I closed with the rear of the taxi. I was five metres from its position when I brought my weapon up once more and started to fire burst after burst after burst into the vehicle. I didn't stop this process until all thirty rounds had been expended from my rifle. During this shooting, my left arm stayed at my side; I didn't have the ability to steady the front-hand grip of the rifle. I lost use of it. I needed it, however, to change my magazine. I dropped to my knee and pressed the magazine release catch with my left-hand thumb. I was able to take control of the magazine and place the adjoining 30-round clip into the magazine housing and operate the cocking handle in order to continue with the engagement. Another thirty rounds went into that car. I recall seeing the bodies of four men (in my words) 'body popping' like break-dancers as another round struck their worthless murdering terrorist bodies.

If I had more rounds on me that day I would have put

more into the taxi. They were going to get everything I could possibly give them. I wouldn't have stopped if one of the wagons hadn't pulled up beside me and opened its back door and Jack grabbed me. He took control of me and guided me into the wagon and into safety. Jack went on to tell me that when the vehicle pulled up to get me, they all noticed I was laughing while filling the taxi with 5.56mm rounds. I was laughing. I don't know why. I don't even recall displaying those emotions. I must have, because the lads confirmed what Jack had seen. It must have been my good old friend adrenaline. It's a powerful thing, adrenaline.

Once in the wagon my breathing once more became painful and laboured. "Stay still, Inni." Jack got access to our significant medical bag and pulled out an FFD (first field dressing). He applied it to my shoulder after cutting off my white T-shirt with a set of scissors. I looked at my stomach to see four pierce wounds on my torso, one 8cm from the right of my belly button, one 3cm above that on my rib cage and two to the left of my rib cage. Rounds had shattered my 50cal vest and penetrated my skin, by a miracle not causing much more damage. I later found out that I had fractured ribs caused by the kick of that raging bull, this being the reason why I found it painful to breathe. The 50cal vest had saved my life. My shoulder was less fortunate; a round had entered it, causing severe damage. The shoulder was a mess. I was administered morphine and a tourniquet was placed underneath to stem the blood loss.

"What about Tim?" I asked.

"He's in the vehicle behind." Jack informed me.

"Is he dead?" The vehicle went quiet. I knew the answer.

Tim, my friend from back in Catterick, had just recently returned from his annual leave. He and his wife had been trying for a family of their own for years with no luck. Tim returned to Kabul announcing that his wife was pregnant and that he would only be doing another six months, then returning to the UK for good. This made the matter even worse. I never met Tim's wife and don't know if he had a little boy or girl. I couldn't bring myself to find out or even visit. I'm sure whatever the case, Tim is looking over his child and is always there!

The two vehicles quickly made their way into the centre of Kabul. We separated. One took the clients back to their accommodation and gave them the once-over to ensure they were OK. My vehicle took me straight to an American medical base by the name Camp Warehouse. I was unloaded and treated for my injury immediately. The doctors attempted to reconstruct my shoulder as best they could but they didn't have a specialist in the area of shoulders. I was to be sent home.

For the following five days I was too ill to move. I was given morphine injections twice daily, and Diazepam and Temazepam to help with the pain. As soon as I took the oral medication I would fall to sleep, wake up after four hours, take some meds and fall once again back to sleep. Apart from being given some food, which I struggled to eat, this would go on until I was fit to fly home. I wasn't too concerned – my plan was simple. Fly home, trigger my medical insurance that Action Group assured us we all had, have an operation or two to fix my shoulder, recover and then return to Kabul. How long could this take? Maybe six months, I thought. I was guaranteed two years' wages while injured in the line of duty. Only trouble being, I now had to pay tax.

A flight home was arranged for me. I said goodbye to the lads in the team and reassured them that I would be returning. I packed up all my belongings and boxed them away in the house. All I took with me was one holdall with my wash kit and other personal belongings. Vince and Dan drove me to Kabul International and waited with me before I climbed onto the UN flight to Dubai, my arm heavily bandaged and still suffering with very painful ribs.

I arrived in Dubai and got a taxi to the hotel. All I wanted to do was sleep. There would be no beer on this trip. Early morning came and I was ferried to Dubai International and placed on my Emirates flight to Birmingham, business class.

Nicola picked me up from the airport in the Audi TT and took me home. I was instructed to telephone Buckingham Gate on return to the UK; here they would give me instructions on what to do in regards to medical arrangements. As soon as I returned to the house, that's what I did. I spoke to a lady in HR who gave me the shattering news.

"Mark, you need to report to your GP. There was a mix-up with your medical insurance that has only just come to light." I couldn't believe what I was hearing. I had spent three years in Kabul working for this company to be told I had no medical insurance! I went mad down the phone.

"Bullshit, a mix-up, you never had me insured in the first place. Do you have the others insured?" I questioned whether they did or not, either way, I wasn't and I was fucked. I had been shot five times only five days ago and these motherfuckers were telling me to report to my GP. I couldn't wait to walk in to see my GP and give him the good news. *"Hello, Mr Inman, what can I do for you today?" "Take a look at this, doc!"*

I skyped Vince that evening and told him that there was a possibility that they were not insured and informed him what I was told to do in regards to report to my GP. The shit went on to hit the fan. One of the lads resigned immediately and moved security companies. The others went on to inform head office that they were not leaving their accommodation until they had in writing their insurance policies and they were checked out for authenticity and accuracy. This caused a complete shutdown of movements for two weeks.

I personally was left with no option; I reported to my GP and joined the queue of our great NHS service. Action Group never paid a penny for my treatment but the National Health

Service took excellent care of me. After all I had done for that company. I protected their clients and saved many of their lives. I had lost friends out there, been involved in a plane crash, two suicide bombings and countless firefights, resulting in fourteen confirmed kills to my name. I was to spend the next two years having operations to fix me physically; this was the easy part. I had no idea I would be about to embark on the biggest and most frightening battle of my life to date. No amount of operations would be able to fix me mentally.

22

THE START OF MY STRUGGLE

Little did I know that the next phase of my life would be so difficult. I would have to fight a different kind of enemy completely. For the first few weeks everything was fine, it just felt as though I was on an annual leave spell. I would wonder how the lads were getting on. I didn't want to Skype as I would be jealous of what they were getting up to out there. I mulled over getting in touch with Tim's wife. I thought about paying her a visit, but then I thought she wouldn't want to see me. I was the one who survived and she no doubt wished it had been the other way around. I wouldn't blame her for feeling that way either. In years to come, I would think the same. I would hold my face in my hands and cry out, "I wish it was me!"

As the weeks went by I started to realise that maybe I wouldn't be going back home – after all, that is what I regarded Kabul to be, and the lads were my family. I had Nicola taking care of me and Bethan would act as a means of taking my mind off things. I started to need a nightlight on when I went to bed, a small light that gave me just enough so when I woke up at night I could figure out where I was. It took me weeks to realise I would never wake up in my room in Kabul again.

I started to become bored very quickly with doing nothing. I would wake up in the morning, take Cassius out for a walk, watch Jeremy Kyle, have an afternoon siesta and then pick Bethan up from school. I started to live a life that I was not designed for, a life that I began to resent.

Early on, I noticed my temper increasing. I would walk down a street in town and have some yobbo look at me with what I felt was disrespect and find myself staring back and asking, "What's your problem?" I thought in my head, *Show me some respect, you have no idea what I've been through or what I can do.* I thought I was better than Joe Civvy. I expected the red carpet treatment everywhere I went. Instances of road rage were becoming more frequent. *How dare anyone mug me off!* If they did they were going to receive the wrath of my threatening tongue. I brought the violent behaviour from the streets of Afghanistan to the harmless area of my local community. If things didn't change I was going to find myself in some serious bother.

I couldn't admit to myself that my career was over, or I was probably too scared to. After all, what was I going to do for a job in the future? Stack shelves in Tesco, deliver pizza or be a second-hand car salesman? I had no trade behind me or skills which were transferable onto Civvy Street. All I knew how to do with my hands was engage in combat, operate weapon systems and lead men into battle. I didn't want to think about it too much. I had two years of wages coming in. OK, it wasn't my full pay – I had to take a 50% cut and pay tax – but it was enough to pay the bills and get by for the time being.

I could only describe the feelings I was encountering as 'mourning'. I had lost something; my identity, my job and my family (the lads). I was starting to feel low in mood. All I wanted was to get a flight to Kabul and join the lads, just to be with them. I missed them dearly. I felt lonely and realised I had nothing to offer Nicola and Bethan. I was good for one thing: on the last working day of the month I had money go into my account to pay bills. Apart from that, I had become a burden to them both. I lost the fire in my belly that had kept me alive in so many circumstances and scenarios over the years. I was no longer that fearless, brave and respected man that I had become accustomed to being. Overnight I had lost everything; I went from hero to zero just like that. I only knew two gears, fifth gear and hold my beer, but now I was operating day by day in first.

Nicola decided that she needed to go back to work and continue with her career in her area of speciality. She very quickly gained employment due to the level of experience she had. She now had a new focus and she didn't need to be around me so much. She could see I was suffering with the odd nightmare, as well as witnessing my temper escalating.

Sadly it wouldn't be long until things became too much. Nicola and I started to argue frequently. I felt that she had no sympathy for what I had encountered in Kabul or the injuries I had sustained while providing financially for her and Bethan. It felt as though I had become a burden to her and she was the first person to show me disrespect when I needed help. I recall our last argument; I remember it because I put my hands through the kitchen door in anger, leaving three distinct holes in it. In her eyes, I was no longer the man she married and truth be told, I had become too selfish to be concerned with my marriage. I wanted to be on my own. We separated. I packed my bags and moved in with my sister who didn't live far away.

Nicola is a good person. I put her through a lot over the years and she deserved better. She always put Bethan's needs first and never stopped me from seeing my angel. I'm happy to say that Nicola moved on with her life. She found someone new, a decent bloke, settled down and had another child. She now lives in a family environment that she deserves. We don't have anything to do with each other any longer. I just hope she doesn't hate me. I am truly sorry, Nicola!

I later moved out of my sister's and rented a room for a short while. I would return to the house that we had bought because Nicola and Bethan had decided to move out in order to be with her new gentleman and start afresh. I didn't want to sell the property, so when the girls left I moved back in and was reunited with my good friend Cassius.

The date for my first operation very quickly came due to the severity of the injury. I still could not move my arm correctly. I was to have further floating bone removed, bone that they failed to retrieve while in Camp Warehouse after the initial incident. On completion of this first operation I would then have another more complex one. It would comprise of reconstructive surgery, which included five pins and a fixable suture anchor plate to secure the shoulder. It was extremely painful. On completion of the operations I was sent home, where I lived just Cassius and me. I could not lie down on a bed due to the pain. The left arm was slung up and strapped close to my chest but even the process of breathing would raise the secured arm, which in return caused severe stabbing pain deep into the shoulder joint. I couldn't sleep until I became so tired that in the end I could get a little before waking up in agony once more. In total it would take six months to recover from the operations. I now had good mobility and wanted to speed the process up.

I decided that I needed some focus instead of wasting away. I joined my local gym and embraced exercise. I trained hard five days a week for up to three hours; during this time I was to gain some significant muscle tone. With this new-found love, I decided to gain qualifications as a fitness instructor and personal trainer. At least while being off injured and recovering, I could be thinking of future employment opportunities.

I began to experience the first of many flashbacks. I was

walking around my local town doing a small bit of shopping. Traffic was around me and pedestrians were going about their everyday business. I was walking with my head down, looking at my feet. I raised my head, and as I did I found myself back on the VCP. I looked down the road to the right-hand side and saw a yellow taxi approaching with four occupants inside. I was back in Bagram. The taxi approached me and drove past with its windows down, firing its AKs in my direction. I froze. As quickly as the vision came to me, it disappeared. I realised where I was; I was stood in my local town. Why had I seen this image? I stood for what felt like half an hour trying to understand what had just happened to me. Was I going crazy? I believed I could even smell the distinct smell of expended ammunition, I could even hear the crack and thump of rounds firing past my head. It was as if I was reliving those few seconds. I came to and began shaking violently, almost as if I had been thrown into a large kitchen freezer and my body was adapting to the freezing temperature. I started to feel nauseous. I just needed to get away as quickly as I could. I felt disorientated and needed to calm myself down in order to function correctly. I realised almost immediately that what had just happened was a flashback. I felt vulnerable in my surroundings. I needed to get back to my car and sit for a while in its safe enclosure. On returning to my car, I sat in the driving seat with my head on the steering wheel, my heart still pounding. I opened the door and proceeded to throw up onto the car park floor.

On returning home I experienced a terrible headache. The flashback continued to concern me; it was all I was thinking about, I couldn't think of anything else. *Was this a one-off or is this going to happen more frequently?* I worried. I decided to go to bed. It was the middle of the afternoon but I felt exhausted, as though I had just been on a ten-mile run. I was emotionally shattered. Cassius joined me in bed. He must have known I wasn't well, he had this knack of knowing when to comfort me; he could almost read my mind.

I quickly fell to sleep. I slept like a baby for hours. I woke up and it was early evening but I still felt tired. I decided to jump into the bath and relax. I stayed in there for thirty minutes, lying back, putting my head under the water so the water was just above my ears. I listened to my heart beating, which had now calmed down. This was the moment I knew something was wrong with me. I didn't know what to do. I didn't want to go to the doctor. *He may think I'm mad.* I was conscious that I needed to seek employment at some point and I didn't want anything on my medical notes which could jeopardise my future. I came to the decision that I needed to keep this to myself. Nobody must know what had happened; it would remain my little secret. Hopefully it was a one-off experience. I woke up that very night screaming. I sat bolt upright and looked at my hands. They were covered in blood. I cried.

23

COUNSELLING

The flashbacks were to become more frequent, almost a twice-weekly occurrence. The flashbacks would manifest in different scenarios. I could be sat at home watching the television and the news would come on; before watching a report about Iraq or Afghanistan, I would rush for the remote control and change television channel. This itself could trigger a memory which resulted in another flashback, be it then or at another point in time. I started to wait for them to happen, knowing they would at some point rear their ugly heads. I was beginning to live in dread of them occurring. When they did, they would not be pleasant. As well as reliving an incident through my eyes, it would destroy the rest of my day. I would be tearful, angry, sad, desperate, lonely and depressed, all these different emotions rolling into one.

Going to the gym would help. I suppose the endorphin and serotonin release would help. Being around people became difficult. *These people weren't like me,* I thought. These were everyday Joe Civvies who had no idea of what I had been through. They lived in their little bubbles of security. The closest they get to violent conflict is watching a movie with popcorn on a Friday night. We were a completely different breed. I was the fucking psychopath who didn't care for his own life and surely didn't care for the people's lives I had taken. These people were the salt of the earth and I was the lad who should be locked up. I believed I was not a nice human being. I didn't deserve to be in their presence. I kept myself to myself. To this day, I struggle to form relationships with people – I fear what they think of me and understand that we have very little in common. I just kept my head down and threw myself into the training, hoping that it would enable me to get an afternoon's sleep due to tiring me out.

Weeks went by and the flashbacks did not subside. I began to feel even worse. My marriage had broken down and I only saw Bethan once a week, and that was if I felt well enough to see her. I didn't want her looking at her father in this state. All I had was Cassius. Life was getting tough, a life that I didn't want any longer. I resigned myself to the fact that I would never return to Kabul or be employed as a bodyguard by any company ever again. I was damaged goods. Who wants to employ a lad that's been shot up? There are lads who are fit and ready to be deployed, not a has-been who's been shot and probably, in their eyes, lost the bottle. What was I going to do with my life? I felt that time was running out. How many more months would I be getting some money coming in?

I still refused to get help from my doctor. I was supposed to be the tough guy, the ultimate soldier. I couldn't show signs of weakness by asking for help. I had to do what I knew best, and that was to continue to fight. I didn't have much left in me though. I continued to hold out the hope that maybe these flashbacks would end and I could start to rebuild my life somehow. I sat in my large three-bedroom house on the living room floor with my back against the sofa. Cassius placed his head onto my lap and looked at me with sad eyes. He knew, he knew that I was not good.

"What's the point, Cass?" I said as I stroked his head and cried once more. This was the first time I contemplated suicide. I spent the evening deciding how I would do it. I remember wishing I still had my Glock 17 pistol with just one round in it, that bullet that I had always saved for myself if the situation arose. *It's here now!*

I decided long ago that I would not be visiting my GP; I didn't want any trace on my medical records of what I was going through. I was already fucked when it came to being re-employed in some sector, never mind having a note about suicidal thoughts and flashbacks on my record for the rest of my life. I did succumb to the fact that I needed some help. I didn't want to talk to family and friends. I had nobody. I decided that I would pay to see a private counsellor just to see if I could get some things off my chest; it may help with the flashbacks.

I visited a really kind and lovely lady by the name of Rita, an Irish lady in her 60s who quickly gained my trust. When booking my first appointment over the phone with her I could tell immediately that she was the one to help and I felt confident. She asked me to briefly describe to her why I felt I needed her help. On ending the phone consultation she said, "Don't do anything stupid, Mark, I will see you soon", in a kind, softly spoken delicate tone. I had never told her at this point that I was considering ending my life but with what I had told her she must have heard triggers to suggest that I was considering this course of action. Rita helped me over the following few months. I would visit her on a weekly basis at her home in a nearby local village. We would spend an hour together talking and going over things I had done and my feelings in regards to actions I had taken. I felt as though it was £30 well spent. I would often drive home after our session and think, *what did we just talk about?* I strangely couldn't remember. I felt a little better though, I had had my 'Rita fix'. I hoped it would keep me going for the next seven days.

Money had started to get tight for me. I was on 50% of my wage and the months of being paid by AG were running out. I was living in this huge house and the bills were mounting up. Another pressure that I was feeling that I just didn't need. The car, my beloved, beautiful black Audi TT, my symbol of having made it, having money and finally being someone, was about to go. I could no longer afford the finance and the car needed a service which there was no way I could afford. I telephoned the finance company and asked for it to be voluntarily repossessed. It was collected from my home. A truck came and took it away. I watched as my trophy was removed on the back of a flat bed, another kick in the bollocks and the first black mark on my credit rating.

With money getting tight I decided to see if there was some avenue that I could use my skills in. I held an SIA (Security Industry Authority) licence in close protection after all, the highest security qualification available. Surely this licence could help me get some work of some description? I walked into town and, for the first time in a long while, into the job centre. Outside there were young lads and girls hovering about dressed in their tracksuits, with the distinct smell of weed lingering. I felt rock bottom. I went inside and felt that everybody was looking at the skinhead with tattoos, judging me as if I was one of those outside. I felt angry; I just wanted to shout the room down. *"I've spent ten years in the army and three years body guarding in Afghanistan."* Where was that going to get me? Chucked out probably. I operated the touch screens and entered 'security' into the search. A job appeared as a door supervisor. *I could do that,* I thought. I spent my days in the gym and was of good muscle tone and strength, and I certainly had no fear. OK, I wasn't the biggest bouncer at 5ft 10 inches but I had good communication skills, intelligence to talk people down, and if it did come down to it, I could fight. *I've been shot, what are these fuckers going to do to me while working on a door?* This would be easy!

I telephoned the number linked to the advertisement; a bloke picked up the call and pronounced his name and the company. "I'm calling about the job advertised." The bloke on the phone at first didn't sound interested. I went on, "I have an SIA licence in close protection, I have just returned from Afghanistan having protected government officials for the last three years, and before that I spent ten years in the army."

"Come and meet me tomorrow," he eagerly said. I had to smile as I rang off. If I hadn't come out with all that shit he wouldn't have been interested, I'm sure.

I met the head doorman and the owner of the security company. I showed them my licence and gave them a copy of my CV. After spending half an hour chatting with them, the owner of the company announced, "Mark, I can't offer you a job, you are too over-qualified."

I went on to say, "How can I be over-qualified when I have never worked a door in my life?" He went on to look at me and smile.

"You start tomorrow, £10 an hour." He continued to shake my hand.

I went on to work Friday and Saturday nights on the door for the following ten years. I hated every single shift but I needed the money to help pay Bethan's maintenance and it also contributed to my counselling with Rita.

My time with Rita felt constructive. I was getting much off my chest; she became my outlet. She was able to come up with reasons as to why I was struggling. She very early on identified that part of my trouble was adrenaline addiction. All the hits I had been getting in my life and especially in Kabul had contributed to me feeling a high which could not be replicated back home in the UK. Therefore, I was on withdrawal. "Mark, you may never experience adrenaline on that level again in your life, adrenaline rushes as you know them may never happen again. Like a drug being withdrawn from an addict, adrenaline has been withdrawn from you and this is one of the reasons you are suffering." This made perfect sense.

With this withdrawal I was also struggling to integrate back into Civvy Street. I didn't want to be a Civvy; I didn't want to be normal. I struggled enormously in accepting that I was no longer Superman, I was just plain old Inman.

I had an appointment with Rita one Thursday evening. I knocked on her door and she let me in. We went straight upstairs into the room in which we had talked for the last nine months. I sat down in the chair facing Rita to start the session.

"Mark, before we start today's session I need to tell you that I have been in touch with my supervisor. She is there for me to contact when I find clients difficult or I need guidance. I phoned her because I feel I can no longer offer you answers or help. I feel it's wrong that you continue to pay me £30 when I feel I can no longer help you."

Who's going to help me? I thought.

Rita continued, "My supervisor says that you are welcome to continue seeing me, even if it's for you to just talk. We both feel that I cannot help you any longer, other than be here to listen to you." I respected Rita for saying this to me, but I was still having flashbacks, still feeling down and, at times, still feeling suicidal. Bottom line – the help I had been getting over the last nine months did not change what was happening. I thought I needed Rita but what I really needed was something else. I left Rita's house that day and never returned. I was on my own again. Maybe I had become too much hard work for Rita.

I drove home. I opened the front door and sat with Cassius on the floor, crying. I held my hands up to my face and asked, "Why me? What have I done to deserve this?" I thought about Tim, I remembered him lying dead on that dusty horrid floor looking at me. I shook my head and with tears rolling down my face cried out, "I wish it had been me." I sobbed for a while. I then got up to make a cup of tea, opening the cupboard door to get my sugar. There in front of me was all my pain medication for my shoulder, probably more than two hundred painkillers. I grabbed the boxes and took them and my tea into the living room. I popped the tablets out of their wrapping and laid them out onto the fireplace. I sat and looked at the tablets; all I had to do was put them in my mouth and swallow. I wouldn't wake up and my war would be over. I stared at the tablets for what felt like a lifetime. I got up and took out four envelopes and paper. I proceeded to write letters. I wrote four that night – one to my sister, Nicola, Nicola's new fella and finally, Bethan. The letters took me an hour to write. As I wrote them, I sobbed uncontrollably. I had no choice. I couldn't continue to live like this. I didn't want to live like this. This way of life was not for me.

I sealed all four letters and left them on the kitchen worktop in clear view. I went back into the living room to end my life. I bottled it. I couldn't do it. I don't know why? I think it was because of Bethan, even though I knew she would be OK and very well looked after. I think I did it because I was holding out for a little hope. Something came into my head that I will never forget and I think of often in tough times:

If I didn't let them beat me in Afghanistan, I can't let them beat me at home!

24

SHE SAVED MY LIFE

Financially, things were becoming worse for me; AG had now ceased paying me. This meant I could no longer afford the mortgage on my property. I had failed to pay three months running and was facing a repossession order. I had already lost my marriage, daughter and car and now was about to lose my home. I was to start preparing myself for this scenario. I went to my local council and was placed on a list for a flat. This time in my life was probably the lowest I got to. From an exciting job with a wife and child and good money, three holidays a year and a flash motor to having nothing apart from the clothes on my back and in my holdall, my medals, photographs and, of course, my best friend Cassius. I was about to be homeless, living on the streets. I have no doubt that my sister would have put me up for a short while and my parents would not have wanted to see me on the streets, but I came to the conclusion that this was my mess and I was not going to be a burden to anybody. I wouldn't even tell them. I would drift away into obscurity to start this phase of my life. I had one worry – Cassius. I didn't want to drag this poor sod along with me. He was now getting old and was suffering with his legs. All of the running he had done with me over the years contributed to his arthritis. I wanted to do what was right by the old man and let him live his final years in security and warmth and, more importantly, with love. I'm sure given the choice he would have stayed by my side but he didn't have the choice, I was making it for him. I produced some posters and asked around if anyone would take him for me. Nicola sadly couldn't because she was living in rented accommodation, which forbade her to house pets. I was not going to settle until I found somewhere.

I had a little money as I was still doing the hours as a bouncer at a local well-known establishment. I didn't know how long it would last for as when the house would be taken, I surely wouldn't be able to administer myself appropriately to present myself as a clean, smart and professional individual. I knew that when the house was gone, employment would be also. It all began a race against time. At what point would I turn up at the house and the locks would have been changed? It could have been any day.

In the nick of time I had a stroke of luck. I applied for a job working for the NHS. An advertisement in the local paper was asking for an advanced fitness instructor to be a part of a team working to help in the area of rehabilitation. I had applied a month earlier and out of over one hundred applicants I secured a job. It would still not be enough money for me to remain in the house, but it increased my options. Combined with the door supervisor work and the full-time job as an exercise instructor, I could just about keep my head above water. Sadly, I would not be home much to spend time with my best friend. He would see me in the evenings Sundays to Thursdays, but be on his own during the day. I felt terrible that I was neglecting him and I could see it was making him sad. I believe strongly he was becoming depressed with being on his own and the pain he was suffering with his arthritis. I continued to try to find him a better home.

I didn't enjoy my new nine 'til five job. In fact, I hated it, but it gave me money and kept me from becoming homeless; because of this, I needed to be grateful and embrace the opportunity I had. It also gave me the grounds to interact with people of different ethnic groups, age ranges and cultures which I had never done before, which in turn helped me to adapt better into civilian life. It wouldn't be long also until I would hopefully hear about a flat that I could call base. If I lost my home in the meantime, I probably just had enough money to get into a bed and breakfast.

Just as things started to look up a little, I had another gift from the gods. While working on the door one Friday evening I noticed two girls. A blonde and a brunette, both immaculately turned out and very pretty. As I walked past the pair, the brunette smiled at me and said hello. I in return smiled and responded. I just thought she was being polite and thought nothing further of it. The girls would later make their way closer to the front door, in view of my colleague and me. The girls shortly left. I opened the door as they exited the bar. I observed them both as they walked across the road with some confidence and swagger. As they both reached the opposite side they halted, proceeded to have a brief discussion and nodded at each other. The beautiful long haired brunette girl scurried away up an alleyway towards a car park where their transport must have been. The blonde navigated across the road towards me.

"Excuse me, do you like my friend Donna?"

Straight to the point, I thought. I responded in a truthful manner.

"She's stunning".

"Would you like her telephone number?"

"No! I will give you mine to pass on," which I did. The

blonde made her way back to her friend and out of view. Within five minutes, I received a text message: *Hello it's Donna x.*

During the next couple of days, Donna and I would text each other. She claimed that she recognised me from the gym. I have racked my brain but I don't recall her – she doesn't like me admitting that! We went on a date and hit it off immediately. She informed me that she was married but separated and going through a divorce. She didn't have children and had recently moved out of her marital home and back in with her parents. We spent a great evening together, we got drunk. She came back to my house where she met my best friend. We both fell to sleep drunk on the sofa, cuddling up. I woke around 1am. I woke Donna up and booked her a taxi home.

The following day I received a phone call from a young lady who had been looking for a family pet for her husband and three children. She had seen a picture of Cassius and asked if she could come and meet him. I felt terrible for him that he was losing his master, and sad for me that my best friend was leaving me. The lady came around the house almost immediately and fell in love with my boy. It was impossible for her not to. The lady asked if she could have him and I agreed. She asked if I could keep hold of him for a couple of days and wait until the weekend, when we arranged to meet up and Cassius would be introduced to his new family. I was happy that he was going to a large family with children. He was the perfect dog for them, soft, kind, loyal and lovable. They were lucky to have him.

Donna drove to my house and picked Cass and I up in her car. We drove to a pub about fifteen minutes away and were met by Cassius' new family. I walked over to the family's car, where Cass was introduced to the children. He was excited at the fuss but, of course, didn't know we were to be separated for good. I picked him up and put him into the boot of their car. I hugged him and gave him a kiss.

"Thank you for being with me, thank you for being my best friend. I'm sorry I couldn't keep my promise to keep you. Be good, I love you!" I couldn't hold my tears back.

"We will look after him well, Mark," the lady assured me. I watched the car drive away and witnessed Cassius look at me through the window of the boot all the way until the car went out of view. I was heartbroken. Something else I had lost.

Donna and I became very close very quickly. Donna lived in a small granny flat adjacent to her parents' house. It was a little home from home and gave her some privacy away from her parents, Pete and Shirley. I would go round to the house and have a good drink with Pete. He would cook us up some tea and the four of us would sit around the dining room table and enjoy each other's company. It was a great time.

Strangely enough, I received an offer from Nicola and her partner. They knew I was about to lose the house and they wanted to make me an offer. If they moved back in with Bethan and their baby son then they would repay the arrears and continue with the mortgage. I agreed and moved out. I was living out of my holdall on a friend's sofa. Donna wasn't happy with this; she wanted me to move into the little granny flat with her. Her parents also wanted me to move in. They saw that we made each other happy and they wanted Donna's fortunes to change. I agreed. I moved my holdall of clothes into the flat. Donna gave me a drawer to put my clothes and photographs into. I looked for my medals, and they had disappeared. I knew they had been stolen by the so-called friend whose sofa I was surfing. I confronted him about my loss, but the coward refused to admit he had taken them. They were all I had left of my time in the forces. I have nothing to pass onto my children. Bethan holds my dog tags above her bed to this day. That's it; I have nothing else.

Donna and I fell in love and spent the following year living with Pete and Shirley in the granny flat. It was a great time in our lives. In the winter it would get so cold in there that as soon as we got home from work we would put the television on, pull out the sofa bed, turn the portable gas heater on and get into bed. Pete used to call us 'John and Yoko'. During the night it would freeze and when we came to open the patio doors they would be frozen shut. How I never got another bout of pneumonia I will never know.

We of course wanted to buy our own property. This would be difficult for me due to having lost my car and not being able to pay the mortgage on my home. Donna though, manged to secure a small mortgage, enough for us to buy a small two-bedroom house that would become our first home. We moved in and within two months she became pregnant.

I had another good turn of fortune. I decided to telephone the lady who had taken Cassius for me. I just wanted to see how he was doing after all this time. I would have phoned earlier but I just didn't have the courage. She informed me that sadly she was looking to re-home him as they were moving away and they were unable to take him.

"I want him back," I immediately announced, all this without consulting Donna first. I knew though that she would support my decision. I telephoned Donna and told her that we could get Cass back. She too was happy, happy for me. I finished work and drove to the lady's house. I couldn't wait to see my best friend. It had been almost eighteen months since I last saw him. She opened the door and I was greeted with barking. He wandered out to me, wagging his tail. He knew exactly who I was.

"I've come to take you home, buddy." I put him in my car. I couldn't believe my luck. I was reunited with my best friend. We were meant to be together. My first stop after picking Cassius up was to drive to see Bethan. "Look who I have." Bethan was overjoyed.

On the 10th February 2012, our son Charlie-Jack was born.

Charlie after my grandfather and Jack after Donna's. CJ, as we call him for short, was and still remains the apple of both of our eyes, a young boy who is full of love. We are truly blessed.

Donna came into my life days before I would become homeless. Thoughts of suicide and flashbacks were still frequent. When she came to me things started to improve. I finally had something positive in my life, a purpose for living again. Somebody sent her to me at that vulnerable point. She took care of me and showed me love. If she hadn't entered my life that Friday evening, I honestly believe I probably wouldn't be here today. She was that little bit of hope I needed and was looking for that night I laid those tablets out to take. Donna, I have no doubt, saved my life. I don't have just one angel now, I'm lucky to have two.

You would think that this would be the end of my problems as life started to change in fortune. No. I would have a huge battle to come, a battle that I am still fighting.

25

POST-TRAUMATIC
STRESS DISORDER (PTSD)

Charlie-Jack had just been born and life was great. Little was I to know that my past was going to creep up on me again. I started to feel unwell. I couldn't quite put my nail on it, but something was not right. I started to have bouts of nausea during the day, coupled with headaches. They would come on for no reason at all and started to happen more frequently. I had not had flashbacks for a good couple of years so the last thing I thought it could be was linked to that. I went to my GP and spoke to him about my symptoms to see if he could come up with any solution. He immediately, without hesitation, went on to say he thought I was depressed and said I appeared agitated and anxious.

"And what do you put that down to, just because I've been to Afghanistan?" I was not happy and left the surgery.

I would find myself sat watching television at the end of the working day when all of a sudden I would jump up and rush to the toilet and continue to be violently sick. I would then sit back down as if it hadn't happened. It started to become such a normal part of my day that even Donna didn't take much notice. It became normality. The head pain was worrying me a little. I had a pain at the rear left side of my head and even to touch the area felt strange. Again, I plucked up the courage to go to the doctor, who yet again said I was displaying signs of anxiety. I responded by saying, "If I came in here with a broken toe you would say I was depressed or stressed. I'm not, I have headaches." The GP conceded and sent me for some tests, including a CT scan on my brain. I was sure it would find something. It didn't.

Finally it would all come to a head. I knew there was something wrong but yet again I didn't want to admit this to anyone or myself. I began to have nightmares and terrors. I couldn't stop them from occurring. I started to go to bed dreading the fact that they would happen. They were violent nightmares which caused me to wake in a sweat with my heart beating ferociously. Each nightmare would be different and put me back into a previous scenario that I had encountered, but this time the outcome was different. I would often wake with the image of Tim's face looking at me.

I would be waking in the middle of the night knowing that I would not be able to fall back to sleep again. I would go downstairs and sit with Cassius. I was going to work tired and agitated due to the lack of sleep. Little things began to make me feel angry. I felt I had a real problem, yet people around me moaned and whinged about trivial things. They didn't have real problems; I would give anything to have their dramas.

I noticed that I needed to have order in my daily routine. Everything had to be in a certain way and when I returned home a serious bout of OCD (Obsessive Compulsive Disorder) would kick in. Everything had to be clean and tidy, put in its correct place, almost as if in a regimental fashion. I couldn't sit on the sofa until all the jobs in the house were complete and up to a standard that was only achievable if I myself did it. Even if a royal butler was to clean, it wouldn't have been at an acceptable level in my mind. I was driving Donna nuts. She felt as though I was moaning at her for not being tidy enough. Looking back, I realise it was my way of having some control and having order in my brain. I could literally not relax until everything was perfect. Donna would say that it was like living with that geezer from the Julia Roberts film, *Sleeping with the Enemy*.

After four nights of nightmares and only a few hours' sleep, I had to accept that enough was enough. The doctors were correct; I needed some help. I could not continue like this. I had already had one marriage fail; I wasn't going to lose Donna and CJ because of the same reason. I went to my GP, accompanied by Donna. I sat in front of the GP.

"What can I do to help?"

I proceeded to tell him, "I haven't slept in almost four days."

While still looking at his computer screen he responded by saying, "Well, that's some sort of world record." I could have got up there and then and left. *You prick,* I thought. I needed help though; I had to go through this bullshit. I decided to give him something to think about.

"I spent three years in Afghanistan and killed many people, I have done some bad things." *That will get his fucking attention,* and it did. His chair turned to face me for the first time. He looked at me and continued to talk all the bullshit I had heard time after time.

"Thank you for your service, thank you for risking your life for the sake…"

Yes, yes, I don't need to hear the fucking shit that I have heard time after time. I'm not interested. Bottom line is I should have never gone out there, and because I did I'm in this fucking shit state predicament.

The GP asked if I thought of self-harm or suicide. I lied and said no. I was of course thinking of my medical records.

I wanted damage limitation on those files. The doc prescribed me some sleeping tablets and anti-depressants. He went on to inform me that the tablets would take a few weeks to get into my system and went on to say that I would gain weight. *Not me,* I thought. *I won't get overweight.*

Within eight weeks I had piled on almost twenty kilograms. I felt terrible. My self-esteem was rock bottom. I looked in the mirror and saw a fat ugly bastard, a far cry from the pretty boy who had the girls chasing him, the athletic physique that stopped fucking bullets with his torso. I was no longer that fine specimen of a man, but a slob. A fucking Joe Civvy working a shit nine to five job, fat, pasty skin, bags under his eyes, a useless oxygen thief. Since taking this medication I felt even worse. I recall one night, having taken my sleeping tablets that I woke up standing over Charlie-Jack's cot, looking at him. As I woke I wondered what the hell I was doing. *Why am I stood over him like this?* It frightened me. I decided that this medication and what was happening to my body had to change.

I went for a check-up at the doctor's request. He noted my weight gain and decided to check some other stats. My blood pressure was through the roof, my cholesterol level up and I was borderline type 2 diabetic. He wanted to place me on more medication. I was on that slippery slope. I made another appointment to see the doctor in six weeks' time and asked if he could delay prescribing the meds. I knew what I needed to do. I needed to take control. I stopped taking the sleeping tablets immediately and decided to start weaning myself off the anti-depressants. I began exercising in order to lose the weight I had gained. I started swimming daily and purchased myself a bike. I began running short distances and with run by run the distance I acheived would increase. I got up to 42km a week, the distance of a marathon. I started to feel much better. My self-esteem was improving with the weight loss. I started to take pride once more in my appearance. I was enjoying the exercise; it felt as though it was really helping my mind as well as my body shape.

I began to sleep better as the nightmares began to subside and my energy levels returned. I actually started to smile and laugh again. I returned to the doctor who again conducted some tests. My blood pressure, cholesterol and blood sugar levels were normal. I was no longer taking the sleeping tablets or anti-depressants. I had escaped the medication.

I recall one Armistice Day taking the day off work having decided to pluck up the courage to visit the National Memorial Arboretum for the first time. I had wanted to go so many times but just couldn't face it. This was a huge moment for me. I went alone to pay my respects and absorb the peacefulness of the venue. Veterans were present, proudly displaying their medals and swapping stories with their comrades. I made my way to the prominent feature *The Wall*, where the names of the fallen are beautifully engraved. I identified lost brothers who I had served with and touched their names with my bare hands. I recalled occasions we had spent together. I felt enormously emotional; I was fighting to hold the tears back. As I walked away, a handsome young man in his mid-twenties was making his way in my direction towards *The Wall*. I immediately noticed his left leg. He had lost it and it had been replaced by a typical metal one. He hobbled proudly. I looked at him and immediately admired him. We never made eye contact; he continued past me. A feeling came over me of shame. Believe it or not, I actually felt jealous. He would receive instant respect from everybody he came into contact with, be recognised as a hero. His terrible injury was visible. Mine, however, was hidden. I had nothing to show apart from the scars on my shoulder, which you can only see when my shirt is off. I feel ashamed to admit this, but I'm sure other sufferers would empathise with me.

I still needed some form of help. I was referred to Combat Stress. I would have frequent visits to my home from a counsellor. I had numerous appointments but truth be told, they didn't help one bit. I was becoming disheartened with the whole process. I was to have a session of EMDR (Eye Movement Desensitisation and Reprocessing) treatment. I was holding some pebble-shaped vibrating units in my hands. It did fuck-all.

I had one session with the counsellor; we spent an hour talking to each other. I told him about the contacts I had been in and the people I had shot. I told him that I didn't give a shit about those people that I had killed and I had no sympathy for them or their families. They had attempted to kill either me or my colleagues, they got what they deserved. I then went on to tell him about the 'wishing well' and my nightmare where Bethan appeared. I got upset and held the tears back. I told him that I wanted to live and provide a good environment for CJ to grow in with love, laughter and security. The counsellor said one thing that made pure sense.

"While talking to you over the last few months, the only time you have showed emotion is when talking of your children." That was it, he was correct, that's all that mattered out of everything – the army, prison in Hong Kong, the accident and Afghanistan – my beautiful children. They were my medicine. At that very point the penny dropped.

As I saw the counsellor out of my house and closed the front door, I decided that I was going to sort this myself. That was the last time I received any form of medical help. Nothing had worked. No amount of medication, counselling or EMDR. I had been talking to muppets who had never been to war or in a combat situation. How could they understand how I was feeling or what I had been through? I needed to gain confidence in myself. There was only going to be one person who could get me out of this terrible situation I found myself in, and that was me.

26

CALM HEAD

Today as I write this chapter I am happy. I am pleased I have got my life story down on paper. Maybe one day my children will pick this up and read about their father and hopefully be proud of what I did with my life. When I sit in my rocking chair I will be able to tell my grandchildren stories about my adventures, just as Charlie did to me.

Life has been tough for me but I am proud of the way in which I continued to fight. I got knocked down so many times but I refused to stay down. I got up. If I hadn't had these life experiences then I wouldn't have turned out to be the person I am today. My time in Hong Kong moulded me to become that tough, hardened individual who accepted whatever life threw in my direction. I never wallowed in self-pity but accepted what I was handed and used it to better myself. I often think back to my early days and Hong Kong, and even though it was tough at the time and tested me as a young man, I am glad it happened. I believe it gave me the foundations of inner strength which I used time after time. It gave me the strength to confront situations that others may have turned away from. It gave me confidence as I accepted nothing in life could ever get as bad as that moment in time. I would say it was my life-defining moment. It made me who I was and who I am. If I had the choice of the incident happening again or avoiding it, I would gladly have it happen again. It possibly saved my life. So to those motherfucking coppers who gave me the kicking from hell, you created a man, and you are damn lucky that we never crossed paths again.

Do I have regrets? Yes, I have two; my first, I regret not getting out of bed that cold, wet morning during SAS selection. I realise that decision cost me my dream. If you have a dream, don't make the mistake I made. Chase that dream and don't let yourself down in its pursuit and, more importantly, don't let anybody tell you that you can't achieve your dream. Focus on it and fight to get it. If you consider giving up on that dream then remember me and remember how it still to this day makes me feel. I hate the fact I quit. I beat myself up over that decision all the time.

My second regret is going to Kabul. It was not my country to go to and impose my bullying presence. I didn't show those Afghans the respect they deserved. I treated those people as though they were inferior to me. How dare I? I had turned into what I despise, I became a bully. I am truly sorry for this. I am not talking about those bastards I shot – they deserved what they got – but those innocent locals who I looked down upon. Those who I bullied out of the way while driving or spoke to with utter disrespect, those I gave the finger to or swore at because they were in my way. What a wanker I was. I went out there for money and excitement. Did I make a positive change? No. Did I achieve anything out there that made my children's lives better? No. When I returned home I thought about it long and hard. Imagine for one moment that your local town had some Afghans driving around your roads, aggressively forcing you off the roads because they felt they were more important, showing their weapons off and thinking they owned the place. What would you do? I know exactly what I would do. I'd be doing everything in my power to hurt these fuckers and regain my country. Maybe we deserved what we got. Maybe my curse for going out there and acting in this way is my PTSD. We reap what we sow.

How am I today? I still suffer with PTSD; I always will to some point. I have, though, climbed the mountain and am on the other side. It does get better as time goes by. Time is a great healer. I have faith in myself that I can beat this. It's just another fight that I have to prepare for and one I am winning and will beat. I find myself hyper-alert. I read vehicle registration numbers, I count the amount of people in a room, and I look at faces and body language to identify a threat. I am so wired that it takes a lot of energy. Certain times of the year I am worse. November is always a tough month. Fireworks destroy me. I absolutely despise them and with every bang, I'm back in Kabul or in a firefight. I have to prepare myself mentally if I am going to take my boy to a fireworks display. After all, I don't want him missing out. I find it so tough though. I come home from the evening's display and am more than likely sick. Donna will open a bottle of prosecco and have to warn me prior to prepare for the pop. I still have nightmares at times but am lucky that the flashbacks have gone.

I would love to help people that suffer with PTSD. I would talk to them and tell them my story and the reasons why I started to suffer, but I would motivate them to trust in themselves and have the belief in their ability that they can recover no matter what, even if all avenues and routes have been previously explored, to have self-belief and remember that they didn't beat you over there; you can't let them beat you at home.

I'm no longer that hothead I used to be. I would like to think I'm a good person who is kind, gentle and shows respect to others. That's all we really need to do as human beings. You won't go far wrong if you treat people how you expect to be treated yourself.

I have people to thank for helping me become this better person: Donna, Bethan and Charlie-Jack. You have taught me to be a better man. OK, I'm no longer that superhero, I am Joe Civvy – I just choose to tuck my red cape in so nobody can see it. It's always there though. I will always have my rocking chair to look forward to, and when I finally find that chair and sit in it, I will once more become Superman.

27

ODE TO MY SON

If you can keep your head when all about you
Are losing theirs and blaming it on you,
If you can trust yourself when all men doubt you,
But make allowance for their doubting too;
If you can wait and not be tired by waiting,
Or being lied about, don't deal in lies,
Or being hated, don't give way to hating,
And yet don't look too good, nor walk too wise:

If you can dream – and not make dreams your master;
If you can think – and not make thoughts your aim;
If you can meet with Triumph and Disaster
And treat those two imposters just the same;
If you can bear to hear the truth you've spoken
Twisted by knaves to make a trap for fools,
Or watch the things you gave your life to broken,
And stoop and build 'em up with worn-out tools:

If you can make one heap of all your winnings
And risk it on one turn of pitch-and-toss,
And lose, and start again at your beginnings
And never breathe a word about your loss;
If you can force your heart and nerve and sinew
To serve your turn long after they are gone,
And so hold on when there is nothing in you
Except the Will which says to them: "Hold on!"

If you can talk with crowds and keep your virtue,
Or walk with Kings – nor lose the common touch,
If neither foes nor loving friends can hurt you,
If all men count with you, but none too much;
If you can fill the unforgiving minute
With sixty seconds' worth of distance run –
Yours is the Earth and everything that's in it,
And – which is more – you'll be a Man, my son!

If, Rudyard Kipling (1895)

GLOSSARY

2IC – Second in Command

50cal vest – body armour

AG – Action Group

AK-47 – 7.62mm Kalashnikov rifle

Beasting – extreme physical fitness/punishment

Bergen – army-issued rucksack

BFA – Blank Firing Attachment (yellow piece placed over a rifle's muzzle when firing blank ammunition)

BG – Bodyguard

Burka – Afghan female dress (usually blue in colour) which covers completely

BV – kettle inside armoured vehicle

C-130 Herc – aeroplane

Cam cream – camouflage cream (military face paint)

Casevac – Casualty Evacuation

CFT – Combat Fitness Test (8 tab, wearing 45lb)

Civvy – Civilian

CO – Commanding Officer

Comms – Communication (radios)

Contact – firefight/shooting or bombing

CNPA – Counter Narcotics Police of Afghanistan

CP – Close Protection

Cpl – Corporal

CSgt – Colour Sergeant

CSM – Company Sergeant Major

CQMS – Company Quartermaster Sergeant

Dip plate – Diplomatic vehicle registration plate

DOMS – delayed onset muscle soreness

DPM – Disruptive Pattern Material (camouflage pattern)

DS – Directing Staff

DZ – Drop Zone

ECM – Electronic Counter Measure

EMDR – Eye Movement Desensitisation and Reprocessing

Endex – End of Exercise

FFD – First Field Dressing

Glock 17 – pistol/weapon

Gonk bag – sleeping bag

GPMG – General Purpose Machine Gun

HALO – High Altitude Low Opening

HK G36 – rifle/weapon

HMRC – Her Majesty's Revenue & Customs

HQ – Headquarters

ID – Identification

IED – Improvised Explosive Device

IRA – Irish Republican Army

ISAF – International Security Assistance Force

ITC – Infantry Training Centre

JNCO – Junior Non-Commissioned Officer

LAW – Light Anti-Tank Weapon

L/Cpl – Lance Corporal

LSW – Light Support Weapon

MFO – Military Forces Overseas (packed belongings which are stored or transported)

Minimi – rifle/weapon

MT – Motor Transport

NAAFI – Navy Army Air Force Institute (shop or bar)

NBC – Nuclear, Biological and Chemical

NCO – Non-Commissioned Officer

Non-tac – non-tactical

OC – Officer Commanding

OCD – Obsessive Compulsive Disorder

Ops room – Operations Room (base)

Pads estate – housing for married soldiers

Player – Terrorist

Provost – Battalion Police

PSBC – Platoon Sergeants' Battle Course

PT – Physical Training

PTI – Physical Training Instructor

PTSD – Post-Traumatic Stress Disorder

QM – Quartermaster

QRF – Quick Reaction Force

R&R – Rest and Recuperation

Recce – Reconnaissance

REME – Royal Electrical and Mechanical Engineers

REMF – Rear-Echelon Motherfucker

Round – bullet

RMP – Royal Military Police

RRW – Royal Regiment of Wales

RSM – Regimental Sergeant Major

RST – Range Safety Team

RTU – Return to Unit

RUC – Royal Ulster Constabulary

RV – Rendezvous

RWF – Royal Welsh Fusiliers

Sangar – manned observation point

SAS – Special Air Service (special forces UK)

Saxon – armoured vehicle used in Northern Ireland

SCBC – Section Commanders' Battle Course

Sgt – Sergeant

SIA – Security Industry Authority

Snatch – small armoured vehicle used in Northern Ireland